War and the State

War and the State

The Theory of International Politics

R. Harrison Wagner

THE UNIVERSITY OF MICHIGAN PRESS

Ann Arbor

For Rosi

2010   2009   4   3   2

A CIP catalog record for this book is available from the British Library.

Library of Congress Cataloging-in-Publication Data

Wagner, R. Harrison (Robert Harrison)
    War and the state : the theory of international politics /
R. Harrison Wagner.
        p.   cm.
    Includes bibliographical references and index.
    ISBN-13: 978-0-472-09981-8 (cloth : alk. paper)
    ISBN-10: 0-472-09981-7 (cloth : alk. paper)
    ISBN-13: 978-0-472-06981-1 (pbk. : alk. paper)
    ISBN-10: 0-472-06981-0 (pbk. : alk. paper)
    1. International relations—Philosophy.   2. War.   3. State, The.
I. Title.

JZ1316.W34   2007
327.101—dc22   2006028159

    ISBN13 978-0-472-02590-9 (electronic)

Contents

Figures

Preface

The central question debated by students of international politics is the relation between organized violence and political order at the global level, and this book is mainly concerned with what political scientists in the United States have had to say about that subject. As current events remind us, however, this is a question that pertains to all politics and not just international politics, and therefore I believe that the distinction between international and domestic politics that underlies the division of intellectual labor among scholars who study them has interfered with our understanding of both and has left us poorly equipped to understand both interstate and intrastate conflicts since the end of the cold war. Thus, although the main focus of this book is the theory of international politics, I hope that it will be of interest to students of comparative politics, history, and political theory as well.

The most influential advocate of distinguishing between international and domestic politics has been Kenneth Waltz, and my objective in writing this book is perhaps most directly comparable to the objective he had in writing his well-known book *Theory of International Politics* (1979). In that book Waltz tried to identify what the subject of the study of international politics was, to state its main properties, and to indicate how our understanding of it could be improved. Those are also my goals.

A great deal has been learned about international politics since Waltz wrote his famous book, but there are still many disagreements about how to understand it. Anyone who wants to understand those disagreements must read widely across the journals and subdisciplines of the social sciences, and some of the relevant literature is inaccessible to people without training in formal modeling or unwilling to take formal models seriously. My goal is to make this material accessible to as broad an audience as possible.

Knowledge progresses by trial and error. Thus intellectual progress requires a common understanding of what counts as a mistake, scholars must make it easy for others to spot their mistakes, and they must be motivated to look for them and correct them. I believe that these conditions are only imperfectly satisfied among students of international politics in the United States. As a result, while there is widespread agreement that much that Waltz wrote must be revised, there is much less agreement about what revisions should be made. This fact not only impedes intellectual progress but also diminishes the ability of scholars in the field to speak with authority to a broader audience. By clarifying many of the issues that divide students of international politics, I would like to foster a more productive dialogue among them.

Many political scientists believe that the answers to the questions that divide them are to be found in the philosophy of science. Unfortunately, philosophers of science disagree about many things, and thus attempts to settle disagreements among political scientists by appeals to the philosophy of science just make those disagreements more intractable. In chapter 1, I argue that this emphasis on the philosophy of science is misplaced and that the main problem is instead the willingness of political scientists to tolerate incomplete arguments. I then reconstruct and evaluate the main arguments offered by the competing schools of thought that have divided students of international politics in the United States.

The central figure in this story is Realism, which has dominated the study of international politics in the United States since World War II to such an extent that it has shaped the thinking even of those who disagree with it. Both Realists and many of their critics assume that the world consists of a collection of independent states, and their disagreements focus on whether and how wars among them might be prevented. Many people assume that, since domestic political institutions can prevent civil wars, interstate wars could only be prevented by political institutions at the global level, and debates between Realists and their critics often focus on whether that is a realistic prospect. One of the main messages of this book is that this framework of thought misleads us. Wars do not require states; they merely require armies. Armies can exist without states, and states are among the possible by-products of conflicts among armies. If states exist, wars can occur within them, between them, or across the boundaries that separate them, and the result can be more states, fewer states, or states with different boundaries. Thus a world of independent states is not a world without a global order—the independent states *are* the global order, and the most important question about war is how effective such an institutional structure can be expected to be as an alternative to violence.

To answer this question, we need to understand the relation between organized violence and political order of any sort. This is a much broader question than the one that has come to be the focus of contemporary Realism and its critics, and I will argue in chapter 2 that it is the central question raised by the intellectual tradition from which modern Realism was derived, which is often called raison d'état, or reason of state. To think productively about it, one must understand both violence and how people organize themselves to engage in it. That is the subject of chapter 3.

   Organized violence makes predation profitable, which in turn leads to violent contests among competing predators. But contests among predators can increase the bargaining power of their prey and thus over time diminish the gains from predation. The European state system, I argue, was the product of such a process. Chapters 4 and 5 discuss why competing predators find it difficult to avoid violent conflicts, and chapter 6 discusses whether the states that emerge from recurring violent conflicts among predators could provide the basis for a peaceful political order at the global level.

   Throughout the book I have tried to indicate not only what we know but also what we do not know, and therefore I have tried both to provide references for readers who want to pursue these topics further and to identify specific questions to which we currently do not have good answers. There are undoubtedly many errors of my own to be found in the following pages, and I can only hope they will be productive ones. Right or wrong, little if any of what follows is original, and the parts that are original, if any, are also the parts that are most likely to be wrong. If a mistake that I have made motivates a reader to figure out exactly what the mistake is and to correct it, then my purpose will have been served.

   I have taken the ideas in this book from so many people that acknowledging them all poses a serious accounting problem, and I apologize if I have inadvertently omitted someone from the footnotes. But footnotes could not possibly convey the extent of my indebtedness to James Fearon and Robert Powell, whose writings have been the source of many of the ideas in this book and who have also repeatedly caused me to experience the bracing sensation of being unambiguously and embarrassingly wrong. Nor can footnotes adequately record my debt to Roy Licklider for inviting me to participate in a project on civil war termination, which first led me to appreciate the cost of separating the study of international politics from the study of domestic conflict.

   I also owe a great deal to a number of remarkable scholars who, while they were my colleagues at the University of Texas, were also my teachers. If any of them should happen to read this book they will recognize their influence at many places in it, and though I will refrain from listing their names here, I would like to express my gratitude to all of them for their intellectual generosity.

   I am also grateful for the comments and encouragement of a number of people who read part or all of the manuscript, and I would like especially to thank Michael Brenner, Scott Gartner, Hein Goemans, and Robert Rauchhaus for their extended comments. I thank also all the students who, over the years, have been involuntary audiences for previews of portions of this book.

A semester's leave from teaching funded by a Dean's Fellowship from the College of Liberal Arts at the University of Texas at Austin helped make my work on this book possible.

Portions of chapter 3 originally appeared in R. Harrison Wagner, "Bargaining and Conflict Management," in *Multiple Paths to Knowledge in International Relations: Methodology in the Study of Conflict Management and Conflict Resolution,* ed. Zeev Maoz et al. (Lanham, MD: Lexington Books, 2004). I gratefully acknowledge permission from Lexington Books to reprint selections from that work here.

Portions of chapters 4 and 5 originally appeared in R. Harrison Wagner, "Bargaining, War, and Alliances," *Conflict Management and Peace Science* 21, no. 3 (fall 2004): 215–31. These passages are reproduced by permission of Taylor & Francis Group, LLC, http://www.taylorandfrancis.com.

CHAPTER 1

The Theory of International Politics

Therefore, the seeker after the truth is not one who studies the writings of the ancients and, following his natural disposition, puts his trust in them, but rather the one who suspects his faith in them and questions what he gathers from them, the one who submits to argument and demonstration, and not to the sayings of a human being whose nature is fraught with all kinds of imperfection and deficiency. Thus the duty of the man who investigates the writings of scientists, if learning the truth is his goal, is to make himself the enemy of all that he reads, and, applying his mind to the core and margins of its content, attack it from every side. He should also suspect himself as he performs his critical examination of it, so that he may avoid falling into either prejudice or leniency.

(Ibn al-Haytham)[1]

Since the end of World War II, debates about the relation between war and the state among political scientists in the United States have been dominated by a body of ideas commonly called Realism and the criticisms those ideas have provoked.[2] Nearly every author who wants to write something portentous about international politics either defends Realism, invents a new species of it, or uses it as a point of departure for some other "ism" that he or she wants to defend. Prominent among these alternatives to Realism have been Liberalism (including what has been called neoliberal institutionalism) and Constructivism.

Because mathematical models based on the theory of games have been used to evaluate the competing claims made by Realists and their critics, debates about Realism have become embroiled in controversies about game theory, the use of mathematics to describe human behavior, and something called "rational choice theory." Some Constructivists have claimed that what is at stake is nothing less than fundamental issues in the philosophy of science or even something called "ontology." The result has been not only to make the controversies provoked by Realism even more

---

1. Quoted in Sabra 2003, 54.
2. I will always capitalize the term *Realism* when I use it to refer to the academic doctrine that goes by that name among students of international politics.

difficult to settle but also to create confusion about what a theory of international politics might consist of or how to evaluate it.

Theories, Arguments, and Explanations

I will argue that the fundamental cause of the unproductive nature of these controversies has been the willingness of political scientists to tolerate incomplete arguments. Indifference to the validity of arguments is often justified by the claim that the issues raised in these debates are fundamentally empirical ones and that therefore they can only be settled by looking at the facts. If what I have to say is to be persuasive, I must show why this common view is mistaken. Let us begin, then, by looking at a few simple examples that will make this clear.

Arguments and Explanations

Suppose you went to the dog pound to look for an inexpensive dog and wanted to make sure that any dog you got had a friendly disposition, was good with children, and would not maul a passing stranger. Suppose the attendant assured you that a particular dog would have those qualities. Skeptical, you might ask, "How do you know that, and why should I believe it?" The attendant might reply that the dog in question was a Labrador retriever. "So?" you might reply, to which the attendant might respond that Labrador retrievers are friendly dogs and are good with children.

The attendant's answers to your questions can be interpreted as an argument, perhaps the simplest possible argument that actually conveys new information. It has two premises: "Labrador retrievers are friendly and good with children" and "This dog is a Labrador retriever," from which it follows that "This dog will be friendly and good with children," which is what you wanted to know. The conclusion "follows from" the premises only because if one accepts the premises and denies the conclusion one would have contradicted oneself, which is why if one believes the premises one must also believe the conclusion. Arguments that have this property are called valid arguments, and reasoning from premises to conclusion in this way is commonly called "deductive reasoning."

However, this little argument would satisfy you only if you were confident that both of the premises were true. If one or both were not true, the argument would remain valid but the conclusion might be false. Suppose, then, that you asked why you should believe that this dog was a Labrador retriever—this is, after all, the dog pound. The attendant might reply that Labrador retrievers had certain recognizable characteristics such as a large, square head, short hair, a wide chest, and a friendly disposition, and this dog had those characteristics.

At first glance this looks like a deductive argument just like the first one: the first premise is that Labrador retrievers have certain recognizable characteristics, and the second is that this dog has all those characteristics. But if so, the argument is not valid, because it does not follow from these two premises that the dog is a Labrador retriever. Such an argument would be an example of a logical fallacy called "affirming the consequent" and therefore could not provide the assurance you were looking for.

But this would be a misunderstanding of the attendant's reasoning. The attendant is saying that the hypothesis that the dog is a Labrador retriever would explain its appearance, and thus its appearance gives us reason to believe that it is a Labrador retriever. There is a deductive argument here, but its premises are that "All Labrador retrievers have certain recognizable characteristics" and "This dog is a Labrador retriever," from which it would follow, if true, that this dog would have the properties of a Labrador retriever. But this is something that one does not have to be persuaded of, since the dog can be inspected directly. The question is, rather, what sort of dog is it? And the reasoning is that, since these premises, if true, would imply that the dog would have the appearance that it does have, the fact that it has that appearance is evidence that the premises are true. This is an example of what is commonly called "inductive reasoning," and the problem of induction is to figure out what justifies an inference of this sort.[3]

But we do not require a justification for reasoning in this way to do it.[4] What is important here is, rather, the fact that the inductive inference from the dog's visible characteristics to its breed is made possible by a deductive inference from the breed to a dog's visible characteristics: if the breed could not explain its appearance, then the breed could not be inferred from the appearance.[5] The problem is that there are other possible explanations of the dog's appearance, some of which might imply that it would be dangerous, and that is why inductive inference requires not just identifying a possible explanation of the facts but also supplying reasons to believe that

3. Probability theory provides a plausible answer to that question, since such an inference can be shown to be an application of Bayes's rule. For a recent discussion by a philosopher, see Howson 2000. For a discussion by a physicist, see Jaynes 2003.
4. A person who did not engage in inductive reasoning would not soon survive, since unlike most animals the behavior encoded in the genes of human beings is inadequate for humans to cope with their environment. Thus there is reason to believe that human beings are endowed with a propensity to engage in it—even infants do it (Ruse 1998; Gopnik, Meltzoff, and Kuhl 1999).
5. In the Bayesian interpretation of inductive inference, the deductive argument tells us that the conditional probability of the conclusion being true, given the truth of the premises, is one.

that explanation is better than other possible ones. Thus inductive inference is sometimes said to be "inference to the best explanation."[6]

Similarly, if you asked why you should believe that Labrador retrievers are good with children, you might be told that many people had had such dogs as pets and this was their uniform experience. Since the hypothesis that all Labrador retrievers are good with children would explain the fact that everyone who had had them as pets found them to be good with children, that fact is evidence that the hypothesis is true. However, a cautious person might wonder if there were other possible explanations of this fact.[7]

In spite of the fact that they are almost trivially simple, these examples illustrate how claims to knowledge are justified. More complex examples could be found in detective stories, murder trials, investigations of the causes of plane crashes, troubleshooting procedures for automobile mechanics or people who service computers, and throughout the natural sciences.

These examples also illustrate the fact that whether we are reasoning from premises to conclusions, or from observable facts to possible explanations of those facts, what is commonly called logical validity is necessary if our reasoning is to affect our beliefs: if the confidence we place in some premises is to be transferred to a conclusion then the conclusion must be implied by the premises, and if some explanation is to be supported by the facts then the facts must be implied by the explanation.[8] In these examples satisfying this requirement is so easy that it is possible to overlook it. Unfortunately, in even slightly more complicated situations it is possible to think one has satisfied it when one has not. We will see that this is true of much that has been written about international politics.

Science, Causes, Variables, and Theories

People who are interested in making the study of politics scientific often consult works on the philosophy of science to tell them what a science is supposed to consist of.[9] Many come away with the idea that the aim of sci-

---

6. C. S. Peirce called inference to the best explanation "abduction," and many writers restrict the word *induction* to inference from a sample to a population. My usage conforms to recent literature that argues that the logic of inference in the two cases is the same (Harman 1965; Thagard 1978; and Lipton 1991).
7. See, for example, Malcolm Gladwell's (2006) comparison between generalizations about the behavior of various breeds of dogs and the development of profiles of potential suspects by police.
8. Or at least the explanation must imply that the facts should have been expected with some probability.
9. For an engaging discussion of this sort of thing, see George Homans's (1984) autobiography.

ence is to identify causal regularities. Since a curve defined by an equation in which a dependent variable is a function of one or more independent variables seems to be a way of representing a causal regularity, statistical techniques for fitting such a curve to numerical data are often the standard by which the study of politics is judged. As a result, even people who do not use statistics couch their explanations in terms of independent and dependent variables, and attempts to explain individual events are commonly described as "small n studies" or "case studies" or are said to commit the statistical sin of "selection on the dependent variable."[10]

But the philosophy of science is mainly about the problem of induction, which is a problem for philosophers, not for scientists, and it is a serious mistake to think that one might find in it a blueprint for doing science. Moreover, the word *science* is not well defined, and the only thing that all the fields of study commonly called sciences seem to have in common is that (1) they all reward people for showing that existing explanations of the phenomena described by the field fail to meet the standards for justifying claims to knowledge discussed above, (2) they give even greater rewards to people who construct nonobvious explanations that survive attempts to discredit them in this way, and (3) they require scholars to make their work as easy to criticize as possible by making the reasoning that supports it transparent (Ziman 2000). Thus a plausible definition of *science* is just that it refers to any enterprise in which scholars compete with each other in constructing nonobvious explanations of the phenomena they study that can withstand concerted attempts to discredit them.[11]

It is not really clear what a "causal regularity" is, but by any ordinary definition of that term much of what is commonly called "science" is more concerned with explaining regularities than with identifying them. Science does not tell us that the sun rises in the east and sets in the west, that the sky is blue, or that the days are longer in the summer than in the winter—it explains those facts. Or, to take a less obvious example, cooks discovered that whipping egg whites into a meringue works best in a copper bowl. The physical sciences explain why that is true. The causal regularity was discovered by cooks; "science" explains it.[12]

---

10. For an influential example, see King, Keohane, and Verba 1994.

11. Many people believe that the philosopher Karl Popper defined at least one test for distinguishing between science and nonscience, and that is the requirement that propositions be falsifiable. However, while genetics may one day provide a means of falsifying the proposition that an anonymous dog at the dog pound has the genes that give Labrador retrievers their characteristic disposition, that is still, apparently, not possible. But that does not make inferences from its appearance to its breed meaningless or unjustifiable (Howson and Urbach 1993; Howson 2000; Ziman 2000, 226).

12. See Derry 1999, 4–6. Note that the explanation also increases our confidence that what cooks say is not just a superstition. See also the physical explanations in Chandrasekhar 1998.

However, what is called science does not just explain regularities, whether causal or otherwise; it also explains unique events, for example, where the HIV virus came from and, if it came from chimpanzees, how it got from animals to people. It is absurd to think that this is an example of a "small *n* study" that would be assisted by an increase in the size of the sample. Rather, the problem is to identify possible explanations of what happened and then to see how many of the known facts each explains.[13]

Consider the problem of explaining plane crashes. People charged with that grisly and important task often know very little about what happened: all the eyewitnesses may be dead, and the plane itself may be smashed to pieces and not fully recoverable. In addition to what can be recovered from the wreckage, they know the pattern formed by the debris, some of the weather conditions when the plane crashed, perhaps some or all of the data on the flight recorders, and sometimes a recording of radar images of the trajectory of the plane as it crashed. Their problem is to find an explanation that accounts not only for the plane crash but also for more of the other information at their disposal than does any other explanation. The plane crash is not a dependent variable whose variation might be accounted for by one or more independent variables. It is a fact, and what is wanted are some propositions from which, if true, that fact could be derived. Thus one must reason backward from what is known to what is unknown, and the only evidence there is for the truth of the investigators' conclusion is that it explains the known facts. However, since more than one explanation might account for those facts, an effort must be made to avoid settling on the first one that comes to mind.

One broad category of explanations for plane crashes falls under the heading of "pilot error." One might wonder if there is a relationship between such things as pilot training or flight schedules and pilot errors serious enough to cause plane crashes. If so, pilot error might be taken as a dependent variable, and one might test for a relationship between it and such independent variables as training procedures or frequency of flying. But such a relationship, if found, could not be said to explain the plane crashes. And to measure the dependent variable one must first have explained all the plane crashes individually, in order to know which ones were the result of pilot error and which were the result of mechanical failure or some other cause—the fact that all plane crashes are in some sense the same does not mean that they can all be explained in the same way. Moreover, to explain any plane crash one must first be able to explain why planes are able to fly.

Contrast this discussion of flight failure with the recent political sci-

---

13. See the account in Kolata 2001.

ence literature on "state failure."[14] In 1994, at the request of Vice President Al Gore, the U.S. government established a State Failure Task Force, composed of prominent social scientists, whose purpose was to determine what conditions were associated with the failure of states. It found three independent variables that accounted for most of the state failures—infant mortality, trade openness, and democracy—and on that basis made a number of policy recommendations to the U.S. government. What is one to make of such a study?

One criticism one might make is that it has not properly identified the dependent variable or that some of the independent variables are really part of the dependent variable (King and Zeng 2001, 654–55). But more serious problems are implied by our plane crash example. It is not clear how one could explain state failure without being able to explain state success, which we are far from being able to do. Moreover, as with plane crashes, there is no reason to think that all state failures (whatever that might mean) can be explained in the same way. And finally, in explaining the "failure" of any state, the problem is not to find independent variables that would account for the variation in some dependent variable but to find a set of propositions from which the facts of interest could be derived. One of those facts would be the relation between the independent and dependent variables reported by the State Failure Task Force.[15]

Some people would say that this implies that to understand state failure we need a theory of state success. But the word *theory* means so many things and has been used in so many different ways by political scientists that that would not be very informative. Any conjecture can be called a theory, and it would not be at all surprising to find a political scientist referring to studies of state failure of the sort just summarized as "state failure theory." Everyone aspires to "do theory," and it is often said that there are many different ways of doing it and we should be tolerant of all of them.[16]

However, while there may be many ways of "doing theory," there are

---

14. See especially the discussion in King and Zeng 2001.

15. Confusion between the relation between independent and dependent variables in a regression equation, on the one hand, and the relation between premises and conclusion in an explanatory argument, on the other, is common in political science, and many political scientists claim that a theory just consists of a specification of the relation among a set of variables. See, for example, Van Evera 1997, 7–48.

16. This usage reflects the influence of postmodernist writings on the study of literature. See the account in Culler 1997, chap. 1, titled "What Is Theory?" Culler writes: "In literary and cultural studies these days there is a lot of talk about theory—not theory of literature, mind you; just plain 'theory'. . . . 'Theory of what?' you want to ask. It is surprisingly hard to say. . . . Sometimes theory seems less an account of anything than an activity—something you do or don't do."

not many ways of constructing valid arguments that can serve as explanations of observed facts. What is wanted is not just anything that might be called a theory but an explanation from which the facts in question can actually be derived. It is that sort of theory that is the subject of this book.

Causality and Meaning

Many people would say that human behavior is too unpredictable for such explanations to be possible. However, after saying that, such people will often literally bet their lives that what they have said is not true by driving a car at seventy miles an hour down a highway while separated from cars traveling at the same speed in the opposite direction only by a painted yellow line. And in buying the car they drive they will have bet a lot of money that wherever they go there will be people willing to supply them with oil and gasoline to keep it running and to fix it when it breaks down. Human behavior is, in fact, very predictable, and if it were not, social organization would be impossible.

Ants seem remarkable to us because their social organization resembles that of humans, and they engage in complex forms of cooperation that look very much like war, gardening, and the domestication of animals.[17] In their famous book about ants, Hölldobler and Wilson say:

> The study of ant social organization is by necessity both a reductionistic and a holistic enterprise. The behavior of the colony as a whole can be understood only if the programs and positional effects of the individual members are both specified and explained more deeply at the physiological level. But such accounts are still far from complete. The information makes full sense only when the colonial pattern of each species is examined as an idiosyncratic adaptation to the natural environment in which the species lives. (1990, 3)

If one substitutes "psychological" for "physiological" in this quotation, one gets something very close to the following statement by the German sociologist Max Weber:

> Interpretive sociology considers the individual . . . and his action as the basic unit, as its "atom." . . . In general, for sociology, such concepts as "state," "association," "feudalism," and the like, des-

---

17. Comparisons between the social organization of humans and the social organization of insects can be found in both Hobbes and Aristotle. For a recent development of the theme, see Skyrms 2004, xi–xiv.

ignate certain categories of human interaction. Hence it is the task of sociology to reduce these concepts to "understandable" action, that is, without exception, to the actions of participating individual men. (Gerth and Mills 1946, 55)

These two quotations touch on two issues that are the source of vast amounts of unnecessary conflict and confusion. These issues have been revived by Constructivists in their quarrel with Realism.

One issue is whether the social sciences should be "reductionistic" or "holistic," to use the terminology of Hölldobler and Wilson. What they say of this in connection with the study of the social behavior of ants seems obviously true of human beings as well: it must be both.[18]

The other is whether substituting "psychological" for "physiological," in the quotation from Hölldobler and Wilson, implies that the scientific study of society is impossible. The basis for claiming that it does is that physiology is about what causes what, while psychology is, as Weber said, about meaning.[19] However, as already mentioned, it is not really clear what "causality" means, and if what we are interested in is finding nonobvious explanations for what happens, then it makes perfectly good sense to speak of social science—though, contrary to what many believe, doing so tells us little about how to proceed. And once it becomes clear that we are interested not simply in whether some dependent variable can be made to jiggle by yanking on some independent variable but in why that might be true, one can see that the same criteria for evaluating explanations apply to both realms.

We are curious about how to explain the complex social behavior of ants because it seems so much like what human beings do. If we are to find nonobvious explanations of human social behavior, we must learn to become as puzzled by what humans are capable of doing as we are by the ants. Thus, instead of looking for new, unsuspected regularities that might be found in human behavior, it might be useful to begin by thinking about whether we can explain the regularities in it that are as familiar to us as the rising and setting of the sun or the progress of the seasons and that we all take completely for granted. For example, instead of being puzzled by what is now called state failure, we should be puzzled by state success, which is actually the rarer phenomenon if, by the word *state,* we mean the

18. See the discussion of controversies about this issue among biologists by Edward O. Wilson (1994). For a very interesting discussion of this issue in the social sciences by an evolutionary biologist, see David Sloan Wilson (2002).
19. For an extended argument of this sort, see Winch 1958, which claims that "the conceptions according to which we normally think of social events are logically incompatible with the concepts belonging to scientific explanation" (95).

modern states, whose leaders are now so concerned about state failures around the world.[20]

Nonobvious explanations are, like nonobvious theorems, not obvious! There is nowhere to look up what they might be and no one to tell us in advance what will work and what will not. Unlike natural scientists, social scientists have the advantage of being able to think like the people whose behavior they want to explain.[21] Moreover, it is counterintuitive to think that one could be part of a social organization without already understanding it. But one can know the important elements of a good explanation without seeing their implications, especially if they imply an explanation that is different from one that everyone already accepts. In Darwin's time, the ideas of Thomas Malthus were widely known and what animal breeders did was familiar to nearly everyone. However, only two people saw that those ideas together implied that complex organisms could have developed without an intelligent designer: A. R. Wallace and Charles Darwin. They would not have done so had they stuck with what seemed obviously true to everyone else. It is also unlikely that they would have done so had they first consulted a treatise on the philosophy of science, or a statistics textbook, before proceeding.[22]

Models: Method or Madness?

A model is just something that is used to represent something else, like a model airplane. Everyone who has used a map or a house plan or an architect's drawing has used a model. The purpose of such models is to facilitate inferences about the thing that is modeled that would otherwise be difficult. You could try to figure out how to landscape your yard or arrange the furniture in your new house just by standing in the middle of it and thinking about how it will look, but you might find it easier to work with a drawing. Similarly, you could give your guests complicated verbal instructions about how to find your house, but it might be more effective to give them a map and let them draw the proper inferences from it.

Whenever we use models such as these we have to worry whether con-

---

20. See the discussion by Paul Seabright (2004) of how remarkable and puzzling the development of large-scale political and economic organizations by human beings really is.
21. This is not a trivial point, and it is important not just for social science but for human social organization as well (Ziman 2000, 107–9). See the fascinating discussion of the psychological literature on this subject in Baron-Cohen 1995.
22. Darwin's reasoning was criticized by some of the leading philosophers of his time for failing to satisfy appropriate standards of inductive inference—see the discussion in Hull 1973. For an account of the development of Darwin's ideas, see Mayr 1991, 68–89. See also Press and Tanur 2001, which contains accounts not only of the development of Darwin's ideas but of many other important scientific ideas as well. For further discussion of the problem of explanation in the social sciences, see the witty and enjoyable analysis in Homans 1967.

clusions that we reach that are true of the model also apply to the thing or things that the model represents. If a drawing of one's house or lawn is not drawn exactly to scale, then things that fit in the drawing won't fit in "the real world," and if roads that look straight on a map are really very crooked, then it may take longer to get to your house than your friends thought. There are always differences of this sort between models and the things they represent, and the question therefore is not whether the model is completely accurate (no model is or can be, or it would not be a model) but whether it is accurate enough for the purpose at hand. A map that is good enough to enable people to find your house might not be good enough to determine how much fiber-optic cable to buy if a company plans to wire your neighborhood or to plot the path of a cruise missile.[23]

The same is true of models of nonphysical things. Formal or symbolic logic, for example, is a system of arbitrary symbols and rules for manipulating them that was designed to represent logical inference. Since the rules for manipulating the symbols are absolutely clear, it is often easier to prove theorems by using them than it is by using words. However, that can lead to controversies about whether theorems that are true in this symbolic language always carry over to the ordinary language that everyone actually thinks in (Strawson 1952). And what is nowadays called rational choice theory, in disputes about theories and methods among political scientists, is really just a way of constructing mathematical models of people's choices, which can lead to similar controversies (Wagner 2001).

Since reasoning about models instead of the real thing can be misleading, there has to be a good reason for doing it. And since we explain people's choices all the time without constructing models of them, the whole idea may seem ridiculous. There are three main ways in which explanations involving human choices can become complex enough that models of them can be useful. One is that the consequences of the choices of many people taken together may not be obvious and may then interact with people's subsequent choices. This is what happens in markets and in electoral systems with competing political parties. A second is that individuals may be faced with uncertainty about the consequences of their choices, so their choices are not implied in any straightforward way by their preferences over final outcomes. And a third is that individuals' choices may be interdependent, in that what one person will choose depends on his or her expectations about how one or more other people will choose and vice versa. It is not possible to understand international

---

23. For a discussion of such issues concerning models in the natural sciences, with examples, see Derry 1999, 69–88. An excellent introduction to the use of models in the social sciences can be found in Lave and March 1993. For an introduction to the use of mathematical models in studying international politics, see Powell 1999.

politics without confronting all these problems, which is why mathematical models have become so important in the study of it.

Formal models have helped us think much more clearly about many
of the questions debated by students of international politics. However,
what one gets out of a formal model depends on what one puts into it, and
therefore game theory is not a ready-made theory of international politics,
and no formal model can compensate for a poorly framed question. Many
criticisms of formal models wrongly attribute the problems they identify to
the use of mathematics, when they are instead the result of the way the
problem has been formulated. The purpose of this chapter and the next
one is to look carefully at how the questions debated by students of international politics came to be formulated in the way that they have been. I
will then argue that they need to be reformulated.[24]

A Guide for the Reader

One impediment to settling the issues raised by Realists and their critics is
that it is not entirely clear what Realism is. There is now an embarrass-
ment of Realisms. There is classical Realism, neoclassical Realism, structural Realism (aka Neorealism), human nature Realism, defensive Real-
ism, and offensive Realism, and it may be undergoing further mutations as
I write. Thus it will be necessary to figure out not only what is distinctive
about each of the main varieties of Realism but also what, if anything,
they all have in common.

Because I am interested in evaluating the current state of the field and
not simply summarizing its historical development, I will begin with recent
varieties of Realism and work backward from there, concluding with an
examination of the origins of Realism. Along the way I will discuss the
criticisms of Realism that have been made by its main competitors. Following the guidelines laid down earlier, I will not try to summarize everything that writers who identify themselves with these "isms" have said but
will instead try to identify the main theses they have advanced and the
arguments they have offered in support of them. In the next chapter I will
examine the origins of these ideas in early modern European political
thought, a subject that is frequently discussed by contemporary defenders
of these competing doctrines but that they have often misinterpreted.

The purpose of these two chapters is to show that all these "isms" are

---

24. Unfortunately, defenders of formal models have contributed to confusion about their
significance by saying that their purpose is to help us think consistently. To be inconsistent is
to contradict oneself. The problem with the arguments made by students of international politics is not that they have been self-contradictory but that they have been invalid, that is,
believing their premises and denying their conclusions would *not* be inconsistent.

collections of bad answers to important questions. An understanding of what is wrong with these answers will, I hope, lead to a better understanding of the questions, which are much broader than is commonly assumed by modern-day Realists and their critics. Beginning in chapter 3 I will investigate what contemporary scholarship has to say about these questions.

Every chapter prior to chapter 6 will lead to a new set of questions, which will be the focus of the following chapter. Following chapter 6 I will try to summarize the implications of the preceding chapters.

Offensive Realism

A recent version of Realism that has received a lot of attention is offensive Realism, and its main proponent is John Mearsheimer.[25] The main thesis of offensive Realism is that even states that want only to be secure act aggressively, because the international system forces them to do so.

> This situation, which no one consciously designed or intended, is genuinely tragic. Great powers that have no reason to fight each other—that are merely concerned with their own survival—nevertheless have little choice but to pursue power and to seek to dominate the other states in the system. (Mearsheimer 2001, 3)

Thus whatever the nature of the component states, international politics "has always been a ruthless and dangerous business, and it is likely to remain that way" (2).

Unlike many writers, Mearsheimer actually lists five properties of international politics that together, he claims, logically imply this conclusion (30–32). They can easily be stated in the form of five premises:

Premise 1: *There is no world government.*
Premise 2: *All states are capable of using force against other states.*
Premise 3: *No state can ever be certain that another state will not use force against it.*
Premise 4: *All states seek to maintain their territorial integrity and domestic autonomy.*
Premise 5: *States are rational actors.*

After listing these assumptions, Mearsheimer says:

---

25. The distinction between offensive and defensive Realism is apparently due to Jack Snyder (1991, 10–13).

none of these assumptions alone dictates that great powers as a general rule *should* behave aggressively toward each other. There is surely the possibility that some state might have hostile intentions, but the only assumption dealing with a specific motive that is common to all states says that their principal objective is to survive, which by itself is a rather harmless goal. Nevertheless, when the five assumptions are married together, they create powerful incentives for great powers to think and act offensively with regard to each other. (32)

Thus Mearsheimer claims to have derived a strong, nonobvious conclusion from premises whose truth it would be hard to deny.

However, he makes no attempt to show that his conclusion follows from these premises. Had he done so, it would have been more obvious that, while his premises are clearly stated, it is far from clear what the conclusion actually is. In the passage quoted earlier, he says that, because of these properties of international politics, states "have little choice but to pursue power and to seek to dominate the other states in the system." And in the passage just quoted he says that these properties "create powerful incentives for great powers to think and act offensively with regard to each other." But, while it is clear that he thinks that these statements may be true even if the only objective of states is to survive, it is not really clear what they mean.

One possibility that is consistent with what he says is the following statement:

Conclusion 1 (Mearsheimer?) *Two states may go to war with each other even though they both want only to survive.*

But, while we may be able to think of circumstances in which this statement would be true, it does not follow from these premises.

Another possible interpretation of what he says is something like this:

Conclusion 2 (Mearsheimer?) *Even a state that wants only to survive will want to have more powerful military forces than all other states combined.*

But not even this statement follows from his premises.[26]

Because Mearsheimer never makes clear exactly what he thinks follows from his premises, the fact that his argument is not valid is not as

---

26. Note that the issue is not whether international politics has in fact often been a "ruthless and dangerous business," as Mearsheimer says, or even whether these hypothetical conclusions are sometimes true, but what would explain their truth and therefore whether they must be true as long as Mearsheimer's premises are true.

obvious to the reader as it might be. Impressed by the seemingly obvious truth of the premises, readers may be unjustifiably impressed by the argument itself.[27]

This is the key to explaining the dominant role that Realism has played in the study of international politics: it claims to derive strong conclusions about the behavior of states from properties of international politics that are difficult to deny. But the claim is unjustified, not just in Mearsheimer's case but in others as well.[28]

Defensive Realism

No Realist of any type would quarrel with any of Mearsheimer's five premises. Nonetheless, as Mearsheimer points out, other Realists do not accept his conclusion (Mearsheimer 2001, 19–22). (This would be more clearly true if it were clearer what his conclusion actually is.) But if Mearsheimer's claim about the implication of these premises is correct, they must have made a mistake in their reasoning. Yet nowhere does he say exactly what this mistake is.

For example, he says of Kenneth Waltz, the most prominent of the scholars he identifies as a "defensive realist," that there is a "status quo bias" in his theory, leaving one with the impression that Waltz merely assumes that states only want to protect the status quo, without seeing that his own assumptions imply something different (20). However, Waltz did not merely assume that states were not interested in aggressively expanding; he argued that even if they were inclined to expand, the very features of the international system that Mearsheimer describes would lead them not to do so. Mearsheimer simply ignores Waltz's argument, asserts a different conclusion, and gives it a distinctive name to emphasize the nature of the difference.[29]

---

27. On the cover of the paperback edition of Mearsheimer's book, Samuel Huntington is quoted as saying of it: "All serious students of international affairs will have to come to grips with its argument." On the back, the *Economist* is quoted as saying that Mearsheimer "demolishes all the main components" of the "happy vision" of international politics that emerged at the end of the cold war.

28. Mearsheimer's third premise is actually far more questionable than it appears to be. I will examine it in chapter 6. But first we must determine why it is important.

29. Schweller (1996) also claims that Waltz assumed that states were only interested in security, not expansion. Waltz is frequently unclear, but he flatly and explicitly says otherwise in more than one place. "Beyond the survival motive," he wrote, "the aims of states may be endlessly varied; they may range from the ambition to conquer the world to the desire merely to be left alone." What he assumed was just that "[s]urvival is a prerequisite to achieving any goals that states may have" (Waltz 1979, 91). Otherwise the argument summarized subsequently would have been unnecessary, and his reasoning would have been not merely invalid but absurd.

Waltz's argument, while no more valid than Mearsheimer's, makes even more apparent the fact that Mearsheimer's argument is not valid either. It rests on the fact that, when there are more than two states in the world, one state cannot expand without giving another an opportunity to expand as well, in which case an increase in one state's absolute level of military capabilities might leave it relatively worse off than it was before. Hence, Waltz claims, the nature of international politics forces all states to focus on preserving their own independence by forming balancing coalitions rather than on maximizing their own power. Thus even expansionist states

> cannot let power, a possibly useful means, become the end they pursue. The goal the system encourages them to seek is security. Increased power may or may not serve that end. (Waltz 1979, 126)

Mearsheimer claims, however, that the nature of international politics forces even satisfied states to be aggressive in order to maximize their power. Yet both claim to have derived their conclusions from exactly the same properties of international politics.

Mearsheimer, as we have seen, makes no attempt to show that his conclusion follows from these properties. This is Waltz's attempt to justify his conclusion:

> Because power is a means and not an end, states prefer to join the weaker of two coalitions. . . . If states wished to maximize power, they would join the stronger side, and we would see not balances forming but a world hegemony forged. This does not happen because balancing, not bandwagoning, is the behavior induced by the system. The first concern of states is not to maximize power but to maintain their positions in the system.
>
> Secondary states, if they are free to choose, flock to the weaker side, for it is the stronger side that threatens them. (Waltz 1979, 126–27)

This is the entirety of Waltz's argument in support of his claim that anarchy leads to "the recurrent formation of balances of power" (119). But it is not valid. A state that joins with the more powerful of two states to fight the third will confront a more powerful adversary after victory, but if it allies with the weaker state instead it will be less likely to be victorious. Without more information we cannot say what it should be expected to do.[30]

---

30. For an extended analysis of the question raised by this passage from Waltz's book, see Powell 1999, chap. 5.

In discussing the difference between offensive and defensive Realism, Snyder says:

> anarchy is not in itself sufficient to predict an expansionist security strategy. Realist scholars argue that the normal response to threat is to form a balancing alliance. Therefore states should expect that expansion will reduce their security insofar as it threatens other states and provokes an opposing coalition. (1991, 22)

This may be what some people who have identified themselves as Realists say. But there is no more reason to believe that it is true than there is to believe Mearsheimer's claim for the opposite view.

Structural Realism

The claim that propositions about the behavior of states can be deduced from properties of the state system is the most basic idea in what is often called structural Realism, or Neorealism. This claim was advanced originally by Kenneth Waltz, but it is accepted by Mearsheimer as well, and therefore offensive and defensive Realisms are both varieties of structural Realism. What is not commonly recognized is that the mere fact that structural Realists disagree about which of these views is correct is enough to call structural Realism itself into question.[31] However, there is more to structural Realism than just the question of whether the international system makes states expansionist or instead curtails any expansionist tendencies they might have.

There are two important structural attributes of a state system, according to Waltz. All state systems, he claimed, are alike in having anarchic rather than hierarchical structures. However, there are also structural differences among anarchic systems as a result of differences in the distribution of power among the constituent states (Waltz 1979, 79–101). The disagreement between defensive and offensive Realists is one of the questions that arise about the properties of all systems with an anarchic structure. The other main issue raised by structural Realism is what differences

---

31. Instead, people who are reluctant to conclude that published works might just be wrong often try to save structural Realism by claiming that disagreements among Realists are the result of differing tacit assumptions made by authors who disagree. However, not only is there no textual basis for doing this, but typically no attempt is made to show that the respective arguments might be valid even with the extra assumptions. For an example, see Brooks 1997.

among anarchic systems can be attributed to differences in the distribution of power within them.[32]

Prior to Waltz, most writers about international politics focused on the question of whether power among states was distributed equally or unequally.[33] Since Waltz's writing, nearly everyone has focused on whether systems were characterized by a bipolar or a multipolar distribution of power. There have been controversies about what sort of state behavior can be expected in each type of system and also about whether other types of "polarity" are possible and what effect they might have. I will have more to say about the effects of anarchy later. First let us consider the polarity of state systems.

Waltz's distinction between bipolarity and multipolarity was a product of debates about how to understand the cold war. During the period between 1945 and 1950, when it gradually became clear that World War II would not, as most people had expected, end like World War I with a comprehensive peace settlement but would lead instead to a protracted conflict between the United States and the Soviet Union, there were two features of the international situation that many people found deeply disturbing. One was the development of nuclear weapons, whose existence was unknown to most people until 1945. The other was the fact that after World War II the major powers seemed to be organizing themselves into two hostile coalitions separated by unbridgeable ideological differences. At some point this second feature of postwar international politics began to be referred to as "bipolarity."

The combination of nuclear weapons with bipolarity led many people to fear that civilization itself was threatened. It is ironic that by the end of the cold war many people had concluded that it was precisely those two features of international politics that had turned the cold war into what some people now call "the long peace" (Gaddis 1987). While Waltz originally accepted the view that nuclear weapons were very dangerous, he was almost single-handedly responsible for convincing many people that bipolarity was good, not bad—good enough, in fact, to compensate for the dangers posed by nuclear weapons (Waltz 1964).[34]

Waltz claimed that people who were concerned about the polarization of the world into two nuclear-armed camps as a result of the cold war had misunderstood the situation. What had happened was not that the world had divided into two cohesive alliances of the traditional sort but rather

---

32. While Waltz was responsible for the idea that international systems could be characterized by their structures, it is important to recognize that a very large part of what Waltz said about the effects of a system's structure on the behavior of states within it was first said by John Herz. Herz's discussion is often clearer than Waltz's. See especially Herz 1959.
33. See, for example, Claude 1962, chaps. 1–3; Sheehan 1996.
34. Later Waltz (1981) also argued that nuclear weapons were actually a good thing too.

that the number of great powers had been reduced to two. And a world in which there are just two great powers, he claimed, is less prone to war than a world in which there are more than two (Waltz 1964; 1979, 168–70). He called a world with just two great powers a bipolar world and a world with more than two great powers a multipolar world, and the names stuck.[35]

Why did Waltz think that a bipolar world was less war-prone than a multipolar world? Because, he claimed,

> States are less likely to misjudge their relative strengths than they are to misjudge the strength and reliability of opposing coalitions. Rather than making states properly cautious and forwarding the chances of peace, uncertainty and miscalculation cause wars. . . . In a bipolar world uncertainty lessens and calculations are easier to make. (Waltz 1979, 168)

Because alliances are important in a multipolar world but are not in a bipolar world, in other words, the sorts of miscalculations that lead to war are less likely in a bipolar world.

Is this a valid argument? Let us try to reconstruct it. Clearly one of Waltz's premises is just a definition:

Premise 1 (Waltz) Definition: *A bipolar world is one in which there are two great powers, and a multipolar world is one in which there are more than two great powers.*

Another premise is:

Premise 2 (Waltz) *Miscalculations of the relative strength or behavior of opposing states or coalitions of states can cause wars to occur.*

A third is:

Premise 3 (Waltz) *States are less likely to miscalculate the strength or behavior of states than of opposing coalitions.*

And the conclusion is:

Conclusion 1 (Waltz) *War is less likely in a bipolar world than in a multipolar world.*

---

35. However, the distinction, as well as the terminology and much of the argument Waltz gave for its significance, had earlier been introduced into the literature by John Herz (1959).

It should be obvious that this is not a valid argument.

What is missing? At the very least we need the following two additional premises:

Premise 4 *The only miscalculations that can lead to war are miscalculations about the relative strength or behavior of the great powers.*

Premise 5 *There is no other possible cause of war that might be more likely to occur in a bipolar world than in a multipolar one.*

If we believe the fourth premise, then reducing the number of great powers to two implies that incorrect expectations about the behavior or performance of coalitions cannot lead to war. And if we believe the fifth then there is no other possible factor that might influence the likelihood of war that we need to be concerned about. However, it is far from clear why we should believe either premise, and Waltz does not say why we should.

Waltz's silence on the fifth premise is an indirect consequence of the more general fact that he has virtually nothing to say about why war occurs at all (his second premise is justified by a reference to an earlier edition of Blainey 1988). This is a point that I will return to later. A close reading of what he says about bipolarity, however, will show that his silence on the question raised by the fourth premise is apparently the result of confusing a reduction in the number of *great powers* in the world with a reduction in the number of *states.* Clearly when there are only two states in the world, uncertainty about who will ally with whom in a conflict between them cannot arise. As Waltz put it:

> Systems of two have qualities distinct from systems of three or more. What is the defining difference? . . . Where two powers contend, imbalances can be righted only by their internal efforts. With more than two, shifts in alignment provide an additional means of adjustment. (1979, 163)

Waltz claimed, in effect, that a reduction in the number of great powers to two was equivalent to a reduction in the number of states in the world to two. But nowhere does he say why this should be true.

Indeed, he could not possibly say that, because he never defines what a great power is. He expresses impatience at the question, saying that "one finds general agreement about who the great powers of a period are, with occasional doubt about marginal cases," but admits that "[w]e should not be surprised if wrong answers are sometimes arrived at." "The question," he says, "is an empirical one, and common sense can answer it" (Waltz 1979, 131). In fact, however, common sense cannot answer the question, since the term *great power* has no standard meaning. Definitions without arguments are often pedantic, but arguments without definitions are often not valid. That is why mathematicians are so picky about definitions.[36]

Thus the seeming plausibility of Waltz's reasoning about the difference between a bipolar and a multipolar world was the result of his equivocation between the number of states in the world and the distribution of power between or among them. As a result, he showed neither that during the cold war there were only two great powers nor, if that were true, that that fact would have the consequences he claimed for it. Moreover, his claim that bipolarity rendered other states unimportant to the United States and the USSR during the cold war would, if true, make it impossible to understand why the cold war occurred at all.[37]

It is a remarkable fact that, in spite of all the discussion and debate about bipolarity and multipolarity, not to mention the possible consequences of "unipolarity" since the end of the cold war, neither Waltz nor anyone else has ever specified what the "polarity" of an international system refers to. And therefore no one has ever presented a valid argument in support of the claim that states behave differently in systems with different polarities.[38]

Anarchy and War

We have seen that offensive Realists believe that the anarchic nature of international politics forces states to be aggressive, while defensive Realists believe that even states inclined to aggression are forced by the anarchic structure of the system to create balances of power instead. All structural Realists agree, however, that interstate wars will continue to occur as long as there is no world government.

Some advocates of world government would agree with this proposition, and their only disagreement with structural Realists concerns the fea-

---

36. For one of the few systematic discussions of how the term might be defined, see Levy 1983, 10–19.
37. For further discussion, see Wagner 1993. On the importance of third states for understanding the cold war, see especially Trachtenberg's (1999) discussion of the role of Germany.
38. Schweller, in an analysis of what he calls "tripolarity," defines a "pole" as a state that possesses "at least half of the resources of the most powerful state in the system" (1998, 46). But he then proceeds to discuss tripolar systems as though they were three-state systems and therefore, like Waltz, confuses the number of states with the distribution of power among them. Moreover, Schweller includes forces in being as part of his measure of military capabilities. But forces in being are a function of the decisions made by states and therefore cannot be part of the structure of an international system, which is supposed to constrain the decisions of states.

sibility and/or desirability of world government. Many other people have thought, however, that peace could be achieved without world government. Trade, democracy, socialism, international institutions that fall short of being a world government, or just a common realization that war is self-defeating have all been advanced as possible causes of peace among states. Structural Realists are pessimistic about these suggestions, not because they have examined each of them and concluded it would not have the predicted effects (though there are, of course, many disagreements about the predicted effects of all these factors) but because they think they have an argument that shows that none of these factors, *or any others that one might suggest,* could possibly eliminate interstate wars. This is a very strong claim. Is there any reason to believe it is true?

The claim is that in any anarchic system wars will occur. *Anarchy* just means that there is no world government, so the implicit premises in the structural Realist argument include at least some of those stated by Mearsheimer:

Premise 1 (Anarchy) *There is no world government.*

Premise 2 (Anarchy) *All states are capable of using force against other states.*

Premise 3 (Anarchy) *All states seek to maintain their territorial integrity and domestic autonomy.*

The justification for thinking that this last premise is part of what is meant by anarchy is, perhaps, that if it were not true states would abandon anarchy and create a world government.

In addition, since our goal is to establish what is the best we could expect from an anarchic system, it makes sense to use another of Mearsheimer's premises:

Premise 4 (Best case assumption) *States are rational actors.*

It is not really clear what *rational* means here, but a case for the possibility of peace that relied on the irrationality of states would not be a very strong case, so let us stick it in here and worry about exactly what it means later.

This appears to me to be about as far as one can go in writing down what is implied simply by saying that the interstate system is anarchic. But what are these premises together supposed to imply about the occurrence of war? Waltz has virtually nothing to say about that in *Theory of International Politics* (1979), which is usually taken to be the canonical statement of structural Realism, and what he does say seems to contradict the claim that anarchy is an important part of the explanation of war. The main claim in that book is, rather, that anarchy leads to balances of power, as we have seen. To see what Waltz thought about the relation between anarchy and war, one must look at his first book, *Man, the State and War* (1959), and a later article entitled "The Origins of War in Neorealist Theory" (1988).

Many people seem to have the impression that Waltz's structural Realism is Hobbes's account of the state of nature in modern dress. But Waltz's inspiration was Rousseau, not Hobbes, and in Waltz's first book he attributes to Rousseau the idea that

> wars occur because there is nothing to prevent them. Rousseau's analysis explains the recurrence of war without explaining any given war. He tells us that war may at any moment occur, and he tells us why this is so. (1959, 232)

The conclusion Waltz expects us to derive from premises that describe an anarchic interstate system, therefore, would appear to be this one:

Conclusion 1 (Structural Realism) *War may at any moment occur.*

But this conclusion plainly does not follow from these premises.

What is missing? The premises obviously imply that in anarchy, as Waltz said, there is nothing to prevent states from using force if they want to, but the conclusion would be true only if at any moment some state may want to. Suppose, then, we added a premise that said, "At any moment some state may want to use force against another state." But this would beg the question! No one would doubt that states can use force whenever they want to. The question we started with was whether trade or democracy or something else might lead them not to want to do so. Structural Realism claims that anarchy makes this impossible, but it turns out that Waltz just assumed that it is. The reason this is not obvious is that Waltz confuses the *possibility* of war, which cannot be doubted, with its *probability,* which is what is in question.[39]

Lest one think I am being unfair to Waltz, the following passage makes crystal clear that that is exactly what he did:

> According to the third image [i.e., structural Realism], there is a constant possibility of war in a world in which there are two or more states each seeking to promote a set of interests and having no agency above them upon which they can rely for protection. But many liberals and socialist revisionists deny . . . the possibil-

---

39. As long as planes fly, plane crashes will be possible. But they are sufficiently infrequent that most people do not worry about them.

ity that wars would occur in a world of political or social democracies. An understanding of the third image makes clear that the
expectation would be justified only if the minimum interest of
states in preserving themselves became the maximum interest of
all of them—and each could rely fully upon the steadfast adherence to this definition by all of the others. Stating the condition
makes apparent the utopian quality of liberal and socialist expectations. (Waltz 1959, 227)

The expectations may possibly be utopian, but if they are, it is plainly not
the absence of a world government that makes them so.

In the passage just quoted, Waltz said that for an anarchic system to
be peaceful it would be necessary not only that no state wanted to use force
but also that all states knew that this was true. To many structural Realists
this is the key to the relation between anarchy and war. It seems to suggest
the possibility of a much stronger and more interesting conclusion than
the one Waltz got from Rousseau:

> **Conclusion 2 (Structural Realism)** *At any moment some state may
> choose to use force against another state, even if no state expects
> to gain from doing so.*

Note the similarity of this conclusion to the first of the conclusions that
one might attribute to Mearsheimer that was discussed previously. As we
have seen, it does not follow from Mearsheimer's premises, and it is not
implied by the premises describing a world of independent states just discussed. Some people believe that it is implied by what is called the security
dilemma.

The Security Dilemma

Although many people associate the notion of a security dilemma with
Waltz's structural Realism, the idea was John Herz's, and it is unclear
from Waltz's own writings exactly what he thought about it. It was first
presented in an article published in 1950, nine years before Waltz's first
book was published. This article defends the same thesis that Waltz
defended in his book but offers a different justification for it. Remarkably, Waltz does not even cite it. Herz claimed that anarchy leads to war,
not, as Waltz said, because in anarchy there is nothing to prevent it but
because

> Wherever such anarchic society has existed—and it has existed in
> most periods of known history on some level—there has arisen

what may be called the "security dilemma" of men, or groups, or
their leaders. (Herz 1950, 157)

But what is a security dilemma? According to Herz, groups or individuals
who "live alongside each other without being organized into a higher
unity"

> must be . . . concerned about their security from being attacked,
> subjected, dominated, or annihilated by other groups and indi-
> viduals. Striving to attain security from such attack, they are dri-
> ven to acquire more and more power in order to escape the impact
> of the power of others. This, in turn, renders the others more inse-
> cure and compels them to prepare for the worst. Since none can
> ever feel entirely secure in such a world of competing units, power
> competition ensues, and the vicious circle of security and power
> accumulation is on. (157)

He goes on to claim that

> families and tribes may overcome the power game in their internal
> relations in order to face other families or tribes; larger groups
> may overcome it to face other classes unitedly; entire nations may
> compose their internal conflicts in order to face other nations. But
> ultimately, somewhere, conflicts caused by the security dilemma
> are bound to emerge among political units of power. (158)

It appears that Herz was an "offensive Realist" long before Mearsheimer
was. We have already seen that Waltz explicitly denied that states seeking
security from attack will, as Herz claimed, be "driven to acquire more and
more power in order to escape the impact of the power of others." However, in his later article "The Origins of War in Neorealist Theory," Waltz
cites Herz's article and says that the security dilemma is the link between
anarchy and war (1988, 619). This adds to the puzzle of what Waltz
thought the connection between anarchy and war really was.

Whatever the answer to that question might be, the more important
question is whether (1) there is any reason to think that anarchy must lead
to a security dilemma and (2) there is any reason to think that security
dilemmas lead to war. Let us begin by looking at what Herz says a security
dilemma is.

The most common interpretation of what Herz had in mind seems
also to be the most plausible one. It can be captured in two premises,
which we can add to the ones listed previously that describe a world of
independent states. The first premise is as follows:

Premise 5 (Security dilemma) *An increase in one state's ability to protect itself from an attack by others will diminish the ability of other states to protect themselves from an attack by the first state.*

This seems to be an obvious consequence of the fact that military power is relative, so that, for example, the number of infantry divisions one state needs to defend itself against another depends on how many infantry divisions the other state has, and so an increase in the size of one state's military forces will reduce the chances of success of its potential adversary.

However, no state would care about the size of another state's military forces if it were certain that the other state would never use them in an attack. And therefore if the fact that power is relative is to have any significance we need the following premise as well:

Premise 6 (Security dilemma) *No state can ever be certain that another state will not use force against it.*

Note that this is identical to one of Mearsheimer's premises discussed earlier.

In fact, we now have a set of premises identical to Mearsheimer's except for the addition of one premise, which merely states the obvious fact that only relative, not absolute, military capabilities are important for a state's security. It is obvious that neither conclusion 1 nor conclusion 2 follows from these premises, any more than the various possible interpretations of Mearsheimer's conclusions followed from his. Thus the security dilemma is of no help whatsoever in showing that it is utopian to think that a world of independent states might be peaceful.[40]

Before moving on, let us notice exactly what is missing in this argument. It is certainly possible that, in a world of independent states, no state would actually expect to benefit from war. Thus if anarchy alone is to lead to war, then war must be possible even if no state expects to benefit from it. But if no state actually uses force against another, then no war will occur no matter how apprehensive states might be about its possibility. Thus if anarchy alone is to lead to war, there must be some reason to expect that anarchy alone will lead a state to use force against another state *merely because it fears that another state might use force against it.* There are obviously occasions when states might do such a thing. Indeed, that is what the United States and Britain did against Iraq in the second war in the Persian Gulf. However, the conditions that make that possible

---

40. As noted earlier, it is far from clear why we should believe that premise 6 is true. The important point to note here, however, is that, even if it is true, structural Realism's main claim about the relation between anarchy and war is still not supported.

are not implied simply by the absence of a world government. Nor, as we will see, would a world government make it impossible for such conditions to exist.

Offense and Defense

In addition to doubting whether the sixth premise is true, one might also doubt whether the fifth premise must be true. Clearly it is true of infantry and tanks. But it does not seem to be true of fortifications: increasing the strength or number of one state's castles does not appear to diminish the effectiveness of another state's castles.[41] Moreover, the condition that came to be known as mutual assured destruction (or MAD) seems to imply that it is not true of nuclear weapons either: once a state with nuclear weapons has a secure second strike capability, it is not obvious that it needs more nuclear weapons or that, if it acquires more, its adversary's ability to protect its independence is diminished.

Examples such as these led Robert Jervis to argue, in one of the most influential articles about international politics ever written, that the truth of the fifth premise depended on two factors: "whether defensive weapons and policies can be distinguished from offensive ones, and whether the defense or the offense has the advantage" (Jervis 1978, 186).[42] Paradoxically, even though Jervis questioned whether the fifth premise was always true, his article nonetheless helped convince many people that the security dilemma was the key to understanding why war occurred. The reason is that his article seemed to explain something that was otherwise unexplained by structural Realism.

Even people who did not ask whether Waltz's structural Realist argument was valid noticed that anarchy was a constant property of international politics, but the frequency of war varied greatly. The only explanation of that fact that Waltz had to offer was the distinction between bipolar and multipolar systems. But he claimed that

> Until 1945 the nation-state system was multipolar, and always with five or more powers. In all of modern history the structure of

---

41. Be careful not to be misled by this example, however: castles are fairly immobile, but fortifications can be constructed as infantry forces advance, and so they are more mobile than they might appear to be. If they can be used to protect troops as they advance against the enemy, then they add to the effectiveness of infantry.

42. The effect of the relation between offensive and defensive capabilities on the likelihood of war was the subject of a book by George Quester (1977) published shortly before Jervis's famous article. Jervis's article helped stimulate a long debate about this question that is still going on. Representative selections from the literature can be found in Brown et al. 2004. For a recent survey, see Morrow 2002.

international politics has changed only once. We have only two systems to observe. (Waltz 1979, 163)

Yet prior to the "long peace" of the cold war, there was the "long peace" of the nineteenth century. The distinction between bipolarity and multipolarity could not account for this. Perhaps what Jervis called the "offense-defense balance" could.

Thus Jervis's discussion of the offense-defense balance only reinforced many people's belief that the most fundamental cause of war is indeed anarchy and the security dilemma, though the security dilemma may be attenuated if military technology favors the defense. There are, however, two problems with this inference. First, as we have already seen, anarchy and the security dilemma alone do not imply that war will occur, even if defensive capabilities are not dominant. Thus anarchy and the security dilemma cannot explain why wars occur even when the conditions described by the security dilemma exist. And therefore, second, there is no reason to believe that changing the offense-defense balance will change the likelihood of war at all.

We have already noted that one of the things missing in Waltz's discussion of the relation between polarity and war is any explanation of why wars ever occur. The same is true of both Herz's and Jervis's discussion of the security dilemma. Without such an explanation it is not possible to say what the effect of the offense-defense balance might be on the likelihood of war. This question will be the focus of subsequent chapters.

Even without such an explanation, however, there are good reasons to doubt Jervis's claim that changing the offense-defense balance will change the likelihood of war. For one effect of a situation in which the defense has the advantage might be that states that fight each other are unlikely to risk being disarmed. If so, then war would be less risky than if the offense had the advantage and therefore possibly more attractive.

It is unlikely, for example, that the Palestinians thought in recent years that they could defeat the Israeli army. At the same time Israel has been unable to disarm the Palestinians. Surely this does not make the armed conflict between them puzzling but instead helps explain why it occurs—otherwise the Palestinians either would never have dared challenge the Israelis or would long ago have been disarmed by them. Similarly, the eighteenth century was characterized by frequent wars, and the nineteenth by a long peace. Yet it seems odd to suggest that the offense had a greater advantage in the eighteenth century than in the nineteenth—in fact, exactly the opposite seems to be true. It seems unlikely, therefore, that variations in the salience of the security dilemma could actually account for the difference between them.[43]

---

43. For a development of this point, see Fearon 1995a.

The Security Dilemma and the Prisoner's Dilemma

In his famous article, Jervis also gave another reason to question whether the security dilemma must have dire consequences. He claimed that it could be represented by the famous 2×2 game commonly called the Prisoner's Dilemma, in which "there is no solution that is in the best interests of all the participants." This would seem to justify pessimism about the ability of independent states to avoid conflict. However, if the Prisoner's Dilemma game is expected to be repeated indefinitely, he said, then cooperation becomes possible, though still not certain. This would imply that violent conflict among states might be avoidable (Jervis 1978, 171).

By offering the Prisoner's Dilemma game as a model for the security dilemma, Jervis seemed to provide additional support for the view that the security dilemma was the key to understanding the recurrence of war among independent states. At the same time, by showing that the security dilemma did not make war inevitable, this model provided yet another way of showing how anarchy, which was constant, could explain the occurrence of war, which was not.

Unfortunately, the only connection between the security dilemma and the Prisoner's Dilemma is that they both have the word *dilemma* in their names. And therefore, like his discussion of the offense-defense balance, the additional plausibility that Jervis's use of the Prisoner's Dilemma gave to the idea that anarchy made peace among independent states unlikely was quite unwarranted.

The security dilemma, remember, is represented by premises 5 and 6. The Prisoner's Dilemma is represented in figure 1.[44] The "dilemma" in the Prisoner's Dilemma is the result of two facts, both obvious from figure 1: (1) each player would want to choose D, whatever he expects the other to do, but (2) if they do that, they will end up with an outcome worse for both than if they had both chosen C.

	C	D
C	(3, 3)	(1, 4)
D	(4, 1)	(2, 2)

Fig. 1. The Prisoner's Dilemma

In thinking about what relation there could possibly be between these two so-called dilemmas, note first that part of the definition of the security

---

44. The first number in each cell is the payoff to the row player, and the second is the payoff to the column player. They merely represent the preferences of the players, with bigger numbers being preferred to smaller ones. The labeling of the choices is conventional and is the result of the fact that they are customarily thought of as "Cooperate" or "Defect." However, the names have no significance whatever.

dilemma is that states are uncertain about what each other's preferences actually are. However, in the Prisoner's Dilemma it is assumed that the players' preferences are commonly known and there is no uncertainty about them. Note second that in the Prisoner's Dilemma the essence of the problem is not the players' preferences but the constraints under which they must choose: they must *independently* choose only once between two alternatives. The security dilemma, however, does not specify what choices states must make or how they will go about making them—that is why one cannot infer from it anything about what choices they can be expected to make. It merely says that, when they choose what military capabilities to have, an increase or decrease in one state's military capabilities will change the relative size of the other's.

Suppose, for example, that states are choosing between arming and not arming. Then, one might think, premise 5 would imply that they would have the preferences represented in figure 1. But if states can observe each other's arms levels and respond to them, their choices would not be restricted to simply arming or not but would include as well the possibility of arming if the other does but not arming if it does not. That would not be a Prisoner's Dilemma, even if states had the preferences represented in figure 1. Moreover, if they did both arm they would be worse off than if they had not, but that does not imply that they would fight each other.[45]

Of course, if the Prisoner's Dilemma is expected to be repeated, then the choice that a state makes in one round can be based on the choice that the other state made in the previous round. But each must still pay the price of the other's defection if that is what it chose. It is not clear why this must be so or even what it would mean in any concrete case. Moreover, if the choice involves war (as it must, if the security dilemma is to explain why wars occur), then it is not clear why states would expect that exactly the same game would be played again after a war occurred. In fact, one might think that if states could expect that they would always be around to play the next stage of a repeated Prisoner's Dilemma game, they would enjoy a far greater degree of security than Herz thought they could possibly have.

Finally, let us note that Jervis claimed not only that the security dilemma could be represented by a repeated Prisoner's Dilemma but also that a repeated Prisoner's Dilemma could be represented by the 2×2 game often called the Stag Hunt. The Stag Hunt is portrayed in figure 2. Note

---

45. Jervis says, "A relatively low cost of CD has the effect of transforming the game from one in which both players make their choices simultaneously to one in which an actor can make his choice after the other has moved" (1978, 172). This is obviously not true. But there is no reason to assume that states must make their choices simultaneously in the first place.

that it is different from the Prisoner's Dilemma only in that the players' preferences between joint cooperation and defecting when the other cooperates are reversed. Now, if one player expects the other to choose C, he will want to choose C as well, whereas each will want to choose D only if he expects the other to choose D. In the lingo of game theory, this means that, instead of each having a dominant choice of D, there are two pure strategy Nash equilibria, CC and DD, and determining which will occur depends on what each expects the other to do.[46]

	C	D
C	(4, 4)	(1, 3)
D	(3, 1)	(2, 2)

Fig. 2. The Stag Hunt

However, while in this game, as in the repeated Prisoner's Dilemma, both joint cooperation and joint defection are equilibria, the Stag Hunt is not the repeated Prisoner's Dilemma but is instead just another one-shot 2×2 game like the one-shot Prisoner's Dilemma. Furthermore, in the Stag Hunt the preferences of the players are common knowledge, and therefore the uncertainty confronted by the players of this game, if there is any, is the result of the existence of more than one equilibrium in the game and not uncertainty about what the other state's preferences might be. But the security dilemma is defined by uncertainty about what other states' preferences might be.

The name "Prisoner's Dilemma" is based on the fact that the game was originally illustrated by a story about two prisoners who were induced to confess to a crime by a clever district attorney who, by separating them, forced them to choose independently between confessing or not confessing. The name "Stag Hunt" is based on the fact that the game with that name seems to represent a situation described by Rousseau in his *Discourse on the Origins of Inequality*, which Waltz had used in his book *Man, the State and War* to illustrate the effect of anarchy (Waltz 1959, 167–71).

However, Rousseau used the story not to make a point about international politics but to illustrate what he thought was the lack of foresight of primitive men, who "were so far from troubling themselves about the distant future, that they hardly thought of the morrow."

---

46. A Nash equilibrium is just a set of plans for making choices (called a "strategy"), one for each individual, such that if everyone expects everyone else to choose the appropriate strategy in this set, no one would have any incentive to choose some other strategy. There is also a mixed strategy equilibrium in this game, but I will ignore it.

If a deer was to be taken, every one saw that, in order to succeed, he must abide faithfully by his post: but if a hare happened to come within the reach of any one of them, it is not to be doubted that he pursued it without scruple, and, having seized his prey, cared very little, if by so doing he caused his companions to miss theirs. (Rousseau 1913, 194)

Rousseau thought that the ugly nature of international politics was the indirect result of the fact that human beings had learned only too well to be more industrious, farsighted, and cooperative than that. And Waltz used the story merely to illustrate the proposition that what is rational for an individual is not always rational for a group (1959, 168–71).[47]

Nonetheless, Waltz's use of Rousseau's story and Jervis's subsequent use of the 2×2 game with the same name have led many people to believe that the Stag Hunt game contains an important insight about the nature of international politics. To add to the confusion, in his *Theory of International Politics,* which was published one year later, Waltz claimed that in international politics "states face a 'prisoner's dilemma'" and cited Jervis's article in support of that claim (Waltz 1979, 109).

Jervis's use of these famous games reflected a more general tendency at the time to think that the family of 2×2 games, each of which differs from the others only by having a different configuration of preferences, were ready-made models of any social situation of interest.[48] However, as we have seen, these games contain hidden assumptions that are very strong. Many people thought their use could be justified by the fact that models are not supposed to be descriptively accurate, which is true. However, the assumptions represented by 2×2 games are frequently inconsistent with other assumptions made by people who use them to justify their conclusions, and therefore the arguments they support are self-contradictory.

What 2×2 games can do is serve as *examples* of the counterintuitive effects of the interdependence of choices that can also occur in more complex social situations. The Prisoner's Dilemma illustrates the fact that mutually beneficial choices may not be made if individuals have an incentive to take advantage of other people's decisions to cooperate. The Stag Hunt illustrates the fact that even if this problem does not exist cooperation may not occur if people are not sufficiently confident that others intend to cooperate as well. These are certainly problems that arise in international politics, but they are not restricted to international politics.

---

47. For a recent development of the idea that the Stag Hunt game, and not the Prisoner's Dilemma, best represents the fundamental problem of human social organization, see Skyrms 2004.
48. For an especially influential example, see Snyder and Diesing 1977.

And it is not obvious what they have to do with the security dilemma defined by Herz.

These early attempts to use game theory as a way of thinking about the security dilemma were hampered by the fact that, at the time, game theory provided no way of thinking about one of the defining features of the security dilemma, the uncertainty of states about other states' preferences. Moreover, equilibrium outcomes in matrix representations of games implied implausible predictions when one looked at the actual sequence of choices represented by a game tree. Subsequent developments in game theory that addressed both these issues have led to the widespread use of game models in extensive form with incomplete information. Ironically, unlike the earlier misleading use of 2×2 games, they are the cause of complaints that trivial models have driven out significant research in political science. But they have only focused attention on all the complexities that models like the Prisoner's Dilemma and the Stag Hunt concealed.[49]

Hierarchy and Peace

If anarchy is the root cause of war, one would expect that government (or "hierarchy," as Waltz called it) should lead to peace. But in his famous book *Theory of International Politics,* Waltz explicitly and emphatically denied that this was true:

> The threat of violence and the recurrent use of force are said to distinguish international from national affairs. But in the history of the world surely most rulers have had to bear in mind that their subjects might use force to resist or overthrow them. If the absence of government is associated with the threat of violence, so also is its presence. The most destructive wars of the hundred years following the defeat of Napoleon took place not among states but *within* them. . . . If the possible and the actual use of force mark both national and international orders, then no durable distinction between the two realms can be drawn in terms of the use or the nonuse of force. No human order is proof against violence. (1979, 102–3)

This passage seems to contradict the main thesis of *Man, the State and War.* Nonetheless, Waltz later wrote:

---

49. For a discussion of what can be learned by analyzing the implications of assuming that participants in a 2×2 game are uncertain whether the other person's preferences conform to the preferences in the Prisoner's Dilemma or to those in the Stag Hunt, see Kydd 2005.

Although neorealist theory does not explain why particular wars are fought, it does explain war's dismal recurrence through the millennia. . . . The origins of hot wars lie in cold wars, and the origins of cold wars are found in the anarchic ordering of the international arena.

The recurrence of war is explained by the structure of the international system. (1988, 620)

But what, then, explains the recurrence of civil wars?

These apparent contradictions are in part yet another illustration of the fact that structural Realism has virtually nothing to say about why war ever occurs anywhere. It is therefore not surprising that structural Realists actually have nothing to say about the connection between either anarchy or hierarchy and the occurrence of war. But these passages also illustrate another important fact about structural Realism: in spite of the fact that its main theme is the difference between anarchic and hierarchical systems, it also has little to say about what that difference is.

Here is what Waltz had to say about it:

The difference between national and international politics lies not in the use of force but in the different modes of organization for doing something about it. . . . A government has no monopoly on the use of force as is all too evident. An effective government, however, has a monopoly on the *legitimate* use of force, and legitimate here means that public agents are organized to prevent and to counter the private use of force. Citizens need not prepare to defend themselves. Public agencies do that. A national system is not one of self-help. The international system is. (1979, 103–4)

But the world is full of governments that are not "effective" in this sense, and yet neither Waltz nor any of his followers have ever suggested that structural Realism might have something to say about them. Moreover, the origins of the U.S. Civil War are not to be found in the fact that in the nineteenth century U.S. citizens could not look to government to protect them against the private use of force.

The end of the cold war has been followed by a period like the one in the nineteenth century described by Waltz, in which the most destructive wars have taken place "not among states but within them." As one might expect from these passages in which Waltz attempted to state the difference between anarchy and hierarchy, structural Realism has been little help in understanding them.

For example, one Realist, Barry Posen, has written that they can be understood as the result of the collapse of governments: when the sovereign disappears ethnic groups are faced with the security dilemma that results from anarchy (1993). John Mearsheimer, however, argued that only partition could resolve the conflict in Kosovo or provide a long-term resolution of the conflicts in Croatia and Bosnia (1998). But even if the security dilemma could explain why war occurs (which, as we have seen, it cannot), it would seem strange to say that in 1860 the U.S. government first collapsed and then the North fought the South because of the resulting security dilemma. And the consequence of partition is to substitute anarchy for a common government. If anarchy has the consequences Mearsheimer claimed for it, how could it lead to peace among warring ethnic groups?[50]

Compare these conflicts with the recent conflicts between India and Pakistan. India and Pakistan are independent states, each with nuclear weapons, and the conflicts between them might be taken to illustrate the dire effects of anarchy and the security dilemma. However, their existence is the consequence of the partition of British India into two states, one predominantly Hindu and the other predominantly Muslim, after it became independent. Would conflicts between Hindus and Muslims in the Indian subcontinent be greater or less if India had not been partitioned? Since the differential effect of anarchy and hierarchy on violent conflict is one of the main themes of structural Realism, one might expect that it would have an answer to that question. But in fact it does not.

In this respect structural Realists are not unique. Virtually everyone takes governments for granted, and this fact is reflected in the division of intellectual labor among American political scientists between students of international politics and students of comparative or domestic politics: international politics is the study of relations among governments, and everything else is the study of politics structured by governments within borders that define their jurisdictions. But governments and borders come and go, the incidence of organized violence within the jurisdictions of governments varies enormously across time and space, and both well-defined borders and governments that resemble the ones in contemporary Europe or the United States are rare and a very recent development. The way political scientists organize their work has created a gap in our knowledge about the central problem of our time: the relation between political institutions and organized violence. Structural Realism is like a rug thrown over this gap that only makes it harder to see it.

This gap in our knowledge not only inhibits our understanding of what is now called "state failure." It also inhibits our understanding of international institutions. In discussing the idea of world government, Inis

---

50. On this question, see also the section of Waltz's *Theory of International Politics* called "The Virtues of Anarchy" (1979, 111–14).

Claude said:

> In the final analysis, it appears that the theory of world govern-
> ment does not *answer* the question of how the world can be saved
> from catastrophic international conflict. Rather, it helps us to
> *restate* the question: How can the world achieve the degree of
> assurance that inter-group conflicts will be resolved or contained
> by political rather than violent means that has been achieved in
> the most effectively governed states? (1962, 271)

Because of the division of intellectual labor between students of domestic
and international politics, we still do not have a good answer to Claude's
question. And therefore we do not know what contribution international
institutions short of a world government might make to the resolution of
interstate conflicts. Structural Realism does not answer this question, it
begs it—as do the advocates of various interstate institutions like the
International Criminal Court, whose main appeal is that they resemble
some of the features of modern states.

Worse than that, we cannot even specify clearly what the difference
between government and anarchy is. Is the European Union a government, and if not, what would suffice to turn it into one? Is there a government in Yemen? Was there a government in Afghanistan under the Taliban? Does an Afghan warlord preside over a government? Does the rebel
group in Colombia known as the FARC, which controls a large segment
of the territory nominally allocated to the government in Bogotá, constitute a government in the territory that it controls? Was there a government
of the United States prior to the U.S. Civil War? How long has there been
a government of France, and when did it first appear? The question that
structural Realism begs is not even well defined.[51]

Realism's Competitors

Structural Realism makes three main claims: (1) the anarchic structure of
international politics leads to the recurrence of war, (2) war is less frequent
in anarchic systems with a bipolar structure than in systems with a multipolar structure, and (3) in anarchic systems with a multipolar structure,
alliances lead to balances of power rather than to a preponderance of

---

51. For an elaboration of this point, see Milner 1991. See also Lake 2003. A good way to
begin thinking about this question is to immerse oneself in Samuel Finer's great posthumous
work, *The History of Government* (1997). For a survey of the anthropological literature on
the development of the state, see Johnson and Earle 1987. An older discussion by an anthropologist that I have found very helpful is Fried 1967.

power. No valid argument has ever been presented in support of any of those claims, which is what makes the disagreement between defensive Realists and offensive Realists possible. Thus the only good reason for continued attention to the works that defined structural Realism is that they provide illustrations of how easy it is to make mistakes in thinking about international politics.

However, in a volume recently published under the auspices of the American Political Science Association describing the current "state of the discipline," Stephen Walt claims that "[t]he bottom line is that realist theory is alive and well. It remains relevant, rigorous, and theoretically fecund" (2002, 222). In support of his evaluation, Walt says that the "utility of a research tradition may be judged by two basic criteria," which he calls "explanatory power" and "internal fertility." Following Van Evera (1997), he says that "explanatory power can be judged by the percentage of variance explained by the independent variable(s), the range of topics covered by the theory, and the prevalence of the phenomena being explained" (Walt 2002, 201). And therefore, he claims that

> debates within the realist family and between supporters of realist theory and those of various rivals should not be resolved by asking who can muster the flashiest abstract argument; rather we should ask which explanation best fits the facts. Determining which theory (or approach) is most useful is an empirical question, and rendering such judgments usually requires careful historical evaluation of the specific causal mechanisms in each theory. (Walt 2002, 224)

These statements illustrate the fact that it never occurs to many political scientists that logical validity is an important criterion in evaluating arguments. Empirical evidence cannot confirm or disconfirm an explanation if the evidence is not actually implied by the explanation. For that, the argument need not be "flashy," but it must be valid.[52]

As these quotations from Walt illustrate, one reason for the low value political scientists place on logical validity is the widespread confusion among them between explanations and regression equations. Another is the tendency to equate a theory with any plausible conjecture. Various buzzwords from the philosophy of science are often invoked as ways of

---

52. For Van Evera's own use of the criteria for evaluating theories listed by Walt, see Van Evera 1999. In an earlier article attacking the use of formal models, Walt (1999) claimed that it was consistency that we should aim for in constructing explanations. But the problem with structural Realism is not that it is inconsistent but that the arguments offered in support of its main claims are not valid. For another influential example of this confusion, see King, Keohane, and Verba 1994, 105–7.

evaluating those conjectures. But ultimately many political scientists believe that it is the job of empirical research to resolve the disagreements among the authors of these conjectures.[53]

This can never happen, because no facts can actually be derived from any of the competing "theories." Thus competing conjectures accumulate. Similar conjectures are grouped into schools of thought and named, and scholars who find them plausible identify themselves with them (as Walt identified himself as a member of the "realist family"). Students in political science courses are then expected to know about these competing families, and if the question of how to evaluate them arises, it is only by asking students to think about how they might be tested empirically. And therefore great academic rewards go to those who succeed in devising a new "paradigm" or "approach," which can then provide the basis for further inconclusive empirical research. Thus, in spite of all the talk about science and scientific method among political scientists, the study of international politics does not satisfy the definition of a science given at the beginning of this chapter.

This is not only sad but ironic, since Waltz's book *Theory of International Politics* was written to counter just such attributes of the field. "Among the depressing features of international-political studies," he wrote,

> is the small gain in explanatory power that has come from the large amount of work done in recent decades. Nothing seems to accumulate, not even criticism. Instead, the same sorts of summary and superficial criticisms are made over and over again, and the same sorts of errors are repeated. (Waltz 1979, 18)

The first chapter of that book is devoted to emphasizing the distinction between a correlation and an explanation, and in it Waltz emphasized that an explanation required a creative guess as to what propositions might imply the facts to be explained. Unfortunately, Waltz's arguments did not satisfy his own criteria, but most people accepted his claim that they did. As a result, many criticisms of Waltz's ideas are criticisms of what some people take to be his assumptions rather than the validity of his arguments.

One reason many people accepted Waltz's arguments so uncritically is probably that they already believed his main conclusions to be true. The

---

53. One favorite criterion for evaluating theories is "parsimony." Note that it is hard to beat a bald general assertion for parsimony. See the recent collection of essays in Elman and Elman 2003, which try to appraise the status of international relations theory by the standards laid down by Imre Lakatos but in which no one asks the simple but obvious question whether the arguments being evaluated are valid. See also James 2002.

idea that states form coalitions to balance the power of other states is one of the oldest ideas in writings about international politics. During the cold war the United States and the USSR were obviously much more powerful than other states, and it seemed very plausible that that fact explained both the conflict between them and their ability to avoid war with each other. And the proposition that violent conflicts were likely without a government to prevent them also seemed obviously true to many people.

Waltz's emphasis on the anarchic nature of the international system seemed especially compelling. It implicitly invoked not only the support of the entire Western tradition of the social contract and its concept of the state of nature but also the theory of the state that had been developed by economists, in which the function of the state was to supply public goods and compensate for market imperfections. And, as the article by Jervis discussed previously illustrated, the Prisoner's Dilemma game had come to be accepted by many people as a persuasive illustration of why government was necessary if people's common interests were to be served and therefore a validation of pessimistic expectations about the consequences of anarchy or the state of nature (Jervis 1978).[54]

Neoliberal Institutionalism

The works of two economists in particular were especially influential in reinforcing the view that the anarchic nature of international politics was the key to understanding what happened in it: Albert Hirschman and Charles Kindleberger. In a book about the prospects for constructing a peaceful international order after World War II, Hirschman pointed out that sovereign states always had the option of interrupting trade with other states, in which case the gains from trade became the losses from the interruption of trade. If those losses were not distributed symmetrically, he claimed, they could be the basis for demanding political concessions, and therefore international trade necessarily had an impact on the ability of sovereign states to exercise influence over each other (Hirschman 1945). And in a book about the Great Depression, Charles Kindleberger argued that, given the lack of an international monetary authority, international monetary stability required a dominant state willing to act as a substitute. Britain, he claimed, had served that function in the nineteenth century; in

---

54. It is ironic that Ruggie has criticized the use of rational choice models to study international politics because they resemble the models found in economics, which he claims (oddly) require the existence of markets; and yet, he claims, they cannot explain where markets come from (1998, 23). But economists have traditionally thought that *governments* were required to make markets work, which makes structural Realism's claim that bad things should be expected in a condition of anarchy seem plausible—a claim that Ruggie wants to dispute.

the twentieth century the only substitute available was the United States, but in the 1930s it was unwilling to assume that role (Kindleberger 1973).

Kindleberger's thesis was one of the bases of what is known as "hegemonic stability theory," which came to be accepted as part of Realism.[55] But the only connection between hegemonic stability theory and structural Realism was that they both purported to be consequences of the anarchic nature of international politics (Keohane 1984, 7–10).

As the economic preponderance of the United States declined, hegemonic stability theory seemed to imply that people should be pessimistic about the future of the international economy. But in an influential book called *After Hegemony,* Robert Keohane (1984) argued that such a pessimistic conclusion did not follow from anarchy alone. Rather, he claimed, independent states could cooperate in an anarchic environment, and international institutions could facilitate such cooperation. The repeated Prisoner's Dilemma was one of the foundations of his argument (65–84). This thesis came to be known as "neoliberal institutionalism," and another "ism" was added to the field's inventory of doctrines.

Keohane claimed to have shown that

> even on the restrictive assumptions of Realism and game theory, gloomy conclusions about the inevitability of discord and the impossibility of cooperation do not logically follow. Egoistic governments can rationally seek to form international regimes on the basis of shared interests. (107)

The first statement is certainly correct—in fact, none of the main claims made by structural Realists follows from their assumptions. It is therefore unclear why, in the conclusion to his book, Keohane praised the "taut logical structure" of Realism and said that it "should not be discarded, since its insights are fundamental to an understanding of world politics," but that "it does need to be reformulated" (245).

In fact, because of structural Realism's lack of a "taut logical structure," it is not even clear that Keohane's conclusions are inconsistent with what Waltz said about the consequences of anarchy. Keohane claimed that

> If there were an infinitely large number of equally small actors in world politics . . . [i]nternational conditions would more closely approximate the Hobbesian model in which life is "nasty, brutish, and short." But as we have seen, the fact that the number of key actors in the international political economy of the advanced

---

55. See also Gilpin 1975, 1981.

industrial countries is typically small gives each state incentives to make and keep commitments so that others may be persuaded to do so. (258)

It is hard to see how this contradicts Waltz's discussion of the benefits of the fact that economic interdependence among states is managed by a small number of great powers.[56]

Nonetheless, members of the Realist family resisted Keohane's attempt to hoist them by their own petard, the Prisoner's Dilemma. Prominent among them was Joseph Grieco, who seems to have coined the term *neoliberal institutionalism* (1993, 335–36). Grieco (1988) claimed that neoliberal institutionalists had overlooked the fact that states in an anarchic environment had to be concerned not just about achieving gains from economic cooperation but also about protecting themselves from the possibility of elimination through war. But, as we have already noted, the possibility that states might be eliminated through war contradicts the assumptions underlying the repeated Prisoner's Dilemma game.[57] And without the repeated Prisoner's Dilemma, neither structural Realists nor neoliberal institutionalists have the basis for making any claims whatever about the consequences of anarchy for the behavior of states.[58]

However, Grieco avoided this modest conclusion and claimed instead that Keohane was wrong about states' *preferences.* Neorealists, he claimed, assumed that states were concerned not about *absolute* gains, as in the standard Prisoner's Dilemma game, but about *relative* gains. But structural Realists had not objected to Jervis's use of the standard Prisoner's Dilemma as a model of the security dilemma. Rather, as we have seen, Waltz was happy to accept it as confirmation of his main thesis. Moreover, Grieco did no more to show how a concern for relative gains could be inferred from premises describing anarchy than Waltz or Mearsheimer have done to support their inferences from them.
The resulting "relative gains" controversy helped make the disagreement between neorealists and neoliberal institutionalists a staple of international relations courses all over the country.[59] Like Walt, Grieco claimed that any resulting disagreements could be resolved by empirical tests.

Neoliberal institutionalism is not based on realist theory; in fact,

---

56. See especially Waltz 1979, 132.
57. This was pointed out by Robert Powell (1991) in response to Grieco's article.
58. Another strand of Liberal thinking about war and the state rests on the empirical observation that democratic states do not fight each other and takes its theoretical inspiration from Immanuel Kant's response to the writings of Hobbes and Rousseau (Doyle 1983). I will discuss Kant's ideas, and what contemporary writers have made of them, in the next chapter.
59. The main contributions to this controversy are reproduced in Baldwin 1993. For an incisive review and critique of the arguments advanced by the participants in this controversy, see Powell 1994.

realism specifies a wider range of systemic-level constraints on cooperation than does neoliberalism. Thus the next scholarly task is to conduct empirical tests of the two approaches. (Grieco 1988, in Baldwin 1993, 131)

But an empirical test of an "approach" is not possible.[60]

Constructivism

Like neoliberal institutionalism, Constructivism takes as its point of departure the fact that structural Realism's conclusions cannot be derived from premises that describe anarchy. However, it also objects to the way in which neoliberal institutionalists have tried to think about what the consequences of anarchy might be, as exemplified by the repeated Prisoner's Dilemma game. In the end, however, it is not really clear what this objection is.

Like structural Realism, Constructivism is more nearly a family of like-minded people than a system of logically related propositions. Two of the most prominent members of this family are John Ruggie and Alexander Wendt. I will focus primarily on Wendt.

"Constructivism," Wendt says, "is not a theory of international politics" (1999, 7). What, then, is it? Like much else about Constructivism, the answer to that question is not entirely clear.[61] Unlike neoliberal institutionalism, Constructivism's critique of structural Realism invokes ideas from philosophy and sociology, which are used to support a version of what Dennis Wrong (1961) called "the oversocialized conception of man in modern sociology."[62] This conception of man and society is then applied to states and international systems and provides the basis for Wendt's claim that "anarchy is what states make of it," that is, that there are no inherent properties of anarchic systems independent of the cultures that define both them and the states they contain—a much stronger claim than Keohane made (Wendt 1992).

Some of what Wendt borrows from philosophy is just the account of inference to the best explanation that I laid out at the very beginning of

---

60. Note that there is a special problem in looking for evidence of a concern for "relative gains": whenever states bargain over the terms of a mutually beneficial agreement, no distinction can be made between a concern for absolute gains and a concern for relative gains, since making one state better off must make the other worse off.

61. The term *social constructivism* means somewhat different things in different contexts. My focus here is on what *Constructivism* generally refers to in the literature on international politics. To make this clear I will capitalize the word.

62. Many Constructivist complaints about structural Realism have their origins in Talcott Parsons's discussion of Hobbes (1937, 43–86). Richard Ashley (1986) was apparently the first to try to interpret structural Realism in this light.

this chapter, which, as I pointed out, is perfectly consistent with Waltz's own account of inductive inference in the first chapter of *Theory of International Politics* (Wendt 1987, 350–55; 1999, 47–91). However, as I also pointed out, we do not need to invoke the authority of philosophers of science to reason in this way, since, as Wendt himself says, "scientists, not philosophers, are the final arbiters of what is 'scientific'" (1987, 351). Moreover, like Waltz, Wendt overlooks one of the most important implications of this description of inductive inference: if facts are to support explanations, the facts must be implied by the explanation.

The reason Wendt thinks it is necessary to invoke the philosophy of science is that he wants to use this literature to support the proposition that social structures really exist, even though they are not directly observable (Wendt 1987, 351–55). And the reason he thinks this is important is that he wants us to believe that structural Realism rests on the assumption of "methodological individualism," that is, that only individual people really exist, and therefore statements about social behavior must be reducible to statements about the behavior of individual people. This is a very odd thing to say, since structural Realism is about the behavior of *states,* not individuals, a fact that should make a methodological individualist profoundly suspicious of it.

The relation between individuals and social structures is the subject of what some sociologists call the "agent-structure" problem. To understand it we need only think about the comparison between humans and ants mentioned earlier. Ant social organization is the product of a complex genetic program. Human social organization is invented by humans, but the social organizations humans invent also shape the people who are part of them in complex ways. Every baby is born into a family, and the adult is the product of both the baby's genetic endowment and the family, a fact that gives rise to the nature-nurture controversy among psychologists. Family organization, however, is not simply the product of a genetic program and therefore can be changed. Families, of course, are part of larger cultures and so forth.[63]

Clearly none of this implies that when individuals encounter each

---

63. Constructivists like to say that social structures determine the "identities" of individuals. The word *identity* is undefined, and it is not at all clear what it means, especially when applied to states (Fearon 1999). Constructivists writing about international politics, for example, like to say that the cold war ended because the Soviet Union changed its identity. The Soviet Union *lost* its identity when it collapsed, but it is not clear what it means to say that it changed its identity, unless it means simply that people with different ideas became influential or that influential political actors changed their understanding of how the world works. But in that case one might say that every book, including this one, is an attempt to change the identity of its readers. For an extended example of this sort of discussion, see Hopf 2002. Other examples of Constructivist writings about this and other matters can be found in Katzenstein 1996.

other outside of their families or other organizations that they belong to (as, e.g., when they trade with each other), or when families and other groups engage in organized conflict with each other, their interactions do not conform to the assumptions of either the one-shot or repeated Prisoner's Dilemma games (Seabright 2004). Thus not only should all this come as no surprise to any reader, but it is irrelevant to the issues debated by structural Realists and neoliberal institutionalists.

Wendt, however, tries to leave the reader with a different impression. For example, he says:

> It is possible for a Hobbesian anarchy to have no culture at all. Here, all knowledge is private rather than shared. . . . The absence of shared culture has an interesting, perhaps counter-intuitive implication: the resulting warfare is not really "war" at all. Killing there may be aplenty, but it is akin to the slaughtering of animals, not war. War is a form of collective intentionality, and as such is only war if both sides *think* it is war. Similarly, a balance of power in this context is not really a "balance of power." Mechanical equilibrium there may be, but actors are not aware of it as such. (Wendt 1999, 266–67)

But this is very misleading. War between organized groups is a "form of collective intentionality" *on the part of each of the warring groups,* but not between them—war is not like a Saturday afternoon game of touch football that people agree to play for their mutual enjoyment. And, unless one simply defines common knowledge as equivalent to a shared culture, whatever level of common knowledge may be required for two groups to form and fight each other, a shared culture, as that word is ordinarily used, is plainly not necessary, either within the two fighting groups or between them.[64]

Wendt says that the subject of his book *Social Theory of International Politics* "was the ontology of international life" (1999, 370). *Ontology* is not a word that any student of international politics should ever have an occasion to use, and therefore it is incumbent on people who use it when talking about international politics to define carefully what they mean by it. Both Ruggie and Wendt use the word freely but never define it. The result can only be to intimidate and confuse the reader.

According to the *American Heritage Dictionary,* ontology is "the branch of metaphysics that deals with the nature of being." It is far from clear how the study of international politics might entangle one in contro-

---

64. The ability of human beings to infer each other's intentions is not supplied by culture, but it is what makes culture possible (Baron-Cohen 1995; Tomasello 1999).

versies about the nature of being. Wendt says that the question of whether social structures really exist is a question about the "ontological status of unobservables" and therefore similar to the question of whether elementary particles really exist (1987, 351). But to ask whether elementary particles exist is not to ask a question about the nature of being but to ask what evidence there is for their existence, and therefore the question should be addressed to physicists and not philosophers. Similarly, the existence or nonexistence of social structures or shared cultures among human beings who interact with each other is not an ontological question but an empirical one, and the knowledge that they are human beings tells one nothing about the answer to it.[65]

Whatever ontology is, Constructivism's fundamental objection to structural Realism is that its ontology is (1) individualist and (2) materialist (Wendt 1999, 1–44, 370–78; Ruggie 1998, 1–39). I have just pointed out how strange it is to call structural Realism "individualist." What could it mean to say that it is "materialist"?

A clue to the answer can be found by looking up the word *materialism* in the dictionary:

> **materialism** n. 1. Philosophy. The theory that physical matter is the only reality and that everything, including thought, feeling, mind, and will, can be explained in terms of matter and physical phenomena. 2. The theory or doctrine that physical well-being and worldly possessions constitute the greatest good and highest value in life. 3. A great or excessive regard for worldly concerns. (*American Heritage Dictionary*)

Social Constructivists complain that structural Realism rests on the assumption that material things like military capabilities, rather than ideas, culture, and social norms, are the only things that influence the behavior of states. This is, perhaps, materialism in the second and third senses of the definition, but it is not clear what it could have to do with something that might plausibly be called ontology. Wendt claims that, since it is materialist, structural Realism emphasizes causality rather than meaning in trying to explain international politics. This might plausibly have something to do with ontology, but it is materialism in the first sense of the definition. Thus Wendt has apparently confused the first meaning of materialism with the second and the third ones. That is why he claims that "[m]aterialists privilege causal relationships, effects, and questions"

---

65. In the field of artificial intelligence, the word *ontology* refers to a conceptual scheme or system of categories. (A number of ontology editors are available for downloading on the World Wide Web.) To find out more about ontology, see the Buffalo Ontology Web site, at http://ontology.buffalo.edu/.

(Wendt 1999, 25) and also claims that theories of bureaucratic politics reflect a materialist orientation (Jepperson, Wendt, and Katzenstein 1996, 33).[66]

Wendt's two complaints about structural Realism can be summarized together by comparing the contrast between ant and human social organization discussed previously, which is summarized in figure 3, with Wendt's typology of social theories (1999, 29–33). The ant column in figure 3 exemplifies causal explanations and the human column represents explanations based on meaning and intentionality. An explanation of social behavior that would be genuinely both individualist and materialist (or "physicalist" as Ruggie calls it) would fall into the lower left quadrant. The corresponding explanation of human behavior would, as Weber said, be based on the choices of "participating individual men" and therefore fall into the lower right quadrant. Structural Realism would have to be placed in the upper right quadrant, since it is based on choices made by organizations of human beings acting as units. However, in a table in Wendt's book whose dimensions apparently correspond to the ones in figure 3, Neorealism (or structural Realism) is placed in the lower left quadrant (Wendt 1999, 32). It is not clear why.

	ant	human
holistic	colonies	state choices
individualist	genetic programs	individual choices

Fig. 3.   Ant vs. human social organization

It is clear, however, why Wendt thinks this strange way of characterizing structural Realism is important. He claims that "[n]eorealism's problematic conclusions about international politics" stem not from faulty reasoning but "from its underlying materialist and individualist ontology." This, he claims, implies that "by viewing the system in idealist and holist terms we could arrive at a better understanding" (Wendt 1999, 370).

In other words, if we see (1) that Waltz confused "social kinds" with "natural kinds" (to use Wendt's terminology), we will conclude (2) that the

---

66. The confusion can be clearly seen throughout Wendt 1999, chap. 3. Actually, it is not clear why structural Realism should be called "materialist" even by the second and third definitions of the term. Cultural or religious differences can lead to military conflicts, and it is not clear what is "materialist" about being concerned about the probability of prevailing in such conflicts. The distinction between "material" and "cultural" explanations is, of course, a staple in debates among sociologists and anthropologists about both Marxism and sociobiology (Johnson and Earle 1987, 8–11). But it is not clear what any of that has to do with structural Realism. However, the anthropologist Marvin Harris's discussion of what he called "cultural materialism" is directly relevant to many of the issues to be discussed in the following chapters. See, for example, Harris 1977.

nature of international politics is determined by the culture that states share rather than by its anarchy (Wendt 1999, 372). The first statement is hard to square with the fact that Waltz's inspiration was Rousseau, and Wendt considers Rousseau to be a precursor of Constructivism.[67] But the second would not follow even if it were true.

On this basis, Wendt identifies three types of international culture that might be possible: a Hobbesian culture, a Lockean culture, and a Kantian culture, the main features of each of which are taken from Hobbes, Locke, and Kant respectively (Wendt 1999, 246–312). Using this typology of cultures, he says, for example, that states would form balances of power, as Waltz claimed, only in a Lockean culture in which no state feared elimination by any other state, and therefore a "Lockean culture . . . is a condition of possibility for the truth of Neorealism" (Wendt 1999, 285). But this is simply asserted, and Wendt makes not the slightest attempt to show that it is true or how Waltz was mistaken in thinking otherwise.[68] Thus Constructivism merely adds yet another collection of invalid arguments with a distinctive name to the field of international politics. Like Liberalism (or neoliberal institutionalism), it is supported indirectly by the inadequacies of structural Realism but fails to identify correctly exactly what those inadequacies are.

In a recent evaluation of Constructivism, Jack Snyder has written that

> Current debates about anarchy and culture have been carried out largely at the level of abstract philosophy and visceral morality. Ultimately, however, the impact of culture on war in anarchy is an empirical question. (2002, 9–10)

He then claims that empirical research by anthropologists investigating whether one could "explain behavior in anarchy solely in terms of either cultural or material causes" is relevant to answering this question (12).[69]

In saying this, Snyder illustrates a common view among political scientists that valid inference is just the concern of "abstract philosophy"; any published conjecture is a theory that has to be evaluated empirically; and any argument, valid or invalid, can be represented as a relationship

---

67. See Wendt 1999, 171. Note that this is the only reference to Rousseau in the index to Wendt's book.
68. If culture alone is sufficient to prevent organized violence at the global level, then one might think that governments are not actually necessary to prevent domestic violence, as structural Realists assume, and wonder why Constructivists are not anarchists. But Wendt does not discuss the problem of domestic order and, indeed, has little to say about organized violence at all.
69. Note that Snyder leaves unclear what the distinction between anarchy and hierarchy refers to in a world of stateless societies or what the connection is between "material explanations" and structural Realists' claims about the effects of anarchy.

between one or more independent variables and a dependent variable. That view will keep Constructivism, along with all the other warring "isms," in business for a long time to come.

Generic Realism

The indifference of most political scientists to the validity of arguments, and the resulting incentive to develop competing brands of "theory," leaves everyone with the impression that there is more to all the theories than is really there. Thus, although the brands are ostensibly in conflict with each other, they all actually give indirect support to each other. A recognition that they all shared the same flaw would mean that they would all have to go out of business, and better answers to the questions being debated might not lead to an easily marketable new brand. Instead, each is given credibility by its criticisms of the others, and a never-ending debate among the competing brands comes to define what the field is.[70] Moreover, ideas can be marketed under a brand name even if they have no logical relationship to each other, as offensive Realism, the security dilemma, and hegemonic stability theory all came to be thought of as part of structural Realism as defined by Waltz, simply because they all focused on the effects of anarchy.

Just as Chevrolet, Buick, and Cadillac are all General Motors brands, so offensive Realism, defensive Realism, hegemonic stability theory, and even structural Realism itself have all been considered brands of Realism, and they all gain some credibility from the common view that, if there is a flaw in this or that brand of Realism, we can nonetheless be pretty confident that, whatever the right answer is, it will turn out to be a Realist answer. But what is Realism?

It is sometimes said that prior to structural Realism there was classical Realism, which tried to explain interstate conflict as the result of an inborn human urge to seek power over other men—not surprisingly, this is sometimes called "human nature Realism."[71] However, this was a mistake, so the story goes, because violent conflicts are caused not by human nature but by anarchy, and therefore structural Realism corrects a mistake made by classical Realists. This is a story often used to explain the importance of Waltz's writings, but it is a story that was first told by John Herz to justify the importance of his contribution to the subject.[72]

However, "human nature Realism" seems on closer inspection to be a

---

70. The typical argument has the following form: (1) Either A or B is true; (2) B is not true; (3) Therefore A is true. The argument is valid, but the first premise is always false.

71. See, for example, Mearsheimer 2001, 18–19.

72. See Herz 1959, 232. In spite of this, both Keohane and Ashley have counted Herz among the classical Realists, and Herz's security dilemma does not even appear in the index to

caricature. Its main academic exemplar is Hans Morgenthau, who wrote a famous textbook about international politics that is generally considered to be the main contribution to Realist doctrine prior to Waltz's *Theory of International Politics*. In the first edition of that book, Morgenthau wrote: "Domestic and international politics are but two different manifestations of the same phenomenon: the struggle for power" (1948, 21). But he also said that "the statement that A has or wants political power over B signifies always that A is able, or wants to be able, to control certain actions of B through influencing B's mind" (14). And that is why, "[w]hatever the ultimate aims of international politics, power is always the immediate aim": anything one wants to accomplish in politics of any sort requires getting other people to do something they would not otherwise want to do (13).

Thus Morgenthau did not say that people have an inborn urge to dominate other people (though admittedly he sometimes used language that could be interpreted in that way); he merely stated the truism that to achieve any political objective, no matter what it was, one had to be able to influence other people. The difference between international and domestic politics in this respect, he said, was that in domestic politics

> Cultural uniformity, technological unification, external pressure, and, above all, a hierarchic political organization co-operate in making the national society an integrated whole set apart from other national societies. In consequence, the domestic political order is . . . more stable and to a lesser degree subject to violent change than is the international order. (Morgenthau 1948, 21)

It certainly sounds as though Morgenthau was talking not about the effects of human nature but about the effects of anarchy.[73]

The other main "classical Realist" in the Realist canon is E. H. Carr, whose book *The Twenty Years' Crisis* (1946) seems to have given Realism

---

Keohane 1986, which is devoted to an evaluation of Neorealism (199, 257). This illustrates once again the confusion about what structural Realists think the explanation of war really is and what role the security dilemma is supposed to play in it.

73. For further evidence on this point, see Frei 2001, 140. There is a similar misinterpretation of Hobbes that is common. Hobbes said: "I put for a general inclination of all mankind, a perpetual and restless desire of power after power, that ceaseth only in death" (1957, 64). But he defined "power" as a man's "present means, to obtain some future apparent good" (56). And the reason men sought "power after power" was not "that a man hopes for a more intensive delight, than he has already attained to; or that he cannot be content with a moderate power: but because he cannot assure the power and means to live well . . . without the acquisition of more" (64). Hobbes was perhaps the first "offensive Realist." Morgenthau's emphasis on the struggle for power was, according to Frei, influenced primarily by the writings of Nietzsche and Weber, a fact that Morgenthau carefully concealed in order to avoid alienating his American audience (Frei 2001, chaps. 5 and 6).

its name. But Carr spelled the word with a lowercase *r*, and the message of Carr's book was that the thinking behind the League of Nations had been utopian and therefore unrealistic. This use of the term is consistent with one of the definitions of the word *realism* given by the *American Heritage Dictionary*, which is simply "The representation in art or literature of objects, actions, or social conditions as they actually are, without idealization or presentation in abstract form." John Herz agreed with this interpretation:

> Strictly speaking, the terms "realism" and "idealism" should not be applied to theories. Theory is either correct or incorrect, depending on how it analyzes what happens in politics, but perhaps it is permissible to call a correct analysis a realistic one. Chiefly, however, the terms apply to actions and actors, those who behave according to "real," that is, existing givens, and those who engage in wishful thinking. (1981, 182)[74]

In the first edition of his famous book, Morgenthau did not mention Realism or identify himself as a Realist.[75] And in *Man, the State and War* and *Theory of International Politics,* Kenneth Waltz did not identify himself as a Realist either—the terms *Neorealism* and *structural Realism* were bestowed on him by others. He did say that his ideas were "closely identified with the approach to politics suggested by the rubric, *Realpolitik*" (Waltz 1979, 117). But the word *Realpolitik* was introduced into the German language by August Ludwig von Rochau, a disillusioned participant in the failed revolutions of 1848, in a book about politics in the German-speaking states (Rochau 1859). The word meant, and still means, no more than the word *realism* means as described in the passage just quoted from Herz: Rochau came to believe that he and other revolutionaries had engaged in wishful thinking.

Thus, generic Realism seems to be nothing more than realism and therefore nothing very specific. If so, then the credibility of the Realist brand is entirely dependent on the inferences Realists have made about the effects of anarchy and the security dilemma, and if those cannot be justified then there is no more general Realist doctrine to fall back on. Any work that focused on war and military capabilities that reflected skepti-

---

74. However, see Herz 1951, where the terms *realism* and *idealism* are applied to theories.
75. He had, however, frequently used in his writings the English words *realism* or *realistic* (as well as their French equivalents) in criticizing writers who, he thought, had overestimated the efficacy of norms and the law in controlling social conflicts (Frei 2001).

cism about the prospect of eliminating war in the near future might call itself realist, but Realism itself would provide no justification for such skepticism.

That possibility seems consistent with the definition of the latest brand of Realism, neoclassical Realism, which was invented by Gideon Rose simply as a way of organizing a review of several otherwise unrelated books. "The works under review here," he says, belong to a school of thought

> which I term "neoclassical realism." It explicitly incorporates both external and internal variables, updating and systematizing certain insights drawn from classical realist thought. Its adherents argue that the scope and ambition of a country's foreign policy is driven first and foremost by its place in the international system and specifically by its relative material power capabilities. This is why they are realist. They argue further, however, that the impact of such power capabilities on foreign policy is indirect and complex, because systemic pressures must be translated through intervening variables at the unit level. This is why they are neoclassical. (Rose 1998, 146)

The authors reviewed did not identify themselves as "neoclassical Realists," but given the importance of brand names in the field of international politics, the gift of a brand can hardly be refused, and thus it is not surprising that the term has had a life beyond Rose's review essay.[76] Instead of inventing new brands of Realism and new counter-Realisms, students of international politics should remove the word from their vocabulary, so that arguments can stand on their own and be evaluated independently of each other.

What Next?

An understanding of the deficiencies of structural Realism supplies us with a list of important questions that need answers. At the heart of all of them is the question of what explains the occurrence of war, whether interstate war or not. An answer to that question would help us understand the relation between government and war, which would in turn help us determine

---

76. See, for example, Schweller 2003. Note Rose's assumption that theories are defined by the "variables" that they focus on.

whether a world of sovereign states is doomed to war or not.[77]

While Realism contains no valid arguments in support of answers to these questions, the works of Carr, Morgenthau, Herz, and Waltz are indeed part of a longer tradition of thinking about them. The proper name of that tradition, however, is not realpolitik but *Staatsräson,* raison d'état, *ragion di stato,* or reason of state. That is the tradition that Waltz claimed to be heir to when he invoked the name of Machiavelli in illustrating what he meant by realpolitik (Waltz 1979, 117). However, that is a tradition of thought not about international politics but about fundamental questions of political order that help us understand where the Western distinction between domestic and international politics came from. Supporters of the various "isms" have left quite a misleading impression of what writers in this tradition actually said. If we are to settle the issues that have been debated in the wars among the "isms," we will have to take a closer look at this tradition. That will be the subject of the next chapter.[78]

---

77. The failure of structural Realism to provide a clear answer to this question is the main theme of Van Evera 1999. However, there is actually no explanation of the occurrence of war in Van Evera's book, which instead contains a number of more or less plausible claims about what influences the probability that war will occur. This is like substituting a weather forecast for an explanation of the occurrence of snow. But if the weatherman does not know why snow occurs, one cannot have much confidence in his forecast. Van Evera claims that the hypotheses he discusses, which he calls "misperceptive fine-grained structural Realism," provide support for the structural Realist "paradigm." But it is actually not clear what they have to do with structural Realism. Many of the factors that Van Evera claims influence the probability of war will be discussed later in the book, beginning with chapter 4.

78. For background reading on this subject, I strongly recommend the following books, *to be read in this order:* Meinecke, *Machiavellism* (1998); Tuck, *The Rights of War and Peace* (1999); and Hirschman, *The Passions and the Interests* (1977). For a discussion of the influence of Meinecke on Hans Morgenthau, see Frei 2001.

CHAPTER 2

Reason of State

The subject of E. H. Carr's book *The Twenty Years' Crisis* was, Carr said, "a fundamental antithesis revealing itself in many forms of thought," the "antithesis of utopia and reality—a balance always swinging towards and away from equilibrium and never completely attaining it." He claimed that

> The two methods of approach—the inclination to ignore what was and what is in contemplation of what should be, and the inclination to deduce what should be from what was and what is— determine opposite attitudes towards every political problem. (Carr 1946, 11)

The word *utopia,* of course, comes from the book with that name by Sir Thomas More and refers to an "impractical, idealistic scheme for social and political reform" (*American Heritage Dictionary*). Many efforts to create ideal or utopian communities have failed. What is it that makes utopian communities utopian?

The concept of an equilibrium, introduced first by John Nash and then developed by subsequent game theorists, provides a way of thinking about this question. To see what it entails, let us look at a simple way of organizing human behavior that works very well.

Classical Realism, Social Norms, and Raison d'État

Perhaps the simplest possible example of a rule that works is the "rule of the road," which says, in some countries, that automobiles should keep to the right of a line drawn down the middle of a road and, in other countries, that they should keep to the left. As already mentioned in chapter 1, this rule works well enough that people everywhere bet their lives every day that everyone will follow it, and there is perhaps no form of human social behavior that is more antlike, not only in the appearance of the resulting lines of traffic but also in its extreme regularity and reliability. However,

53

this behavior is not genetically determined, and people are actually free to drive where they please. Moreover, if drivers fall asleep or are intoxicated they may deviate from the rule, and a head-on collision may result.

If our concern were merely to establish regularities in human behavior, this would have to be listed among them. However, no one would be impressed by our discovery of it.[1] But explaining it, while not difficult, is not quite as straightforward as it might at first appear to be. Making clear what the explanation is will help us think about behavior that is harder to understand, including situations where rules do not work.

Rules and Equilibria

The part of the explanation that is obvious is that, if each driver sees everyone else driving on one side of the road, he or she will want to do likewise, since otherwise there will be a head-on collision. But to explain why everyone else is driving on the same side of the road we must assume that each driver expects everyone else to do that as well. And if other drivers are to expect me to drive, say, on the right side, then they must believe that I expect them to do so as well, and so forth.

We could summarize this reasoning in the following premises:

Premise 1 (Individual preferences) *Drivers prefer to avoid head-on collisions with oncoming traffic.*

Premise 2 (Expected outcome of choices) *If all other drivers drive on one side of the road, someone who drives on the other side will experience a head-on collision.*

Premise 3 (Expectations of others' choices) *In the United States, each driver expects other drivers to drive on the right-hand side of the road.*

Premise 4 (Common knowledge) *Premises 1–3 are common knowledge among drivers in the United States.*

These premises imply that we should expect the fact to be explained to be true:

Conclusion 1 (Equilibrium outcome) *In the United States, automobiles keep to the right of oncoming traffic.*

These premises together exemplify what is meant by the concept of an equilibrium in the theory of games, and the situation exemplifies what is

---

1. Peter Kincaid's book *The Rule of the Road* (1986) describes this regularity in detail, but it is not considered to be a notable contribution to social science.

often called a coordination problem.[2] Premises 1 and 2 are represented in a more general form in figure 4, which makes obvious the fact that if one driver expects another to keep right he will prefer to keep right and that if he expects the other to keep left he will want to keep left. It also abstracts from the details of the driving situation and therefore applies to any situation that has the same structure. What figure 4 does not tell us is what will happen. To know that, we have to know what each expects the other to do and that those expectations are common knowledge.[3]

	R	L
R	(1, 1)	(0, 0)
L	(0, 0)	(1, 1)

Fig. 4.   A coordination game

Note that this explanation does not mention the government or the fact that the law prescribes that drivers should drive on the right-hand side of the road. That is because the fact that one might get a traffic ticket if one drives on the left is a far less significant incentive to stay to the right than the fact that one will run into oncoming traffic if one does not. And in fact, rules of the road like this one were supported by conventions before the conventions were underwritten by governments (Kincaid 1986, 1–42). The function of government is not to give drivers an additional incentive to drive on the right (premises 1 and 2) but to make sure that everyone expects the same thing and that these expectations are common knowledge (premises 3 and 4). And while governments can, with considerable effort, change these expectations (as the government of Sweden did in 1967, when Sweden switched from driving on the left to driving on the right), it is obviously much easier and less costly for governments merely to ratify prevailing conventions than to try to change them (Kincaid 1986, 159–62).

Moreover, pedestrian traffic is often regulated by such conventions even when governments do not try to control it. In the United States, pedestrians generally keep to the right. In the United Kingdom people drive on the left, but pedestrians in London include many people from countries where everyone is used to staying to the right. At street intersec-

---

2. Readers who still think that explanations must identify causal relationships might ask themselves what causes what in this explanation.

3. Game theory clarifies this problem but has little to say about how common knowledge emerges. For an accessible introduction to the subject, see Chwe 2001. The emergence of conventions like the rule of the road is discussed in Young 1996. Thomas Schelling (1960) was important in defining the coordination problem. A classic treatment is by Lewis (1969). For a very clear and helpful discussion of the relevance of game theory and decision theory to many of the issues discussed in this chapter, see O'Neill 1999.

tions in London, therefore, there are instructions in the pavement telling pedestrians which way to look before crossing, and anyone using the stairs in a London underground station at rush hour will quickly notice what happens when there is no convention about pedestrian traffic that is common knowledge.

Rationalism, Materialism, and Social Norms

This simple example of the rule of the road is pregnant with implications for current controversies about the relation between culture or social norms and what is variously called classical Realism, realpolitik, or raison d'état. Explanations of social behavior like the one just offered for the power of the rule of the road are sometimes criticized for being "individualist" or "rationalist" or for focusing entirely on self-interest as a motive for action.[4] But, while the explanation of the behavior of drivers focuses on the decisions made by drivers, it is not strictly individualist, since it shows clearly that what drivers do is a function of the convention that tells them what to expect other drivers to do. This convention could well be described as a social norm, and a pedestrian who violates it and runs into another pedestrian might provoke an indignant response from the injured party. Since the consequences of running into a pedestrian are much less severe than a head-on automobile collision, a desire to avoid such a rebuke might be a significant incentive to watch where one is going while walking, whereas it plainly is insignificant in enforcing the norm for automobile traffic.[5]

The explanation could be said to be rationalist in that it exaggerates the extent to which drivers think about what to do. One might claim instead that the rule of the road is an institution that organizes people's behavior so that they do not have to think carefully about what they do.[6] But a rule that relied on people not thinking carefully about what they were doing would not be very reliable, since one day they might pay attention to what they were doing and do something different, or they might drive where the rule of the road was different and have an accident because they could only do what they were accustomed to doing. It is precisely because the rule of the road passes the "rationalist" test that people do not

---

4. See, for example, the works of social constructivists referred to in the previous chapter.
5. On the other hand, if there is no such norm, there will be more collisions, but the interdependence of people's decisions will still be common knowledge to them, and they will do something. (One might think about whether the mixed strategy equilibrium in the game in figure 4 is a plausible model of such a situation.)
6. See, for example, March and Olsen 1989.

have to think about it and can instead think about something else while they are driving.[7]

One might say that the explanation was self-interested (or even materialist in at least one sense of that ambiguous word) because of premise 1. Note, however, that premise 1 does not say *why* drivers want to avoid head-on collisions—perhaps they are suicidal but do not want to harm other people. The explanation only relies on their having that preference. As long as people are free to choose, they will have preferences, and it is a mistake to confuse explanations based on people's preferences with explanations based on their self-interest.

However, it is plausible to think that the desire to avoid personal injury to themselves is a more reliable reason for expecting drivers to satisfy premise 1 than the desire to avoid harming others, and that helps explain why the rule itself is so effective. Moreover, if the opposite of self-interest is taken to be not altruism but the "internalization" of a social norm, then if the social norm is to drive on the right, people who have internalized it become a menace to others when they drive in countries where the norm is to drive on the left. And if the norm they have internalized is just to follow the local rule, whatever it is, then (1) there is still a coordination problem in specifying the local rule and (2) everyone would surely feel more comfortable knowing that drivers had a stronger reason to follow the local rule than a norm that they might or might not have internalized that tells them to follow it.

Note that everyone benefits from the existence of the rule of the road, but that benefit is not the motive that sustains the rule. The motive that sustains the rule is just each individual driver's desire to avoid a collision with the automobile coming in the opposite direction. Moreover, the social benefit can be achieved merely by the individual actions of every driver or pedestrian.

A utopian scheme for social organization, by contrast, would be a scheme that everyone would benefit from but that lacked an incentive for the people whose behavior was to be organized to conform to it or required them to cooperate in ways that were not feasible. The expectations associated with the rule, in other words, would not constitute an equilibrium.

An example would be a proposal to finance the U.S. defense budget entirely by voluntary contributions. One might argue that that would be

---

7. When such a convention does not exist or there is uncertainty about whether it is common knowledge, premise 1 implies that people have a big incentive to think carefully about what they are doing. When the rule was changed in Sweden, the accident rate actually went down for a while, because people were more careful about what they were doing. However, the number of head-on collisions nonetheless increased (Kincaid 1986, 161).

better than a system of compulsory taxation, since, unlike taxation, it would mean that no one would ever have to contribute more than he or she wanted to. One reason that scheme would be utopian is that people would have a strong incentive to contribute little or nothing, since the effect of each individual's contribution would be imperceptible. The Prisoner's Dilemma game is a plausible representation of this problem. But that is only one part of the difficulty. Another is that even if people were willing to contribute something, perhaps because they had internalized a norm that said that they should, they would still somehow have to determine what would be their share of the total burden, and there would likely be a lot of disagreement about that and no feasible way to resolve it. And a third is that it is unlikely that there would be unanimous agreement as to what the actual consequences of any particular total amount of money spent on defense would be.

There are other, more subtle and less immediately obvious reasons why attractive-sounding schemes for social organization may not work. When, for example, it is necessary to create artificial incentives for individual behavior to substitute for an incentive like the one stated in premise 1, this may require some supplementary form of social organization that proves in turn to be infeasible. And one reason it could be infeasible is that it violates some other social convention. In a society, for example, in which conventions against killing people are enforced by family feuds, the establishment of a police force to find and prosecute killers according to government laws may prove to be ineffective, as when the police chief in Tropojo, Albania, resigned so that he could "avenge a family murder" and was "reported by his former colleagues to have killed, or ordered the killing, of eight men . . . for the murder of his brother" (Perlez 1998).

This example already takes us very close to the reason why people like Carr argued that the League of Nations was a utopian scheme. It also illustrates why both Carr and Herz thought that all of political thought consisted of a permanent tension between idealism and realism. As Herz put it:

> Political thought may in general be reduced to two major "ideal types," one or the other of which each individual theory approaches to a now greater now lesser degree but which to some extent, and in one form or another, is always present. These types will be called Political Realism and Political Idealism. (1951, 17)

The idealist sees that the existing social order has terrible consequences for the people governed by it and tries to invent a new one that would improve their lives; the realist sees that existing social conventions are very powerful and very stable, and therefore they cannot be changed merely by such actions as opening a police station, hiring some people to sit in it, and giving them uniforms. But without idealism, Carr said, we would all be fatalists:

> we cannot ultimately find a resting place in pure realism; for realism . . . does not provide us with the springs of action which are necessary even to the pursuit of thought. . . . The impossibility of being a consistent and thorough-going realist is one of the most certain and most curious lessons of political science. (1946, 89)

This is not a statement that contemporary Realists tend to quote.

We can now see more clearly the relation between Realism and realism. Carr and Herz thought that the tension between idealism and realism characterized thought about both domestic and international politics. Waltz, on the other hand, was interested in creating a theory of international politics, and he thought that in order to do that he had to say what the difference between international and domestic politics was (Waltz 1979). He claimed that the difference was in their institutional structures, which he called anarchy and hierarchy. In doing this he took the existence of these institutional structures for granted and therefore was unable to explain how they emerged and changed. As a result, he was also unable to explain "domestic" political behavior in institutional environments that did not conform to his definition of *hierarchy* or analyze the possible effects of international institutions on the behavior of states. After Waltz was labeled a Realist, "Realism" became the study of the behavior of governments in an anarchic environment.

This is not realism in the sense of Carr or Herz, nor would they have considered it to be necessarily "realistic."[8] It was therefore a mistake to think that Waltz, Herz, and Carr were all doing the same thing, a mistake caused by the proclivity of political scientists to group writers into schools of thought, which are then labeled and discussed together, as though the common label implied adherence to a common "theory" or "paradigm."

Carr and Herz both claimed that utopian thought was always unrealistic in the same way. For Carr, the mistake was to overlook the role of self-interest in human behavior and the insufficiency of morality as a way of overcoming it (1946, 95). For Herz, the mistake was to overlook the security dilemma (1951, 18). But the example of the rule of the road illustrates the fact that the possible divergence between self-interest (or "egoism") and the common good is not restricted to the problems posed by violent conflicts, nor is the security dilemma necessarily relevant to

---

8. Carr, for example, did not think that the international order would necessarily long remain "anarchic" (1946, 224–39).

understanding it. And neither morality nor coercion, the two correctives that Carr focused on, is necessarily helpful in aligning the two.

There are two features of the rule of the road that make it so effective. One is that, given expectations that are common knowledge, the rule is self-enforcing. The other is that, once one rule has been established, no one has an interest in changing it for the other one. As already noted, more difficult problems arise when rules are not self-enforcing—it is in that context that Carr's discussion of morality versus coercion becomes relevant. But difficult problems also arise when the rule would be self-enforcing, but people have conflicting preferences as to what it should be. Precisely because the rule would be so effective, there might be intense conflict about what rule is to be followed. Instead of determining what side of the road people should drive on, for example, the question might be what language they should speak.[9]

The question raised about international politics by both Carr and Herz, then, is this: If the League of Nations was a utopian scheme for reducing the number of violent conflicts, what would be realistic? Both Carr and Herz saw that this is a question that applies to what is now considered to be "domestic politics" as well as to international politics. To answer it we would need to be able to explain why violent conflicts occur. But the closest either Carr or Herz came to an answer to that question was Herz's definition of the security dilemma, and we have already seen that that is not an adequate answer.

Social Norms, Equilibrium Institutions, and Raison D'état

Imagine a place where people had, in the course of many years of experience with pedestrians and horse-drawn vehicles, developed a variety of different conventions as to what to do when they passed each other when traveling in opposite directions. These conventions included not only what side of the road they should keep to in order to avoid colliding with someone traveling in the opposite direction (which might be dependent on whether the travelers were pedestrians or horse-drawn vehicles or some combination of the two) but also what to do in case of collisions and who was responsible for various kinds of damages that might result. Suppose as well that there were conventions about how to proceed in case someone failed to follow such a convention, for example, if a person suffered some damage as a result of a collision with another person and the other person

---

9. In that case, the game in figure 4 becomes the game commonly called "Battle of the Sexes."

ran away instead of offering the compensation that was prescribed by convention.[10]

Suppose also that different conventions had developed in different localities, with the result that when people from different localities encountered each other they might each violate the other's expectations as to what should be done. Then, since the conventions were in conflict, each might look for some higher principle that would justify his or her own convention as to the right way of behaving in order to show that the other was in the wrong.[11] But there might be disagreement about these principles or disagreement about how to apply a principle to any given collision.

As long as the vehicles were slow and traffic was sparse and mainly local, these collisions and the ensuing disagreements might be a tolerable inconvenience to most people. Suppose, however, that there was a rapid increase in both the volume of traffic and the speed and power of the vehicles encountering each other. Then the number of collisions might increase rapidly, along with a rapid increase in the number of disagreements about how to deal with their consequences and about what principles should be used to resolve those disagreements. Moreover, new situations might arise that were not covered by any existing convention, and the new vehicles might give the people who owned and operated them an opportunity to take advantage of other people in ways that had earlier not been feasible. They might, for example, be able simply to drive certain kinds of traffic off the roads entirely.

In those circumstances some people might continue to try to extend existing conventions to the new situation by inferring general principles from the prior conventions and then applying those principles to the new problems. But there would be two difficulties with this response. One, as already mentioned, is that there might be disagreement about how to define those principles or to apply them to particular cases. Another is that the new principles might not be supported by effective conventions as to how to enforce them—a man could be expected, with the assistance of friends and family, to chase down a hit-and-run driver and extract compensation from him when the most powerful vehicle was a horse-drawn carriage, but not if the offender was driving a fast car.

These two difficulties could then provide the stimulus for an alternative approach, based on (1) an attempt to elicit support for new, artificial

---

10. The blood feud, exemplified by the actions of the police chief in Tropojo mentioned previously, is an example of such a convention. For a systematic description, see Boehm 1987. For an illustration of how game theory can be used to model such social conventions, see O'Neill 1999.

11. Examples can be found in the development of the common law tradition. See Holmes 1991 and Levi 1949.

conventions by emphasizing the dire consequences of continuing disagreement and (2) an examination of how new conventions could be arrived at and then enforced. Because of the general disagreement about both the appropriate conventions and the general principles that might justify them, this alternative approach would have to appeal to motives that did not rely on prior agreement about either the conventions that should govern behavior or the principles that might justify them.

One reason this discussion of traffic problems may seem silly is that we take for granted the fact that governments are available to deal with such problems. But modern governments are a side effect of the response of Europeans in the early modern period to violent conflicts. I believe that thinking about these possible responses to the hypothetical problem of regulating traffic can help us understand the responses of European thinkers in the early modern period to the problem of the increasing scale and intensity of violent conflicts that occurred at that time.

The hypothetical attempt to derive more general principles from existing conventions in my little story about traffic problems corresponds roughly to the development of the idea of natural law as a way of regulating conflict. The attempt to devise new, artificial conventions for regulating violent conflict that did not require prior agreement on general principles is sometimes called raison d'état, and the motives to which writers in this tradition appealed came to be known as people's "interests," which referred roughly to what is now commonly called "rational self-interest."[12]

As noted earlier, sometimes self-interest is contrasted with altruism and sometimes with a commitment to norms or ethical principles. However, contrary to what many people assume, the term *self-interest* itself has no standard meaning. It is not clear, for example, whether one should say that parents who devote most of their income to preparing their son for medical school, and then insist that he attend even after it becomes clear that he would prefer to be a rock musician instead, are altruistic or self-interested. An appeal to people's "interests," in the context discussed here, means just an appeal to strong motives that everyone can be counted on to have, regardless of their ethical commitments. These would include a desire to feed and clothe and to avoid death and personal harm to both oneself and one's family. Other motives might also be important in particular contexts, for example, the desire to be esteemed by others. There is no

---

12. For an extended discussion of the meaning of the term *interests*, and the reason for its use among European political thinkers in the early modern period, see Hirschman 1977. For a discussion of the subsequent development of the concept, see Swedberg 2003.

reason to think that a person's "interests," in this sense of the term, could not include a concern for the well-being of other people.[13]

The term *rational* also does not have a well-defined meaning. Indeed, decision theory and game theory are largely devoted to defining what it means in contexts where its meaning is especially unclear. The reason it is associated with the word *interest* is that if political organization is to be based on people's interests then people's interests need to be stable and reliable (Hirschman 1977, 42–54). Thus "interest" (or "rational self-interest") refers to what people would want to do if they thought carefully about what they were doing and therefore represents what one might call, borrowing a term from the political philosopher John Rawls, a "reflective equilibrium."

That is why the concept of rational self-interest has always had both a descriptive and a normative component. Decision theory is, in part, an attempt to determine whether such a reflective equilibrium always exists for individual choices, while game theory is an attempt to determine whether an equilibrium always exists if the choices of rational individuals are interdependent. However, neither decision theory nor game theory is restricted to the analysis of people's *interests*, but both focus instead on their *preferences*, a better defined and more general idea. They reveal that non-self-interested preferences are not the solution to all social problems.[14]

Of course, if people are to think carefully about what they are doing, they must have an incentive to do so, and therefore interests are most effective as a mechanism for supporting an equilibrium when, like the rule of the road, people have a strong incentive to think carefully about how their interests are affected by their actions. That will be true when (1) the

---

13. See George Homans's discussion of individual self-interest in Homans 1950, 95–96. Homans writes: "If we examine the motives we usually call individual self-interest, we shall find that they are, for the most part, neither individual nor selfish but that they are the product of group life and serve the ends of a whole group and not just an individual. What we really mean . . . is that these motives are generated in a different group from the one we are concerned with at the moment." For an extended discussion of how the difference between self-interest and altruism could be rigorously defined, see the papers collected in Katz 2000.

14. Some of the most intense family conflicts I have witnessed were conflicts over who was to pay the bill for a family meal in a restaurant, where neither party to the conflict wanted the other to pay but each wanted to pay the whole bill himself. People claiming to be acting to protect unborn babies have killed doctors who perform abortions. And it is hard to see how a suicide bomber could be acting out of pure self-interest. The distinction between people's interests and their preferences is the basis for ongoing controversies about whether people's preferences are entirely socially determined or reflect at least in part something that might merit the term *human nature*. For an interesting discussion of this question by an evolutionary biologist, see Wilson 2002.

interests that are at stake are important to them and (2) the consequences of their actions will have a significant impact on those interests.

The raison d'état tradition has led to recurring controversies about the relation between the interests required to sustain a rule, or system of rules, and prevailing mores or standards of ethical behavior. This issue is exemplified by current debates about whether honesty on the part of corporate executives in the United States requires, or can best be achieved by, a commitment to ethical behavior on the part of the executives or a system of financial rewards and/or penalties that would rely on their interests instead. In that context, the "realist" view would be that interests are more reliable than ethics.

But as the rule of the road example illustrates, artificial rules are most effective if they rely on existing conventions, and solutions that violate prevailing standards of morality may not work—the police chief in Tropojo may have been motivated by what he considered to be an ethical principle (Boehm 1987, 65–89). That is why Carr claimed that the "realist answer to the question of why law is regarded as binding" contains only "part of the truth":

> no community could survive if most of its members were law-abiding only through an ever-present fear of punishment. . . . there is plenty of evidence of the difficulty of enforcing laws which seriously offend the conscience of the community or of any considerable part of it. (Carr 1946, 176–77)

The reason Carr thought the League of Nations was utopian was not just that it was not backed by sufficient military force but also that it was not supported by the conscience of a community.

As the behavior of the police chief in Tropojo also illustrates, however, ethical principles do not just exist in people's heads. They are embedded in social conventions, which are enforced in turn by actions that impinge on violators' interests. The police chief may have been motivated by what he considered to be right, but he also had to take into account what other members of his family expected him to do and how they would treat him if he failed to comply. Similarly, the corporate executive must be concerned not just with the monetary consequences of his behavior but also with what his wife and children will think about what he does and what they will do as a consequence.

The reason writers in the raison d'état tradition emphasized interests over social norms or ethical standards is that in Europe in the early modern period, as in contemporary Albania, prevailing social norms and ethical standards came to be seen as part of the problem rather than part of the solution to it. And that was not just because there were deep disagreements about social norms but also because the social norms of that time actually helped make large-scale violent conflict possible by sustaining the organizations that participated in it. The nobility consisted of a privileged class of warriors, and prevailing conventions gave them a license to profit from violence.[15] The Roman Church had come to be seen by many as a protection racket, which had acquired great wealth by selling protection from God's punishments. Efforts to reform it led to competing religious organizations, which threatened to undermine the conventions that supported the established social and political order. These rival religious groups were opposed by forcible means, and commitments to alternative systems of norms were then invoked as incentives to participate in the ensuing violent conflicts.[16]

Because of the development of trade and the resulting revival of money, all of this took place in the context of increasing wealth, which made participation in organized violence not just justifiable but also profitable for large groups of people.[17] And in response to these incentives, new modes of military organization and new forms of military technology were developed, which led to organized violence on a scale that had not been possible before.[18]

The State of Nature

A writer who wanted to emphasize the need for new rules of the road would paint a dire picture of the traffic problems that would arise without them. Without any commonly known rules, he might argue, drivers would have to concentrate on protecting themselves from collisions. Since no one could know what other drivers might do, each might want to have maximum flexibility in responding to oncoming traffic, which would mean that everyone would drive down the middle of the road, leading to many head-on collisions. To avoid this outcome, each might want to find a way to signal to others what side of the road he intended to use. One way of doing this would be for drivers to join together in groups driving on one side of

15. For example, a promise by a captured nobleman to pay a ransom in order to be released was considered to be a valid contract. For a discussion of medieval conventions regulating looting and the use of booty, see Redlich 1956, 1–5.
16. See the graphic picture of life in Europe in the fourteenth century painted by Barbara Tuchman (1978). For a recent discussion of the prevalence of organized violence in early modern Italy, see Jones 1997, 333–650. For a general discussion of the problem of order in early modern Europe, see Rabb 1975.
17. See Fritz Redlich's (1956, 1964–65) studies of looting and mercenary armies in early modern Europe.
18. The literature on the effects of changes in military technology and organization in early modern Europe is immense. For recent introductions to it, see Keen 1999 and Parker 1996.

the road in hopes that oncoming traffic would be compelled to drive on the other side. To minimize the damage from collisions, larger and better-protected vehicles might be developed. Since this would only increase the damage done to others in a collision, others would feel compelled to develop better-protected vehicles in response.

Note that none of this behavior would require that drivers be unconcerned about the damage they did to others. Rather, even drivers who suffered severe remorse from it would be unable to avoid it without a commonly known set of rules to govern the behavior of all of them.

My stories about traffic problems are, I fear, growing more and more fanciful. Nonetheless, I think they offer some insights into early modern European political theories, which continue to influence everyone's thinking about the relation between war and the state.

One might say, using terminology that became common in early modern Europe, that drivers in the conditions I have described were in a state of nature with respect to each other (Tuck 1999, 1–15). If so, note what that would, and would not, mean. It would not mean, as already noted, that they did not care about each other's welfare or even that they did not want their behavior to be governed by rules or had no idea what rules should be followed were they to adhere to them. It also would not mean, as some people have said about men in Hobbes's state of nature, that they lived "outside of society" (Tuck 1999, 8). It would mean simply that there were no rules to regulate their behavior such that (1) it was common knowledge that each would have an incentive to follow the rules if he or she expected others to do so as well and (2) it was also common knowledge that each in fact expected the others to follow them.

A possible interpretation of Thomas Hobbes's political ideas, then, is that he described what he thought were two equilibria, one of which (the equilibrium that characterized behavior in the state of nature) was much worse for everyone than the other (the equilibrium that characterized behavior in a commonwealth). In the state of nature, men are "in that condition which is called war."

> Whatsoever therefore is consequent to a time of war, where every man is enemy to every man; the same is consequent to the time, wherein men live without other security, than what their own strength, and their own invention shall furnish them withal. In such condition, there is no place for industry; because the fruit thereof is uncertain: and consequently no culture of the earth; no navigation, nor use of the commodities that may be imported by sea; no commodious building; no instruments of moving, and removing, such things as require much force; no knowledge of the face of the earth; no account of time; no arts; no letters; no soci-

ety; and which is worst of all, continual fear, and danger of violent death; and the life of man, solitary, poor, nasty, brutish, and short. (Hobbes 1957, 82)

If men are to avoid such a condition, Hobbes claimed, they require "a common power, to keep them in awe, and to direct their actions to the common benefit." And

[t]he only way to erect such a common power, as may be able to defend them from the invasion of foreigners, and the injuries of one another, and thereby to secure them in such sort, as that by their own industry, and by the fruits of the earth, they may nourish themselves and live contentedly; is, to confer all their power and strength upon one man, or upon one assembly of men, that may reduce all their wills, by plurality of voices, unto one will: which is as much to say, to appoint one man, or assembly of men, to bear their person; and every one to own, and acknowledge himself to be the author of whatsoever he that so beareth their person, shall act, or cause to be acted, in those things which concern the common peace and safety; and therein to submit their wills, every one to his will, and their judgments to his judgment. This is more than consent or concord; it is a real unity of them all, in one and the same person, made by covenant of every man with every other man. (Hobbes 1957, 112)

In the state of nature, Hobbes wrote,

we find three principal causes of quarrel. First, competition; secondly, diffidence; thirdly glory.
   The first, maketh men invade for gain; the second, for safety; and the third, for reputation. The first use violence, to make themselves masters of other men's persons, wives, children, and cattle; the second, to defend them; the third, for trifles, as a word, a smile; a different opinion, and any other sign of undervalue, either direct in their persons, or by reflection in their kindred, their friends, their nation, their profession or their name. (81–82)

"The passions that incline men to peace," by contrast, "are fear of death; desire of such things as are necessary for commodious living; and a hope by their industry to obtain them" (84).
   From the passions that incline men to peace can be inferred rules for right behavior, which Hobbes calls "laws of nature," which can all be summarized in the maxim "Do not that to another, which thou wouldest not

have done to thyself" (103). However, men are not obliged to obey these laws of nature in the state of nature, since doing so would put their lives at risk, and everyone has a natural right to defend himself. Thus the laws of nature become obligatory only in a commonwealth.

It is because of his claims about equilibrium behavior in the state of nature that it is unclear whether Hobbes should be considered a writer in the natural law tradition or a writer in the tradition of raison d'état. He claimed that self-defense was not only a basic *interest* but also a *natural right* and that as long as it was not common knowledge that everyone would obey the laws of nature people had the right to defend themselves. Moreover, what sustained the natural law equilibrium in a commonwealth was the realization that violation of those laws would propel people back into the state of nature.[19]

According to Tuck, the explanation for this dualism is that Hobbes was looking for a firm foundation for morality in a time of general skepticism about the foundations of all knowledge.[20] Like other writers on natural rights at the time, he took "the jurisprudence of war which had developed among humanist lawyers, and derived a theory of individual rights from it" (Tuck 1999, 11). Thus the analogy that Hobbes and others drew between the relations among individuals in the state of nature and the relations among sovereigns was meant to be taken literally. The raison d'état tradition, on the other hand, was heavily influenced by Tacitus, who saw all politics as at least potentially civil war. And therefore there was a close relation between ideas about natural rights and the raison d'état tradition in early modern Europe (Tuck 1999, 1–15).

This analogy between sovereign princes and sovereign individuals has been the source of confusion ever since. For if Hobbes's description of equilibrium behavior in the state of nature was accurate, then one might expect it also to be a description of equilibrium behavior in the relations among states. And, indeed, this is where offensive Realism comes from, by way of Herz's security dilemma. But Hobbes himself did not make this inference. He wrote:

> But though there had never been any time, wherein particular men were in a condition of war one against another; yet in all times, kings, and persons of sovereign authority, because of their independency, are in continual jealousies, and in the state and

---

19. Some people have thought that the Prisoner's Dilemma provides a way of understanding what Hobbes wrote about the state of nature. But there is little support for this in Hobbes, and we will see that there are better ways of understanding what he may have had in mind. For a discussion of Hobbes and the Prisoner's Dilemma, see Tuck 1989, 106–9.

20. See Tuck 1989. For a brilliant description of the social conditions that give rise to such skepticism, see Mannheim 1936, chap. 1.

> posture of gladiators; having their weapons pointing, and their
> eyes fixed on one another; that is, their forts, garrisons, and guns
> upon the frontiers of their kingdoms; and continual spies upon
> their neighbors; which is a posture of war. But because they
> uphold thereby, the industry of their subjects; there does not fol-
> low from it, that misery, which accompanies the liberty of partic-
> ular men. (Hobbes 1957, 83)

But if wars in the state of nature were only conflicts among "particular
men," they could not be very severe: civil wars are conflicts among armies,
just as wars among sovereign princes are. Thus it is not clear why wars
among sovereigns should have less serious consequences than civil wars.

This is one of the great questions posed by the development of the
European system of states beginning with the Renaissance. In early modern Europe, sovereign political authorities came to be seen as the solution
to pervasive violent conflicts. But the creation of sovereign political
authorities led to violence among them on a scale that dwarfed what had
been possible earlier. This raised the question of whether the process that,
in retrospect, we can see led to the construction of the modern state would
stop with the construction of multiple independent sovereigns and, if so,
whether the cure for the violence of early modern Europe might be worse
than the disease.

Hobbes does not have an answer to this question, in part because his
main concern was with civil war, not interstate war. Perhaps the closest he
came to saying something relevant to it was this:

> a great family, if it be not part of some commonwealth, is of itself,
> as to the rights of sovereignty, a little monarchy: whether that
> family consist of a man and his children; or of a man and his ser-
> vants; or of a man, and his children, and servants together:
> wherein the father or master is the sovereign. But yet a family is
> not properly a commonwealth; unless it be of that power that by
> its own number, or by other opportunities, as not to be subdued
> without the hazard of war. For where a number of men are man-
> ifestly too weak to defend themselves united, every one may use
> his own reason in time of danger, to save his own life, either by
> flight, or by submission to the enemy, as he shall think best; in the
> same manner as a very small company of soldiers, surprised by an
> army, may cast down their arms, and demand quarter, or run
> away, rather than be put to the sword. (Hobbes 1957, 133–34)

Hobbes clearly thought that it was enough that a sovereign be able to
defend his subjects "from the invasion of foreigners" as well as from "the

injuries of one another," and therefore it would be wrong to seek in what he wrote an answer to the questions that have occupied modern-day Realists (Hobbes 1957, 112).

A more basic reason for Hobbes's lack of an answer to these questions is that his arguments, like the arguments advanced by modern-day Realists, were incomplete. And, therefore, not only did he not say what he thought the answer was, but it is also not possible to infer it from what he said. For it is not only unclear from what Hobbes wrote why relations among sovereigns should not be as bad as relations among individuals in the state of nature; it is also unclear why the state of nature must be as bad as Hobbes said it was.

Nor is it clear what sustains a commonwealth. Hobbes wrote that the laws of nature were not binding in the state of nature, because "covenants, without the sword, are but words, and of no strength to secure a man at all" (1957, 109). But one man's sword is not enough to enforce the agreement that sustains Leviathan, the artificial man that is the commonwealth, nor can the existence of the commonwealth be threatened by one man acting alone. Both rebellion and opposition to it require cooperation and therefore agreement. And if agreement can only be sustained by force, then both the commonwealth and rebellion would appear to be impossible, and we are left with a world of solitary individuals.

Some writers have claimed it was Hobbes's individualism that prevented him from providing a clear account of what might hold a commonwealth together. As Meinecke wrote:

> Mere egoism and that which is merely useful, in however rational
> and knowledgeable a manner it might be advocated (as in the case
> of Hobbes), will never serve as an internal connecting-link to hold
> great human communities together. Some sort of higher feelings
> of moral and intellectual values must be superadded to thought
> and action which is in accordance with *raison d'état,* if the latter is
> to lead on to its climax [i.e., the modern state]. (1998, 216)

This view is reflected in Talcott Parsons's discussion of Hobbes (1937, 43–74). Like Meinecke, Parsons claimed that Hobbes's ideas showed that "individualism" and "utilitarianism" were incapable of explaining social order. And there is a straight line from there to the criticisms of structural Realism made by Ruggie, Wendt, and other Constructivists.[21]

---

21. For a survey of the literature by sociologists on the Hobbesian problem of order, see Wrong 1994. Note, however, that what Hobbes wrote about contracts makes it hard to explain not only social order but any sort of collective action, including both war in the state of nature and rebellion against the sovereign. And therefore any solution to the Hobbesian problem of order might lead to more social disorder than order.

The example of the rule of the road suggests, however, that the problem with Hobbes's account of the Leviathan is not that he focused on the interests of individuals but that he lacked the idea of an agreement that was self-enforcing because it was part of an equilibrium set of expectations that were commonly known (Hardin 1991). Given such an equilibrium set of expectations, the "passions that incline men to peace" might be enough to hold a great human community together.

Note well, however, that whatever sustains the commonwealth, the difference between the state of nature and a commonwealth cannot be that in the commonwealth the contract that binds men together is enforced by the sword. The sword of Leviathan may be used to enforce contracts between individual men but not to enforce the contract that takes men out of the state of nature. And this is true even if the sovereign is established by force rather than by agreement, since the force of an individual person alone could never be sufficient to compel the agreement of large numbers of people.

The Prince

Hobbes wrote that sovereign power that is acquired by force

> differeth from sovereignty by institution, only in this, that men who choose their sovereign, do it for fear of one another . . . : but in this case, they subject themselves, to him they are afraid of. (1957, 129–130)

Whether established by "institution" or by "acquisition," as Hobbes called it, the outcome is the same, a power "as great, as possibly men can be imagined to make it" (136):

> His power cannot, without his consent, be transferred to another: he cannot forfeit it: he cannot be accused by any of his subjects, of injury: he cannot be punished by them: he is judge of what is necessary for peace; and judge of doctrines: he is sole legislator; and supreme judge of controversies; and of the times, and occasions of war, and peace: to him it belongeth to choose magistrates; and to determine of rewards, and punishments, honour, and order. (130)

But if the power of the sovereign is so great, why should people who are subjected to it expect that life in a commonwealth will necessarily be better than life in the state of nature?

The first great question posed by the development of the European state was whether the resulting violent conflicts among states would be worse than the violence within them that they supplanted. The question just stated is the second: whether the new Leviathans that emerged in Europe would themselves be a greater or lesser threat to the well-being of their citizens than violence within them had been. While Hobbes does not have an answer to the first question, he does have an answer to the second, and it has the merit of recognizing that the idea of a social contract provides no answer to it—whether a sovereign authority is the result of voluntary agreement or the exercise of force, the outcome is the same: a sovereign authority that is no longer constrained by the circumstances that led to its creation. To determine whether the creation of Leviathan will improve people's welfare, therefore, we must examine the interests that will shape the behavior of the sovereign once it is in place.

Hobbes claimed, of course, that life in the state of nature would be very bad indeed, and therefore it would not take much for the creation of a sovereign to make it better. That is why Hobbes's critics asked why this must be so: it would appear that the worse the state of nature is expected to be, the less the sovereign must fear rebellion and therefore the worse the life of the citizen would be. But this overlooks a factor that is the main focus of Hobbes's own answer to the question: the dissolution of the commonwealth plunges the sovereign into the state of nature along with everyone else, and therefore the worse the state of nature is expected to be, the more the sovereign would fear the consequences of the dissolution of the commonwealth as well. That is why the "laws of nature," which reason derives from the "passions that incline men to peace," are as binding on the sovereign as they are on his subjects.

Moreover, the role of the sovereign is not just to provide everyone (the sovereign included) with security against the "injuries of one another" but also with security "from the invasion of foreigners." Thus, Hobbes claimed,

> the greatest pressure of sovereign governors, proceedeth not from any delight, or profit they can expect in the damage or weakening of their subjects, in whose vigor, consisteth their own strength and glory; but in the restiveness of themselves, that unwillingly contributing to their own defence, make it necessary for their governors to draw from them what they can in time of peace, that they may have means on any emergent occasion, or sudden need, to resist, or take advantage on their enemies. (1957, 120)

This passage illustrates a connection between the two great questions posed by the development of the European system of states that is one of the themes of the raison d'état literature but that the division of intellectual labor in modern political science makes it easy to overlook: the sover-

eign's interest in securing his position against other princes who would like
to take it from him gave him an additional incentive to preserve the
"vigor" of his subjects, which was the source of his own "strength and
glory." Thus the extent of the domestic welfare-enhancing effect of
Leviathan was in part a function of the extent of the potentially welfare-
reducing effect of the state system that was Leviathan's by-product.

This link is exemplified in a striking work written by a near-contem-
porary of Hobbes, a French Huguenot nobleman named Duke Henri de
Rohan, called *De l'interest des Princes et Estats de la Chrestienté,* which
was published in 1638 and translated into English in 1663 (Rohan 1663).
As Meinecke wrote of this work, "There are sentences here which will
make even the modern reader's heart beat fast" (1998, 168). Were it not for
the archaic English into which it was translated, one might think it had
been written by a modern student of international politics. But it was written about European politics before the emergence of the modern European state, and it illustrates the fact that the development of the European
state cannot be separated from the development of the European state system.

The preface to this work is often quoted. It begins with the arresting
statement:

> The Princes command the People, & the Interest commands the
> Princes. The knowledge of this Interest is as much more raised
> above that of Princes actions, as they themselves are above the
> People. (Rohan 1663, preface)

However, "[t]he Prince may deceive himselfe," or "his Counsell may be
corrupted,"

> but the Interest alone can never faile. According as it is well or ill
> understood, it maketh States to live or die. And . . . it alwaies
> aimeth at the augmentation, or at leastwise the conservation of a
> State. (preface)

Rohan's purpose in this work is to use the interests of the main actors in
European politics at the time to explain what they were doing, in order to
help the French king to understand what the protection of his interests
required. He thereby illustrates both the descriptive and normative content of the notion of "interests" discussed previously.

The reason this is relevant in the current context is that Rohan had
been one of the main military leaders of the French Protestants, whose
military power the French monarch had set out to destroy. Yet in this treatise he seeks to instruct the king of France as to how best "to augment, or
at least conserve," the French monarchy. One reason for this is that the

Huguenots had been defeated and Rohan was trying to ingratiate himself with the king's chief minister, Richelieu, and preserve a military role for himself in the service of the king. But he also wanted to argue that the threat to France posed by Spain meant that it was in the king's own interest to follow a policy of toleration toward the Huguenots, in order to elicit their support against Spain.[22]

Since Rohan's own future was at stake, and since this treatise was written to seem persuasive to Cardinal Richelieu, Rohan's reasoning reveals a great deal about the way men of affairs thought about these questions in the seventeenth century.[23] In the preface he says that "to consider well the Interest of the Princes of this time"

> one ought to lay for a ground, that there be two Powers in Christendome, which are as the two Poles, from whence descend the influences of peace and warre upon the other States, to wit, the Houses of France and Spaine. This of Spain finding itself augmented all at once, hath not been able to conceale the designe she had to make her selfe Mistresse, and cause the Sun of a new Monarchie to rise in the West. That of France is forthwith carried to make a counterpoise. The other Princes are annexed to the one, or the other, according to their Interest. (Rohan 1663, preface)

One should probably resist the temptation of calling this the first reference to a bipolar international system.

Rohan's argument is that the Spanish Habsburgs had sought to use Catholicism, "as that for conscience sake doth make people to undertake anything," as a way of stabilizing their control of Spain and extending it elsewhere (4–5). It was therefore in the interest of the Spanish monarch to establish himself as the protector of the "Catholik Religion" everywhere, which had the effect of making allies of the pope and Catholic princes and weakening potential opponents such as France and England by fomenting discord between Catholics and Protestants within their territories.

From this it follows, Rohan wrote,

> that if the first maxime of the interest of Spaine be, to prosecute the Protestants, for to grow by their spoils: the first interest of France is, to make the Catholikes perceive the venom hidden under the same. Especially to let the Court of Rome understand that the hopes which Spaine gives her to augment her treasures by the ruin of the Protestants; is not but to further her designe

---

22. For a discussion of Rohan's career and writings, see Meinecke 1998, 162–95.
23. For Richelieu's own thinking, see Church 1972.

towards the Monarchie, where she can no sooner arrive, but the Pope must become her Servant. (19–20)

Rather, the authority of the pope "never hath more lustre, then when the power of Christian Princes and States is ballanced."

Moreover France should make shew to the Protestant Princes and States, that although she be of a diverse Religion to theirs, yet shee would rather their conversion, then their destruction, assuring them that this shall not at all hinder her that shee contribute not of her owne to conserve them, and to aide them freely against all those that would trouble or change any thing in their States and liberties. (20)

Implicit in this argument was the inference that the Huguenots should not seek the support of Spain against the French king but should support the French king against Spain.

One implication of this interpretation of the interests of the Huguenots is that the strength of the French king's army is not a complete explanation of his ability to disarm them. The fact that they could have sought the assistance of Spain perhaps explains the willingness of the French king to maintain a policy of tolerance even after they had been disarmed, while the fact that he could be expected to do so may in turn help explain their willingness not to seek Spanish assistance. Nonetheless, eventually a French king reversed this policy of toleration, whereupon many Huguenots fled to England and became a source of strength for the English monarchy.

The passage just quoted refers to "Protestant Princes and States," but both Rohan's argument and his own position in the world illustrate the fact that no European prince in the seventeenth century had the power that Hobbes said a sovereign must have, and therefore no "state" was a commonwealth in the sense that Hobbes used the term. When Hobbes spoke of the "state of nature," therefore, he likely had in mind not some thought experiment or historical condition prior to civilization but the condition of Europe in the seventeenth century.

One of the myths that sustain modern Realist accounts of international politics is that the Peace of Westphalia, which ended the Thirty Years' War, ushered in a system of sovereign states.[24] If Europe during

---

24. On this point see Osiander 2001. For a fascinating discussion of how Westphalia came to be seen as the foundation of the European state system, see Keene 2002. Keene argues that this was the product of attempts by German scholars to find a legal foundation for opposition to revolutionary France and Napoleon. Works by these scholars were subsequently accepted as authoritative characterizations of the European state system by the founders of what is commonly called the "English school" of international politics (Keene 2002, 14–22).

Hobbes's time was in the "state of nature," then one might think that after the Peace of Westphalia it consisted of a collection of Hobbesian commonwealths. This is far from the truth. Rather, "the restiveness of themselves, that unwillingly contribut[ed] to their own defence," to use Hobbes's words, continued for many years to prevent European princes from "draw[ing] from them" what they needed, and the inability of the French monarchy to finance its army by nonviolent means out of the resources available to it within its own borders eventually led to its demise in the French Revolution (Lynn 1993).

Students of international politics today look at the Balkans or Afghanistan and are puzzled, and this puzzlement has produced the growing literature on "state failure." But Europe in the sixteenth and seventeenth centuries was much like the Balkans or Afghanistan today, and the important puzzle is how it came to be so different. The process by which states with the properties of Hobbes's commonwealth were created in Europe was a long and violent one. The question it poses for us today is whether people now living in the "state of nature" must follow the same long and violent path out of it that Europeans did and whether the outcome will ultimately be as welfare enhancing as Hobbes claimed it would be.

The path the Europeans followed is not well described by either of the ways Hobbes said a commonwealth might be created: "institution" or "acquisition." It was, rather, a long, drawn-out mixture of both, in which at times princes attracted sufficient support from some "little monarchs," to use Hobbes's term, to intimidate others, as the French king had done to the Huguenots, and at other times held out sufficient inducements to all to attract voluntary cooperation, as illustrated by Rohan's argument for supporting the French monarch against the one in Spain. But in all cases what was crucial was the relationship among princes, warriors, and the people who produced the goods that fed and armed them all. The effect of the outcome on the welfare of citizens depended heavily on the distribution of bargaining power among these three groups, which was in turn heavily influenced by the recurring military conflicts among would-be sovereigns that characterized modern European history.[25]

A World of Leviathans

Hobbes's *Leviathan* was published in 1651. Almost one hundred years later, Rousseau wrote a work that he originally called *That the State of*

---

25. Useful surveys of the literature on this process can be found in Porter 1994 and Glete 2002. A classic contribution to it is Tilly 1992. A useful account of this process as it developed in England can be found in Brewer 1989.

War is Born of the Social State but that became simply *The State of War* (Rousseau 1991a). In it, as the original title indicates, Rousseau argued that Hobbes had things exactly backward: "Far from the state of war being natural to man, war springs from peace, or at least from the precautions that men have taken to ensure a lasting peace" (45). "Let us contrast these ideas," Rousseau wrote, "with Hobbes's horrible system, and we will find the very reverse of his absurd doctrine."

> As individual men we live in a civil state subject to laws; as people we enjoy a natural liberty: this makes our position fundamentally worse than if these distinctions were unknown. For living simultaneously in the social order and in the state of nature we are subjected to the inconveniences of both, without finding security in either. (44)

As we saw in chapter 1, Rousseau's writings are one of the main sources of what came to be known as structural Realism.[26]

In the hundred years between the publication of *Leviathan* and Rousseau's writings about war, the religious conflicts of the seventeenth century were replaced by conflicts among princes over territory and foreign trade, and independent mercenary armies were replaced by armies that were controlled by monarchs. However, as already noted, the European state in Rousseau's day was still a work in progress, and therefore rule was still largely hereditary, the rights of inheritance were still subject to dispute among quarreling princes, monarchs still had difficulty financing the military forces they controlled, and war continued to be a way of financing war (Lynn 1993, 310).

Different as eighteenth-century Europe was from the seventeenth century, it was still radically different from Europe today. And therefore it is not clear whether the frequency of war in the eighteenth century is best explained by the fact that Hobbes was wrong to be optimistic about the consequences of creating a world of commonwealths or by the fact that the modern commonwealth was still under construction. By adopting uncritically Rousseau's answer, structural Realism conceals the question from us.

Rousseau's thinking about international politics was at least in part stimulated by a proposal for a European confederation written by Charles Castel, Abbé de Saint-Pierre, early in the eighteenth century. After Saint-Pierre's death, his family asked Rousseau to edit and abridge his writings.

---

26. Constructivists fail to emphasize this fact and, following Talcott Parsons, concentrate their fire on Hobbes. But Rousseau was much more pessimistic about international politics than Hobbes was, and it would be hard to portray Rousseau as an individualist, materialist, or utilitarian. For a discussion of Rousseau's ideas about international politics and their relation to the ideas of Hobbes and Kant, see Hoffmann 1963.

Rousseau produced instead an abstract of Saint-Pierre's project, written in his own words, and a separate evaluation or "Judgement" of it that was not published until after his death. In Rousseau's abstract of Saint-Pierre's ideas and his evaluation of them we find many of the issues debated by Realist students of international politics and their critics.

As described by Rousseau, at the heart of Saint-Pierre's proposal was a system of collective security, consisting of "a perpetual and irrevocable alliance" among the nineteen principal sovereigns of Europe, which would "guarantee to each of its members the possession and government of all the dominions which he holds at the moment of the treaty, as well as the manner of succession to them, elective or hereditary, as established by the fundamental laws of each province" (Rousseau 1991b, 69). All future disputes among the members were to be settled by arbitration by a permanent diet consisting of representatives of all of them, "to the absolute exclusion of all attempts to settle the matter by force or to take arms against each other under any pretext whatsoever." Moreover, "all the confederates shall arm and take the offensive, conjointly and at the common expense," against any sovereign who fails to abide by the provisions of the treaty, and "they shall not desist until the moment when he shall have laid down his arms, carried out the decisions and orders of the diet, made amends for his offence, paid all the costs, and atoned even for such warlike preparations as he may have made in defiance of the treaty" (70).

Three questions could be asked about such a proposal: (1) Was it utopian; that is, would the behavior the proposal is intended to induce actually be an equilibrium, in the sense discussed earlier? (2) Was it realistic to think that the rulers who would be governed by it would agree to it? (3) If the proposal was not adopted, how pessimistic should one have been about the prospects for peace?

Even when Rousseau spoke for himself, it is often difficult to figure out what he meant to say. The problem of determining Rousseau's answer to these questions is compounded by the fact that he tried to make the most persuasive case he could for Saint-Pierre's proposal, while at the same time criticizing it as unrealistic. He appears to have thought not that the scheme was utopian but that it was unrealistic to expect that it would be adopted:

> though the scheme in itself was wise enough, the means proposed
> for its execution betray the simplicity of the author. . . . this good
> man saw clearly enough how things would work, when once set
> going, but . . . he judged like a child of the means for setting them
> in motion. (Rousseau 1991b, 94)

A federation of Europe, he wrote, could only be established by force. "That being so," he said, which of us would dare to say whether the league of Europe is a thing more to be desired or feared? It would perhaps do more harm in a moment than it would guard against for ages. (100)

Since it could not be adopted, the reasons given for thinking it would be desirable made Rousseau pessimistic about the prospects for a peaceful European order.

However, there are good reasons to believe that the scheme was utopian and therefore would not have made much difference even if it had been adopted. The idea behind it was that, while princes would retain their ability to make war, none would choose to do so because each would expect to be opposed by an overwhelming coalition of forces if he did, and therefore "the thought of conquests will have to be given up from the absolute impossibility of making them." Moreover, "the very thing which destroys all hope of conquest" would relieve all princes "at the same time from all fear of being attacked," and therefore there could be no purely defensive reason to go to war either (Rousseau 1991b, 74). The function of such a treaty, then, would be, like the rule of the road, to enable states to avoid costly conflicts by creating a set of equilibrium expectations that would be common knowledge. But there are good reasons to think that the behavior predicted would not in fact be an equilibrium.

Suppose that the agreement were violated by a single prince, and consider whether each of the others would choose to join forces in opposition to it. It would be costly to join such a coalition, and therefore if a prince's own interests were not threatened by the violation he might choose not to do it. Moreover, failing to join would be costless unless this failure were itself subject to punishment of some sort. But this punishment would require that all the others cooperate, and now there would be two states to punish, and the costs of punishment for all the others would be even higher. The same reasoning would apply to each successive noncooperative prince in turn, with the cost of joining the punishing coalition greater each time. But this implies that the initial violator could not be confident enough of punishment to deter him from violating the agreement in the first place. Obviously, the cost of punishing an initial violation of the agreement would be even higher if two or more princes joined together to violate it.

The League of Nations was a similar scheme, and this is why realists like Carr and Morgenthau thought that it and other such schemes were utopian.[27] But even if this were not true, and any violation of the agreement were expected to be met by a coalition of all the other princes, this might not be enough to deter violations. The treaty said that the members

---

27. The commitment to collective security required by the charter of the League of Nations was actually both vaguer and weaker than the commitment in Saint-Pierre's scheme.

of the opposing coalition "shall not desist until the moment when [the violator] shall have laid down his arms, carried out the decisions and orders of the diet, [and] made amends for his offence" (Rousseau 1991b, 70). But while it was carrying out this provision, the violator could offer to accept a compromise settlement instead. Since the treaty gives the diet full power to settle all disputes by arbitration, members of the opposing coalition might be sorely tempted to agree to a revision of the prewar status quo as a way of ending such a costly conflict. But then a prince might violate the agreement with the expectation that the violation would lead the diet to take his claims more seriously than it otherwise would.

Rousseau's abstract of Saint-Pierre's reasoning says that "the powers of Europe stand to each other strictly in a state of war, and . . . all the separate treaties between them are in the nature rather of a temporary truce than a real peace" (Rousseau 1991b, 60). "The causes of the disease, once known," he writes,

suffice to indicate the remedy, if indeed there is one to be found. Everyone can see that what unites any form of society is community of interests, and what disintegrates is their conflict; that either tendency may be changed or modified by a thousand accidents; and therefore that, as soon as a society is founded, some coercive power must be provided to co-ordinate the actions of its members and give to their common interests and mutual obligations that firmness and consistency which they could never acquire of themselves. (Rousseau 1991b, 61)

Thus Saint-Pierre, like Hobbes, assumed that, if individuals were to avoid the evils of the state of nature, they required, as Hobbes said, "a common power, to keep them in awe." The problem his proposal was meant to solve was how to construct such a common power over the sovereigns of Europe without subjecting all of Europe to a common Leviathan, which was not only unrealistic but, many believed, undesirable.

However, the reason just given for thinking that Saint-Pierre's scheme might not lead to peace even if a punishing coalition were expected to form is a reason for questioning that assumption. For if princes could influence the decisions of Saint-Pierre's diet by threatening to use force if it did not alter the status quo, then dissatisfied groups within commonwealths could do the same in order to influence the decisions of the sovereign. And therefore, as Waltz recognized, "[i]f the absence of government is associated with the threat of violence, so also is its presence" (1979, 103).

In our examination of structural Realism we saw that, without an understanding of why violent conflict occurs, it is not possible to say what the connection is between a commonwealth (or hierarchy) and peace, or the state of nature (or anarchy) and war, and that structural Realism did not have an answer to that question. Neither does Hobbes, Saint-Pierre, or Rousseau. Thus we must rely on our own resources in thinking about it. A possible answer to it is that Hobbes, Saint-Pierre, and Rousseau all had everything backward—that it is the expectation of peace that makes commonwealths possible, rather than the other way around, and the possibility of war that preserves the state of nature.

Moreover, the arguments of both Hobbes and the Duke de Rohan illustrate the possibility that it is the expectation of war between or among groups that creates reliable expectations of peace within them and that peace, therefore, not only makes large-scale war possible (as Rousseau claimed) but is also just a means of waging it. Since such peace makes war possible on an ever more violent scale, this would be a very pessimistic answer to the question indeed. However, it would be premature to conclude that that answer is the right one.

The Balance of Power

Saint-Pierre, as represented by Rousseau, argued that the condition that made his proposal both possible and realistic was the fact that there was a stable balance or equilibrium among the nineteen sovereigns of Europe.[28] It was realistic to think that his proposal might be accepted, he claimed, because the balance of power made it impossible for any sovereign to expect to make major alterations in the status quo:

> so that if the princes who are accused of aiming to universal monarchy were in reality guilty of any such project, they gave more proof of ambition than of genius. How could any man look such a project in the face without instantly perceiving its absurdity, without realizing that there is not a single potentate in Europe so much stronger than the others as ever to have a chance of making himself their master? (Rousseau 1991b, 62)

Moreover, this same condition implied that, if all the states of Europe but one acted together, they would be overwhelmingly more powerful than a single state that violated the confederation's prohibition of the use of force, and so the existence of a balance of power also made a collective security agreement among the sovereigns of Europe possible.

"[T]his much-vaunted balance," as Saint-Pierre called it, is one of the

---

28. For a list of these sovereigns, see Rousseau 1991b, 72.

pervasive themes of the raison d'état tradition, a theme that, like that tradition itself, has its origins in the warring northern Italian city-states of the Renaissance. In the words of Garrett Mattingly:

> In the 1440's there began to form in certain Italian minds a conception of Italy as a system of independent states, coexisting by virtue of an unstable equilibrium which it was the function of statesmanship to preserve. This conception was fostered by the peninsula-wide alliances whose even balance of forces had ended every war of the past twenty years in stalemate. It recommended itself increasingly to statesmen who had accepted a policy of limited objectives, and had more to fear than to hope from a continuance of an all-out struggle. (1964, 71)

Here we have a concise statement of both the main subject of the modern discipline of international politics and some of the most important issues debated by students of it, which is why Kenneth Waltz wrote that "[i]f there is any distinctively political theory of international politics, balance-of-power theory is it." Yet, he said, "one cannot find a statement of the theory that is generally accepted" (Waltz 1979, 117). Unfortunately, this is still true even after Waltz's attempt to provide one.

As Waltz said, this conception of "a system of independent states" assumed that states,

> at a minimum, seek their own preservation and, at a maximum, drive for universal domination. States, or those who act for them, try in more or less sensible ways to use the means available in order to achieve the ends in view. These means fall into two categories: internal efforts (moves to increase economic capability, to increase military strength, to develop clever strategies) and external efforts (moves to strengthen and enlarge one's own alliance or to weaken and shrink an opposing one). (1979, 118)

Waltz claimed that "[b]alance-of-power theory is microtheory precisely in the economist's sense" and that these assumptions implied that we should expect "the formation of balances of power" (118). He wrote:

> Balance-of-power theory claims to explain a result (the recurrent formation of balances of power), which may or may not accord with the intentions of any of the units whose actions combine to produce that result. To contrive and maintain a balance may be the aim of one or more states, but then again it may not be. According to the theory, balances of power tend to form whether

some or all states consciously aim to establish and maintain a balance, or whether some or all states aim for universal domination.
(119)

But there was no theoretical work on the balance of power prior to Waltz
that established that this conclusion follows from the premises Waltz
listed, nor, as we have seen, did Waltz's own argument show that it does.
Thus the "balance-of-power theory" described by Waltz, like many of the
"theories" that populate the literature of political science, is a mythologi-
cal creature.

According to Waltz, the central proposition of balance-of-power theory is that "balances of power tend to form." But what does that mean? If
there are just two states, to say that their power is balanced would mean
that their military capabilities were equal. But why should we think that
the military capabilities of two states in a two-state world would tend to be
equal? The answer is not clear.

When there are more than two states, the proposition becomes
ambiguous. It could mean that, as in a two-state world, the military capabilities of all states would tend to be equal to each other. But it is even less
clear why that would be true if there are many states than if there are just
two. And the implications of such a condition, were it to exist, are even less
clear, since, as Saint-Pierre pointed out, it would imply that there were
coalitions of states that would be much more powerful than their opponents.

Waltz interpreted the proposition to mean that, when there are more
than two states, weak states would prefer to ally with other weak states,
leading to alliances whose military capabilities were approximately equal
to each other. As we saw in chapter 1, his argument for that proposition
was not valid, and some people have claimed that, while states seeking
only their own preservation would behave in that way, expansionist states
would not. This would be consistent with Mattingly's statement, quoted
earlier, that it was "the function of statesmanship" to preserve a balance,
an idea that "recommended itself . . . to statesmen who had accepted a policy of limited objectives." It would also be consistent with the Duke de
Rohan's analysis of the interests of the French monarchy summarized earlier. In the passage just quoted, however, Waltz explicitly denied that this
was true, claiming that balances would form "whether some or all states
consciously aim to establish and maintain a balance, or whether some or
all states aim for universal domination."

I will return to this question in a later chapter. However, whatever the
right answer to it might be, let us take note of two facts. First, even if
Waltz's answer is correct, it is not clear what its implications are for either
the likelihood of war or the long-run stability of a system of states. For it

is possible that two evenly matched coalitions might fight each other, and
therefore it is possible that over time wars in such systems would lead to
the defeat of all states but one.[29]

Second, for Waltz's answer to be possible, the distribution of military
capabilities among individual states cannot be so unequal that one state
could defeat all the others. As already noted, there is no reason to assume
that this will always be true. The fact that it was true of Europe over a
period of centuries may have been what distinguished that area from other
parts of the world.

Moreover, it is this condition that many European writers, including
Saint-Pierre, had in mind when they wrote of a balance of power. Saint-
Pierre wrote:

> The lie of the mountains, seas, and rivers, which serve as frontiers
> for the various nations who people [Europe], seems to have fixed
> forever their number and their size. We may fairly say that the
> political order of the continent is, in some sense, the work of
> nature. (Rousseau 1991b, 62)

However, he said, "[t]his does not mean that the Alps, the Rhine, the sea,
and the Pyrenees are in themselves a barrier which no ambition can sur-
mount; but that these barriers are supported by others which either block
the path of the enemy, or serve to restore the old frontiers directly the first
onslaught has spent its force" (64). Among these other, supporting, barriers was the fact that no prince, nor any two or three princes, could raise an
army that could defeat all the others.

Saint-Pierre also claimed, however, that if several joined together to
try and had some success,

> that very success would sow the seeds of discord among our vic-
> torious allies. It is beyond the bounds of possibility that the prizes
> of victory should be so equally divided, that each will be equally
> satisfied with his share. The least fortunate will soon set himself to
> resist the further progress of his rivals, who in their turn, for the
> same reason, will speedily fall out with one another. I doubt
> whether, since the beginning of the world, there has been a single
> case in which three, or even two, powers have joined forces for the
> conquest of others, without quarreling over their contingents, or
> the division of the spoil, and without, in consequence of this dis-

---

29. As we have seen, Saint-Pierre, as represented by Rousseau, believed that if war is to be
prevented states that initiate it must expect to be opposed by superior force, not a force of
equal size.

agreement, promptly giving new strength to their common enemy. (Rousseau 1991b, 64)

Here is an argument for the stability of the European balance that is different from Waltz's but equally incomplete. It illustrates the complexity of the issues raised by the European literature on the balance of power.[30]

War

Saint-Pierre claimed that

> the established order, if indestructible, is for that very reason the more liable to constant storms. Between the powers of Europe there is a constant action and reaction which, without overthrowing them altogether, keeps them in continual agitation. Ineffectual as they are, these shocks perpetually renew themselves, like the waves which forever trouble the surface of the sea without ever altering its level. The nations are incessantly ravaged, without any appreciable advantage to the sovereigns. (Rousseau 1991b, 65)

But if the waves that troubled the surface of the sea gave no appreciable advantage to the sovereigns, what caused them? If, as Saint-Pierre claimed, "it appears improbable that, under any supposition, either a king, or a league of kings, is in a position to bring about any serious or permanent change in the established order of Europe" (64), why was it necessary to create a collective security agreement whose sole purpose was to guarantee the stability of that order? Why wasn't the balance of power alone enough to deter states from using force? This is one of the recurring issues in the literature on the balance of power.[31]

One has to look hard to find an answer to that question, either in Rousseau's abstract of Saint-Pierre's ideas or in his presentation of his own, in part because both apparently thought the answer was so obvious that it required little or no justification. As Saint-Pierre put it in discussing "the perpetual quarrels, the robberies, the usurpations, the revolts, the wars, the murders, which bring daily desolation" to Europe:

> But, in truth, what else was to be expected? Every community without laws and without rulers, every union formed and main-

---

30. A useful collection of other European writings on this subject can be found in Wright 1975. See also Sheehan 1996.
31. For an overview of what writers on the balance of power have said about this question, see Claude 1962, 51–66, 88–93.

tained by nothing better than chance, must inevitably fall into quarrels and dissensions at the first change that comes about. (Rousseau 1991b, 59–60)

This, as we have seen, is the foundation on which structural Realism was built. But, as we have also seen, not only is it not an answer to the question, but it is also contradicted by the fact that even communities with laws and rulers often have the properties that Saint-Pierre attributed to the nascent European state system. Moreover, in both Rousseau's abstract of Saint-Pierre's reasoning and in his own evaluation of it one can find arguments that are inconsistent with this explanation of war in eighteenth-century Europe.

According to Saint-Pierre, the fundamental problem was that all agreements among princes were guaranteed only by the contracting parties, there were many disagreements about the principles that should govern those agreements, and those disagreements could only be settled by force of arms. Thus the wars among European princes that so concerned Saint-Pierre and Rousseau were the result not of attempts to overturn the European balance of power but of attempts to compel agreements about the terms of what Saint-Pierre called "the public law of Europe" (Rousseau 1991b, 60).

But, of course, the perpetual agreement that he proposed as the solution to those problems was also to be guaranteed only by the contracting parties, and there would still be disagreements among them. And therefore the question raised by Saint-Pierre's analysis is why there could not be a perpetual agreement reached by the parties to all these individual disputes, which, once settled, would lead to peace among them. The answer he gives is that (1) there were always fresh disagreements to be settled (partly because the nature of the states themselves was constantly changing) and (2) the parties to the agreements were free to use force to renegotiate them "as soon as a change of circumstances shall have given fresh strength to the claimants" (Rousseau 1991b, 60–61).

This, of course, is a reason for thinking that, if Saint-Pierre's scheme were not utopian, the princes of Europe would not accept it, since it would require them to renounce the use of force as a way of settling disagreements that Saint-Pierre assumed they preferred to settle by force. But it is also a reason for thinking that if the range of disagreements among European princes eventually narrowed, and they ceased to expect marked changes in their relative military capabilities, they might be able to avoid the use of force in settling any remaining disagreements among them.

And therefore, one might conclude, the fundamental cause of war among European princes in the eighteenth century was not that they were in a state of nature (or a condition of anarchy) but that they lacked agreement on the principles that should govern their relations with each other and their relative military capabilities were in a constant state of flux. Perhaps in more stable circumstances they would be able to achieve such an agreement, in which case neither a collective security agreement nor a European Leviathan would be necessary to avoid military conflicts among them.

In his *Judgement* of Saint-Pierre's proposal, Rousseau claimed that it was the interests of princes that made agreement among them difficult:

> The whole life of kings, or of those on whom they shuffle off their duties, is devoted solely to two objects: to extend their rule beyond their frontiers and to make it more absolute within them. (1991b, 90)

"From these two fundamental maxims," he wrote, "we can easily judge of the spirit in which princes are likely to receive a proposal which runs directly counter to the one and is hardly more favourable to the other":

> anyone can understand that war and conquest without and the encroachments of despotism within give each other mutual support; that money and men are habitually taken at pleasure from a people of slaves, to bring others beneath the same yoke; and that conversely war furnishes a pretext for exactions of money and another, no less plausible, for keeping large armies constantly on foot, to hold the people in awe. (90–91)

Thus wars among princes were a means of sustaining and increasing their control over their subjects, which in turn was a means of extracting the resources required for further wars. It was war that sustained the political order of Europe, and therefore war could not be eliminated without threatening the interests of rulers.

But this implies that European rulers were actually in a state of war with their subjects, and therefore, as already noted, the states of Europe in the eighteenth century were not Hobbesian commonwealths. Thus it does not imply that a world of Hobbesian commonwealths could not be peaceful. On closer inspection, therefore, Rousseau's explanation of war in the eighteenth century was not, as he claimed, "the very reverse of [Hobbes's] absurd doctrine."

Why was this not obvious both to Rousseau and to his readers? The reason is that Rousseau, along with many other readers of Hobbes, understood Hobbes's state of nature to consist of isolated individuals. But violent conflicts among individuals, Rousseau said, are necessarily limited, because (1) the damage that individuals can do to others is limited, (2) the appetites of individuals are limited, and (3) there is a limit to the inequality of strength of individuals and therefore to the extent to which they must fear each other.

"The state, on the other hand,"

> being an artificial body, has no fixed measure; its proper size is undefined; it can always grow bigger; it feels weak so long as there are others stronger than itself. Its safety and preservation demand that it makes itself stronger than its neighbors. It cannot increase, foster, or exercise its strength except at their expense; and even if it has no need to seek for provisions beyond its borders, it searches ceaselessly for new members to give itself a more unshakeable position. For the inequality of men has its limits set by nature, but the inequality of societies can grow incessantly, until one of them absorbs all the others. (Rousseau 1991a, 38)

Wars between states, then, are wars between artificial persons, not individual men:

> Basically, the body politic, in so far as it is only a moral being, is merely a thing of reason. Remove the public convention and immediately the state is destroyed, without the least change in all that composes it. . . . What then does it mean to wage war on a sovereign? It means an attack on the public convention and all that results from it. . . . If the social pact could be sundered with one blow, immediately there would be no more war; and by this one blow the state would be killed, without the death of one man. (42)

In such struggles between artificial persons, states' objectives far exceed those that individuals would have:

> Land, money, men, all the booty that one can carry off thus become the principal object of reciprocal hostilities. As this base greed imperceptibly changes people's ideas about things, war finally degenerates into brigandage, and little by little enemies and warriors become tyrants and thieves. (40)

But this is a good description of life in Europe in the sixteenth and seventeenth centuries, and it is probably what Hobbes had in mind when he spoke of life in the state of nature. Because Hobbes's sovereign, unlike the eighteenth-century sovereigns described by Rousseau, would be able to make peace without undermining his own position, a world of commonwealths would not necessarily have those properties.

The Market

Rousseau's description of war "in the social state" could actually have been taken directly from Hobbes's description of the state of nature in *Leviathan.* Hobbes wrote that

> in all places, where men have lived by small families, to rob and spoil one another, has been a trade, and so far from being reputed against the law of nature, that the greater spoils they gained, the greater was their honour. . . . And as small families did then; so now do cities and kingdoms which are but greater families, for their own security, enlarge their dominions, upon all pretences of danger, and fear of invasion, or assistance that may be given to invaders, and endeavor as much as they can, to subdue, or weaken their neighbors, by open force, and secret arts, for want of other caution, justly; and are remembered for it in after ages with honour. (Hobbes 1957, chap. XVII, 109–10)

The state of nature that Hobbes described was not a world of isolated individuals but a world in which great families, with their servants and dependents, engaged in violent contests for wealth and then tried to secure their wealth by further violence.[32] When writers in the raison d'état tradition wrote of the interests of princes, it was the interests of the heads of these great families that they had in mind. As Mattingly wrote of Italy in the sixteenth century:

> The sixteenth-century struggle for power had a dynastic, not a national orientation. The kingdom of Naples and the duchy of Milan were wealthy and famous provinces; the conquest of either would increase the apparent strength of the prince who could effect it, and indubitably increase, for a time, the benefits he would be able to bestow on his captains and counsellors. Whether such conquests would be worth to his people the blood and treasure they would cost was an irrelevant, absurd question. Nobody expected they would. (1964, 140)

These words could have been taken directly from Rousseau's characterization of the interests of rulers in the eighteenth century in his critique of Saint-Pierre's proposal.

---

32. Hobbes translated Thucydides into English and was no doubt struck by the parallels he saw between Thucydides' descriptions of the breakdown of political order in ancient Greece and conditions in Europe during his time. For recent discussions, see Johnson 1993 and Rogers and Sorell 2000.

One way writers in the raison d'état tradition thought that interests could provide the basis for political order was that the increasing scale of conflicts among the heads of ruling families might align the interests of rulers with the interests of their subjects. It was out of this alignment of interests that the modern concept of the "national interest" emerged.[33] The idea that competition among predators might protect the interests of their prey became increasingly common and is reflected in the design of the U.S. Constitution (Hirschman 1977).

Adam Smith's "invisible hand" of market competition, which protects consumers from producers who seek to exploit them, was another example of the same idea. But even a producer who overcharged his consumers due to lack of competition from other producers would be better than a predatory nobleman who merely confiscated the fruits of people's labor and provided them nothing in return. And therefore another way that the interests of predators could be aligned with their prey was to substitute trade for predation as a way of accumulating wealth.[34]

In a chapter of *The Wealth of Nations* called "How the Commerce of the Towns Contributed to the Improvement of the Country," Adam Smith wrote that, "though it has been the least observed," the most important contribution by far of the development of commerce and manufactures was that they

> gradually introduced order and good government, and with them, the liberty and security of individuals, among the inhabitants of the country, who had before lived almost in a continual state of war with their neighbors, and of servile dependency upon their superiors. (1937, 385)

This was an effect that was especially striking to contributors to the Scottish Enlightenment such as Smith, who saw clearly the difference between life in the commercial towns of Scotland and life in the Scottish highlands and the borderlands between Scotland and England.[35]

Smith wrote:

> In a country which has neither foreign commerce, nor any of the finer manufactures, a great proprietor, having nothing for which he can exchange the greater part of the produce of his lands which

---

33. For a description of this process in England, see Brewer 1989.
34. This is the main theme of Hirschman 1977.
35. Life in the Anglo-Scottish borderlands might well have been described as "solitary, poor, nasty, brutish, and short." It is the area that contributed the word *blackmail* to the English language, where its original meaning was what would now be called "protection money." For a description of life in the borderlands, see Fraser 1995. For a recent discussion of the Scottish Enlightenment, see Herman 2001.

is over and above the maintenance of the cultivators, consumes the whole in rustic hospitality at home. If this surplus produce is sufficient to maintain a hundred or a thousand men, he can make use of it in no other way than by maintaining a hundred or a thousand men. He is at all times, therefore, surrounded with a multitude of retainers and dependants, who having no equivalent to give in return for their maintenance, but being fed entirely by his bounty, must obey him, for the same reason that soldiers must obey the prince who pays them. (385)

Moreover, "the occupiers of land were in every respect as dependent upon the great proprietor as his retainers," and this was the foundation of "the power of the ancient barons."

They necessarily became the judges in peace, and the leaders in war, of all who dwelt upon their estates. They could maintain order and execute the law within their respective demesnes, because each of them could there turn the whole force of the inhabitants against the injustice of any one. No other person had sufficient authority to do this. The king in particular had not. (386–87)

The feudal law was not the source of this authority but rather an attempt by the king to restrict it. But

[a]fter the institution of feudal subordination, the king was as incapable of restraining the violence of the great lords as before. They still continued to make war according to their own discretion, almost continually upon one another, and very frequently upon the king; and the open country still continued to be a scene of violence, rapine, and disorder.

"But what all the violence of the feudal institutions could never have effected," Smith wrote, "the silent insensible operation of foreign commerce and manufactures gradually brought about" (388).

Foreign commerce and manufactures provided the proprietors of the great landed estates something to spend their wealth on that they preferred to the limited services provided by their retainers. As a result, both retainers and unnecessary tenants were dismissed, and therefore

the great proprietors were no longer capable of interrupting the regular execution of justice or of disturbing the peace of the country. Having sold their birth-right, not like Esau for a mess of pottage in time of hunger and necessity, but in the wantonness of

plenty, for trinkets and baubles, fitter to be play-things of children
than the serious pursuits of men, they became as insignificant as
any substantial burgher or tradesman in a city. A regular government was established in the country as well as in the city, nobody
having sufficient power to disturb its operations in the one, any
more than in the other. (390–91)

Like the more famous "invisible hand" of market competition, this was a
"revolution of the greatest importance to the public happiness, . . .
brought about by two different orders of people, who had not the least
intention to serve the public."

> To gratify the most childish vanity was the sole motive of the
> great proprietors. The merchants and artificers, much less ridicu-
> lous, acted merely from a view to their own interest, and in pur-
> suit of their own pedlar principle of turning a penny wherever a
> penny was to be got. Neither of them had either knowledge or
> foresight of that great revolution which the folly of one, and the
> industry of the other, was gradually bringing about. (391–92)

However, the great landed proprietors did not just become consumers
of "trinkets and baubles." Some of them, of course, became commercial
and manufacturing magnates and therefore a different sort of "robber
baron." One could argue that this was nonetheless preferable to the real
thing. Others, however, became officers in the king's army or administra-
tors of his empire and therefore the indirect beneficiaries of predation on a
larger scale. If the process described by Adam Smith led to the replacement of Hobbes's "little monarchs" by big monarchs, one must ask why
these big monarchs would not just be bigger predators.

Indeed, one could argue that the effect of commerce and manufacturing was not just to provide nonagricultural sources of wealth but also to
increase the optimal scale of predation. When agricultural production that
is consumed locally is the source of all wealth, then whoever controls an
agricultural estate controls the wealth that it produces. Trade and manufacturing, on the other hand, lead to economies of scale in predation, and
the existence of money provides a means of sharing the gains among
predators without dividing large tracts of territory among them.[36]

It was such large-scale predators that Rousseau had in mind when he
argued that European sovereigns would not be impressed by arguments

---

36. This is the basis of Henri Pirenne's (2001) argument that European feudalism was the
product not of the barbarian conquest of Rome but of the disruption of Mediterranean trade
caused by the rise of Islam.

"drawn from the interruption of commerce, from the loss of life, from the financial confusion and the real loss which result from an unprofitable conquest."

> It is a great miscalculation always to estimate the losses and gains of princes in terms of money; the degree of power they aim at is not to be reckoned by the millions in their coffers. The prince always makes his schemes rotate: he seeks to command in order to enrich himself, and to enrich himself in order to command. . . . it is only in the hope of winning them both in the long run that he pursues each of them apart. If he is to be master both of men and things, he must have empire and money at the same time. (Rousseau 1991b, 92)

Anticipating recent arguments about the importance of relative gains, he also claimed that

> the advantages to commerce from a general and lasting peace are in themselves certain and indisputable, still, being common to all states, they will be appreciated by none. For such advantages make themselves felt only by contrast, and he who wishes to increase his relative power is bound to seek only such gains as are exclusive. (93)

However, Europe is no longer ruled by princes, and rule is no longer a means of acquiring great wealth. Thus Rousseau's reasoning does not necessarily apply to states such as the ones that exist in modern Europe.

What accounts for the change? Part of the answer is that competition among the predatory rulers of early modern Europe meant that the resources that were required to maintain their positions greatly increased over time. Thus as more and more of the wealth of Europe was produced by traders and manufacturers rather than by great agricultural estates, means had to be devised to convert this new form of wealth into military capabilities. But, as Adam Smith wrote,

> A merchant . . . is not necessarily the citizen of any particular country. It is in a great measure indifferent to him from what place he carries on his trade; and a very trifling disgust will make him remove his capital, and together with it all the industry which it supports, from one country to another. (1937, 395)

And therefore merchants and manufacturers were in a stronger bargaining position than people tied to the land when predatory rulers sought to capture their resources to support their own wealth and power. In modern totalitarian states rulers have tried to exploit the wealth of commerce and industry without having to compromise with its producers, but, to the surprise of many, states in which the rulers were weaker have proved so far to be militarily stronger. Military competition among states, therefore, has had an important influence on the interest rulers have taken in the economic well-being of their subjects.[37]

Recurring War, Perpetual Peace

It is a short step from the idea that interests are a more reliable way of providing for the common good than morality to the idea that the actions of individuals in pursuit of their interests can have nonobvious consequences for human social behavior. And it is a short step from there to the idea that explanations of the collective behavior of human beings might resemble explanations of natural phenomena.

The ideas of Adam Smith illustrate the first step. One of the people who took the second was Immanuel Kant, who wrote:

> No matter what conception one may form of the freedom of the will in metaphysics, the phenomenal appearances of the will, i.e., human actions, are determined by general laws of nature like any other event of nature. . . . Thus marriages, the consequent births and the deaths, since the free will seems to have such a great influence on them, do not seem to be subject to any law according to which one could calculate their number beforehand. Yet the annual (statistical) tables about them in the major countries show that they occur according to stable natural laws. . . . Individual human beings, each pursuing his own ends according to his inclination and often one against another (and even one entire people against another) . . . unintentionally promote, as if it were their guide, an end of nature which is unknown to them. They thus work to promote that which they would care little for if they knew about it. (1784, 116–17)

Even though "men . . . do not act like animals merely according to instinct, nor like rational citizens according to an agreed plan" (117), it is possible, Kant claimed, that there is an order to human affairs that human beings could uncover.

"[N]ature," he wrote, "produced a Kepler who figured out an unex-

---

37. For extended presentations of this argument, see Jones 1987 and McNeill 1982.

pected way of subsuming the eccentric orbits of the planets to definite laws, and a Newton who explained these laws by a general cause of nature." Kant claimed to have discerned an order to human history, though he said he "would leave it to nature to produce a man who would be capable of writing history" in accordance with it (117). The order he claimed to have discerned could be characterized as a theory of the evolution of human society, which he outlined long before Darwin's theory of biological evolution.[38]

Darwinian evolution takes place through the biological process of the inheritance of traits of organisms, and individual animals have only limited means of responding to changes in their environments. Kant's idea was that human beings were endowed with greater means of inventing ad hoc responses to their environment than were animals, but this adaptation

> requires trials, experience and information in order to progress gradually from one level of understanding to the next. Therefore every man would have to live excessively long in order to learn how to make full use of all his faculties.

Thus, in humans, "those natural faculties which aim at the use of reason shall be fully developed in the species, not in the individual," and therefore, we might now say, human evolution takes place at the social level as well as, or instead of, the biological level (Kant 1784, 118).

There are three elements to the Darwinian theory of evolution: (1) a mechanism that randomly produces new traits in animal populations; (2) a mechanism that selects some traits to be reproduced at greater rates than others; and (3) a mechanism of reproduction that leads to repeated operations of the first two mechanisms. In any theory of social evolution, the mechanism that produces diversity must obviously be human inventiveness, while the mechanism of reproduction must be just the transmission of culture and social organization from one generation to the next.

What is striking about Kant's theory of social evolution is that the mechanism that selects some social inventions over others is conflict, which leads to violence and war.

> The means which nature employs to accomplish the development of all faculties is the antagonism of men in society. . . . I mean by antagonism the asocial sociability of man, i.e., the propensity of men to enter into a society, which propensity is, however, linked

---

38. Kant was interested in eighteenth-century ideas about biology, and some scholars have claimed to find in his writings about biology ideas that anticipate Darwin's. For a skeptical discussion of these claims, see Lovejoy 1910 and 1911.

to a constant mutual resistance which threatens to dissolve this society.

"This propensity," he wrote, "apparently is innate in man."

> Man has an inclination to *associate* himself, because in such a state he feels more like a man capable of developing his natural faculties. Man has also a marked propensity to *isolate* himself, because he finds in himself the asocial quality to want to arrange everything according to his own ideas. He therefore expects resistance everywhere, just as he knows of himself that he is inclined to resist others. (Kant 1784, 120; emphasis in original)

According to Kant, man's "asocial sociability" leads to an evolutionary process that might be compared to the process by which American professional football has evolved. Teams, seeking to defeat other teams, invent strategies and formations that their opponents have difficulty coping with. Such successful strategies are either copied or countered by newly invented strategies, and over time, therefore, the game of football gradually changes.[39]

The development of football, of course, is constrained by rules that define the game. The evolution of human society, however, is not constrained by rules, and therefore any rules that constrain conflict must be endogenous to the evolutionary process that is driven by recurring conflicts.

Kant's description of human nature resembles Hobbes's, and like Hobbes he thought that "[m]an *needs* a master who can break man's will and compel him to obey a general will under which every man could be free" (Kant 1784, 122; emphasis in original).[40] However, as we saw in our discussion of Hobbes, the creation of a "master" (or sovereign) entails a problem, which Kant states very graphically:

---

39. It is interesting to compare what Kant said about the evolution of human society with modern writings on the same subject by evolutionary biologists. For examples, see Diamond 1997 and Wilson 2002. Also relevant is Bingham 1999. A useful recent survey of evolutionary thinking in the social sciences, with a focus on the development of economic institutions, can be found in Bowles 2003. See also the collection of papers, with accompanying commentaries, in Katz 2000. I have found the work of the anthropologist Christopher Boehm useful in thinking about what "asocial sociability" might mean as a way of characterizing human nature—see Boehm 1987 and 1999. Kant's ideas about social evolution have been given remarkably little attention by evolutionary social scientists. For recent discussions, see Fukuyama 1992; Wright 2000; and Cederman 2001a and 2001b. For a discussion of Wright's book by an evolutionary biologist, see Wilson 2000. Some of William McNeill's writings lend themselves to interpretation in these terms. See especially McNeill 1980 and 1982.
40. On Kant's Hobbesianism, see Tuck 1999, 207–25.

But where is he to get this master? Nowhere but from mankind.
But then this master is in turn an animal who needs a master.
Therefore one cannot see how man, try as he will, could secure a
master . . . who would be himself just. . . . One cannot fashion
something absolutely straight from wood which is as crooked as
that of which man is made. (122–23)

There are two parts to Kant's solution to this problem. One is to "organize
a group of rational beings"

in such a way that, in spite of the fact that their private attitudes
are opposed, these private attitudes mutually impede each other
in such a manner that the public behavior . . . is the same as if they
did not have such evil attitudes. (Kant 1795, 453)

"Such a problem," he claimed, "*must* be solvable."
But the solution to it would seem to require both a designer with the
appropriate motivation and a willingness to accept what the designer recommended. Hobbes, as many people have pointed out, was unclear how
people were supposed to get from the state of nature to a commonwealth,
and Rousseau argued that European rulers would never accept the scheme
for regulating violence proposed by Saint-Pierre. Kant's solution to this
problem is analogous to Darwin's argument that intelligent design is a by-
product of the evolutionary process:

if I say of nature: she wants this or that to take place, it does not
mean that she imposes a *duty* to do it . . . but it means that nature
itself does it, whether we want it or not.

And the mechanism by which nature does it is war: "If internal conflicts
did not compel a people to submit itself to the compulsion of public laws,
external wars would do it" (Kant 1795, 452). "We have to admit," Kant
wrote, "that the greatest evils which oppress civilised nations are the result
of war."

But if this constant fear of war did not compel even heads of state
to show this *respect for humanity,* would we still encounter the
same culture, or that close association of social classes within the
commonwealth which promotes the well-being of all? Would we
still encounter the same population, or even that degree of freedom which is still present in spite of highly restrictive laws? We
need only look at *China,* whose position may expose it to occasional unforeseen incursions but not to attack by a powerful

enemy, and we shall find that, for this very reason, it has been stripped of every vestige of freedom. (Kant 1786, 231–32)[41]

Biological evolution does not have a goal or end state toward which it is directed. Kant claimed that there was reason to believe that social evolution does:

> a union of nations wherein each, even the smallest state, could expect to derive its security and rights—not from its own power or its own legal judgments—but only from this great union. . . . However fanciful this idea may seem and as such may have been ridiculed when held by the Abbé St. Pierre and Rousseau . . . it is, nevertheless, the inevitable escape from the destitution into which human beings plunge each other. (Kant 1784, 124)

Thus, he claimed:

> All wars are . . . so many attempts (not in the intention of men, but in the intention of nature) to bring about new relations among the states and to form new bodies by the break-up of the old states to the point where they cannot again maintain themselves alongside each other and must therefore suffer revolutions until finally, partly through the best possible arrangement of the civic constitution internally, and partly through the common agreement and legislation externally, there is created a state which, like a civic commonwealth, can maintain itself automatically. (Kant 1784, 124–25)

Thus Kant claimed not only that "war made the state," as modern scholarship on the development of the European state tells us (Tilly 1992; Porter 1994), but also that it would eventually produce a peaceful global order.

Recent writings about Kant by students of international politics have mainly focused on his characterization of the properties of a peaceful global order, which some have seen as an alternative to Realism as a theory of international politics.[42] However, Kant's understanding of the basic problem of political order was nearly indistinguishable from Hobbes's, and his understanding of international politics in his time was not very different from Rousseau's (Tuck 1999, 197–225). What distinguished him

---

41. For Kant's analysis of how external wars lead to internal justice, see Kant 1784, 128; and Kant 1795, 448–55. It is replete with biological analogies.
42. See especially the influential articles on Kant by Michael Doyle (1983).

from Rousseau was his belief that a global Leviathan was not necessary for peace, and what distinguished him from Hobbes was his belief that peace among commonwealths required that commonwealths be republics.

Even though Kant thought that a global Leviathan was not necessary for peace, he wrote that

> the state of peace must be *founded;* for the mere omission of the threat of war is no security of peace, and consequently a neighbor may treat his neighbor as an enemy unless he has guaranteed such security to him, which can only happen within a state of law. (Kant 1795, 436; emphasis in original)

Therefore peace required a treaty that embodied specific commitments. This treaty would establish

> a union of a particular kind which we may call the *pacific union* . . . which would be distinguished from a *peace treaty* by the fact that the latter tries to end merely *one* war, while the former tries to end *all* wars forever. This union is not directed toward the securing of some additional power of the state, but merely toward maintaining and securing the *freedom* of each state by and for itself and at the same time of the other states thus allied with each other. And yet, these states will not subject themselves (as do men in the state of nature) to laws and to the enforcement of such laws. (444; emphasis in the original)

But if such commitments are not backed up with force, what guarantees that they will be kept? Kant's answer is "mutual self-interest."

> It is the *spirit of commerce* which cannot coexist with war, and which sooner or later takes hold of every nation. . . . In this way nature guarantees lasting peace by the mechanism of human inclinations. (455; emphasis in original)

Human interests, then, would enable such an agreement to "maintain itself automatically," as Kant put it, or, as we would now say, make peace an equilibrium. Thus we might now conjecture that the function of the treaty would be to make the expectations that supported the equilibrium common knowledge. But in the absence of such a commitment, it is not clear that Kant thought that peace would be an equilibrium.

Both the states that make up the international system and the network of agreements that define it have changed considerably since Kant's time. Structural Realism assumes, without any supporting argument, that nothing important has changed since then. Enthusiasts for Kant's ideas are inclined to believe that the conditions that Kant specified for peace among the states of Europe have been achieved. But that would have seemed a plausible claim in the middle of the nineteenth century as well, when the greatest amount of violence was yet to come. And Kant seems to have thought that revolutionary France might form the nucleus of a peaceful international order (Tuck 1989, 221–25).

The problem is that Kant's theory of social evolution suffers from some of the same limitations as Marx's theory of economic evolution: (1) it is not clear exactly what properties the end state of the process is supposed to have; (2) therefore it is not clear how far off the achievement of the end state is; and (3) it is not clear whether the actions of human beings can influence when the end state might be reached. Modern scholarship provides strong support for Kant's claim that war is the mechanism that drove the creation of the modern European state. But without a better understanding of what explains violent conflicts it is not possible to say what implications the current properties of those states have for the likelihood of future conflicts.

From Raison d'État to Realism

As Kant's writings illustrate, the origins of modern social science are to be found in the raison d'état tradition.[43] The idea that people's behavior is to be explained by their interests, arguments that show that the consequences of this fact can be both complex and nonobvious, and efforts to design institutional arrangements that channel competing individual interests in directions that serve the common good are all fundamental to both modern economics and modern political science. Moreover, current controversies about the relative importance of interests and social norms or culture in explaining social behavior echo early criticisms of writers in the raison d'état tradition.[44]

Since the theory of games has been most enthusiastically embraced by economists, many people have the impression that game theory is just economics, and since economists are not much interested in norms or culture, they conclude that game theory cannot have much to say about the relation among culture, norms, and the interests of individuals. But, as the example of the rule of the road discussed at the beginning of this chapter illustrates, this is wrong (O'Neill 1999, 259).

---

43. As they also illustrate, this is where the modern Western conception of the morally autonomous individual comes from as well (Tuck 1999).

44. See the discussion in Tuck 1999. For an interesting argument that even religion can be explained as a way human beings have managed to organize themselves for collective action to serve human interests, see Wilson 2002.

The two fundamental insights of game theory are (1) that one cannot specify what actions are in an individual's interests without also specifying what would be in the interest of other individuals (this is the problem of strategic interdependence) and (2) that in any given social situation there will often be multiple combinations of rational choices by individuals, all of which are both stable and individually rational (this is the problem of multiple equilibria). The second insight provides a way of understanding how norms and culture help explain the behavior of individuals. But the first insight illustrates the fact that cultural explanations are usually incomplete, in that they fail to explain why individuals must do what their culture requires, even when it appears contrary to obvious human interests.[45] Thus it seems unlikely that we will be able to resolve the issues raised in debates between writers in the raison d'état tradition and their critics without an answer to the questions that game theory has always focused on.[46]

If "realism" is raison d'état, it is just modern social science and not a theory of international politics. Why, then, is realism thought by so many people to be a doctrine that is only relevant to international politics?[47] At least part of the answer lies in the fact that the central concern of writers in the raison d'état tradition was to control violence by using political institutions to channel people's interests in peaceful directions. Because the European state proved to be such a successful means of doing that, such states are now taken for granted. They are considered as natural as the rivers and mountain ranges that often separate them. Many people now project the states of the second half of the nineteenth century back onto earlier periods in European history, when they did not actually exist. As a result, domestic violence now seems abnormal or unnatural, the civil wars in the United States and Spain aberrations, and violence within territories demarcated by international agreements to be the consequence of "state failures" rather than the absence of states that have the properties of the ones that developed in Europe.

This is why, when Kenneth Waltz set out to write a book about the causes of war, he took for granted that his subject was interstate wars, and

---

45. For an investigation of this question by an anthropologist in an analysis of one particular set of social norms, see Boehm 1987. For a more general discussion, see Wilson 1998. For an extended discussion of the incompleteness of cultural explanations of human behavior, see Homans 1967.

46. The importance of social norms for understanding human behavior was part of game theory from the beginning. See the discussion of "standards of behavior," and their relation to social organization, in von Neumann and Morgenstern 1944, chap. 4. For recent discussions of how game theory can be used to illuminate the relation between culture and individual behavior, see Wilson 1998; O'Neill 1999; Chwe 2001; and Bowles 2003. See also Aoki 2001 and Greif 2006.

47. Unfortunately, the recent book about the relation between Realism and raison d'état by Jonathan Haslam (2002) mainly serves to reinforce this impression.

it seemed natural to him to group the possible causes of war into three categories: those pertaining to the nature of man (the first image), those pertaining to the nature of states (the second image), and those pertaining to the nature of the interstate system (the third image) (Waltz 1959). This would have made little sense to Europeans in the seventeenth century, to whom Hobbes's writings were addressed.

Thus contemporary Realism simply assumes that the problem that concerned Hobbes has been solved and then turns our attention to the implications of the existence of a world of commonwealths. But Hobbes's problem has not been solved in many places, and even where solutions seem to have been found, we cannot assume that they will last forever (Seabright 2004).

Contrary to what many people assume, Waltz had very little to say about Hobbes, and what he did say implied that Hobbes's characterization of the state of nature rested entirely on a pessimistic interpretation of human nature. According to Waltz:

> because for Hobbes there is no society, nothing but recalcitrant individuals on the one side and government on the other, the state must be a powerful one. (1959, 85)

This reflects Rousseau's reading of Hobbes. But we have seen that Hobbes wrote things about the state of nature that are inconsistent with this interpretation and that his contemporaries were very unlikely to have understood him in that way. The state of war that concerned Hobbes and his contemporaries was not a condition populated by individuals outside of society but one populated by warring groups, and thus the wars that concerned Hobbes and his readers were neither armed conflicts among individuals nor wars between or among states.

Waltz also claimed that liberals in the eighteenth and nineteenth centuries

> were as individualistic as Hobbes, but they rejected usually Hobbes's view of human nature and always his opinion of the social results of selfishly motivated behavior. Most of them believed, on the one hand, that man is generally pretty good and, on the other, that even though individual behavior may be selfishly oriented, still there is a natural harmony that leads, not to a war of all against all, but to a stable, orderly, and progressive society with little need for governmental intervention. (1959, 85–86)

But if there is a disagreement between writers like Adam Smith and Hobbes, it is not a disagreement about human nature but about the extent to which increasing the opportunities for trade will reduce the relative attractiveness of predation as a means of satisfying people's interests. In the absence of trade and economic growth, the only means to achieve great wealth is to seize it by force. It requires neither an optimistic view of human nature nor belief in a natural harmony of interests to think that increasing the opportunities to gain from trade will reduce the incidence of economic predation or that the self-interest of both rulers and ruled could motivate them to acquiesce in arrangements that had that effect.

Modern Realism's analysis of the implications of the existence of a world of commonwealths is an eclectic mixture of Hobbes's characterization of the state of nature and Rousseau's characterization of interstate politics in a world of predatory rulers. But there is no foundation in what Hobbes wrote for Realism's characterization of a world of commonwealths, and no valid reason has been given why Rousseau's characterization of his own time applies to a world of states whose rulers more closely resemble Hobbes's sovereign than the rulers of the eighteenth century.

What Next?

Thus Waltz, in trying to construct an explanation of war on the foundations laid by writers in the raison d'état tradition, started in the wrong place. One must begin not with a world of sovereign states but with a world in which people are free to organize themselves in order to profit from the use of force. That is where Europe found itself in the early modern period, and that is where much of the world finds itself today. Violent conflicts among such organizations may continue for long periods of time, as they did in Europe in the early modern period. However, out of them may emerge, as eventually happened in Europe, institutional arrangements that substitute for the use of force. These arrangements may take the form of common institutions, or they may take the form of separate institutions with jurisdictions over separate territorial areas. The division of intellectual labor in modern political science underemphasizes the problem of explaining which of these outcomes occurs. And modern Realism begs the question of which should be expected to be the most stable substitute for violent conflict.

Beginning with the next chapter, then, I will consider what violence might be good for and what that implies for the ways in which human beings organize themselves.

CHAPTER 3

Violence, Organization, and War

What is a war? That is a question that is harder to answer than many people assume. At a minimum it is a contest in which organized groups compete in killing and wounding each other or destroying things they value. But why would any group expect to benefit from harming members of another group?

Often such contests take the form of an attempt by one group to destroy the military forces of another, and many people tacitly, but incorrectly, assume that that is the point of all military contests. But what would be the benefit of doing that, even if one were successful? A common answer is that it would prevent the other group from using its military forces against one's own. But that only raises the question of why the other group would profit from doing it: if it is common knowledge that no group would benefit from disarming another group, then no one could expect to profit from destroying another group's means of disarming one's own.[1]

The effect of one group's disarming another is just that the victorious group can then kill or wound the members of the other group, or destroy things of value to them, without forceful opposition. Moreover, contrary to what is commonly assumed, in many violent contests neither side has any prospect of destroying the military forces of the other side, and even if they did, neither seems to try seriously to do it. Thus our primary task must be to explain why one group would expect to benefit just from killing or wounding the members of another group or destroying their property.

We saw at the beginning of chapter 1 that John Mearsheimer (2001) claimed that international politics was "tragic." What he meant was that war is inefficient, though admittedly the word *inefficient* seems hardly adequate as a way of describing war. I use the word *inefficient* here in the way that it is used in economics, where it describes a consequence of the choices of two or more people that leaves them worse off than they would have

---

1. Note that that would appear to describe a world of Hobbesian commonwealths, in which it would be common knowledge that the function of sovereigns, to use Hobbes's words, was simply to provide security to their citizens from the "injuries of one another" and "from the invasion of foreigners."

been had they chosen differently.[2] To say that war is inefficient means that there is an alternative to war that would be better for the participants than the prewar expected value of fighting.[3]

But why would a war ever occur if all the parties to it would be better off avoiding it? One possible answer is that strong emotions or cognitive errors of some sort have prevented them from seeing their true interests, and this seems to be what is implicitly assumed by much of the literature on conflict management. However, game theory provides compelling examples of situations in which rational individuals choose outcomes they would all have been better off not choosing. One is the coordination game discussed in the previous chapter. Two others, the Prisoner's Dilemma and the Stag Hunt, have been especially popular as ways of understanding why much of what happens in international politics seems to be contrary to everyone's interests, as we saw in chapter 1. However, all these games are far more plausible as explanations of a failure to cooperate to achieve common interests than as explanations of war. And if people are unable to cooperate, there can be no armies and therefore no wars.

Kenneth Waltz wrote, "The threat of force internationally is comparable to the role of the strike in labor and management bargaining" (1979, 114). This suggests another explanation of inefficient choices that is a much more promising way of understanding wars than the Prisoner's Dilemma or the Stag Hunt but one that Waltz never developed.

In a strike an organization of employees seeks to increase employees' gains from a contract by preventing the owners from profiting from the firm or industry until they agree to terms that are more favorable for the employees. However, in doing this the employees also harm themselves. Thus whatever the terms of the agreement that ends a strike, the strike itself is costly for both sides, and both would have been better off accepting the agreement before the strike rather than after it. This is often true of wars as well.

Strikes are commonly regarded as examples of bargaining, and therefore one might hope that an understanding of bargaining would help one understand why strikes occur. If Waltz is right, then an understanding of bargaining might also contribute to an understanding of wars.

Strikes, of course, may be accompanied by violence. However, there are two attributes of strikes that distinguish them from most violent

---

2. More precisely, an outcome is inefficient if there is another feasible outcome that at least one person would prefer and that would leave no other persons worse off.

3. The classic discussion of the tragic nature of interstate conflict is Butterfield 1951. But Butterfield's main example is the struggle between East and West over the future of Germany in the aftermath of World War II, which did not lead to war. It is instructive to read Marc Trachtenberg's (1999) discussion of this issue in the context of Butterfield's analysis. See also Wagner 1980.

conflicts, and if we are to understand violent conflicts we must bear these differences in mind. One is that even if force is used by labor or management, a wage contract leaves them both better off than they would be without one. In the context of war, however, force is used in an attempt to make one's adversary worse off. Second, wage contracts are typically enforceable, whereas the parties to an agreement made in the context of the use of force must usually be concerned about whether the agreement will in fact be carried out.

These two differences are more closely related to each other than they may at first appear to be. Whether some contract makes one party better off or not depends on the baseline used for comparison. In adverse economic circumstances management may succeed in getting labor to agree to a wage agreement that leaves workers worse off than they were before, and the workers may therefore feel no different from someone who surrenders something valuable to someone else at gunpoint. Distinguishing between the two cases requires a distinction between what one possesses and what one owns. But this distinction rests on a definition of property rights, which may be contested and in any case has to be enforced.

We should not exaggerate the enforceability of contracts even when the definition and enforcement of property rights can be taken for granted. Wage bargains often include complex stipulations concerning working conditions and management prerogatives that can be evaded without provoking external sanctions. However, bargaining theory takes the enforcement of agreements for granted, and if we are to understand violent conflicts we must consider what the consequences might be if agreements can be violated. First, however, we must think about how to understand bargaining.

Bargaining

A strike is, at least in part, a dispute between labor and management about how to divide up the revenues of a firm. Thus it can be helpful in thinking about strikes to think first about a simpler situation in which two people are offered a sum of money if they can agree on how to divide it between them, but if they cannot agree they get nothing. We can ask two questions about such a situation: (1) What division will the two bargainers agree to? and (2) How long will it take them to agree?

These simple questions lead to two surprisingly difficult puzzles, which are the subject of a very large literature. The first is the result of the fact that rationality and self-interest alone are not enough to answer the question of what division the bargainers will accept. The second puzzle concerns the relation between the two questions just stated: if it is clear what division the bargainers should accept, then they should accept it immediately. But if that were true then bargaining as it is commonly understood (including strikes) would never occur.

Why Haggle?

Since it seems plausible that rational bargainers will not throw the money away and therefore will certainly agree to something, the question of what they will agree to may seem unimportant. However, the question of how long it will take them to agree is very important, since even temporary disagreement can be extremely costly. A plausible answer is that agreement on a division of the money requires some information that the two bargainers may not initially possess, and if they do not have it the bargaining process provides a way of getting it. Thus the costs associated with delay in reaching agreement are the price that must be paid for the information required to reach it. However, an understanding of what that information might be requires a solution to the first puzzle, which is therefore more important than it first appears to be. Let us see how it arises.

Since by assumption each bargainer prefers more money to less but neither will get any unless the other agrees, each bargainer's decision about what division to accept depends on her expectation of what the other will agree to. This is the sort of problem that game theory was invented to solve, and the answer to it was supplied by John Nash and is therefore called the Nash equilibrium. But all that the Nash equilibrium requires of rational bargainers is that their expectations be consistent, in the sense that, given some expectation as to what each will do, neither should have an incentive to deviate from it. And if each bargainer is free to demand any amount as a condition for his or her agreement then every possible division of the money satisfies this requirement. Thus game theory seemed at first merely to justify the common belief that any division of the money would be consistent with rational behavior, and therefore nothing could be said about what rational bargainers would agree to.[4]

Two types of solution to this puzzle have been offered.[5] One is that, since every division would be a Nash equilibrium, the problem is, as in the coordination game discussed in the previous chapter, to coordinate the

---

4. For an example of a Nash equilibrium, see the discussion of the coordination game in chapter 2. It is important to distinguish the Nash equilibrium, which is a necessary condition for rational behavior when decisions are interdependent, from the Nash bargaining solution, which was Nash's own attempt to answer the question of what bargainers should agree to. Unfortunately the Nash bargaining solution requires special axioms whose relation to individual rationality is by no means clear. Thus not even Nash thought that the Nash bargaining solution was a definitive answer to the bargaining problem.

5. For a more extended discussion and references to the literature, see Kreps 1990, 551–71.

bargainers' expectations on one division rather than another. This implies that the bargaining problem is at its core just another example of a coordination problem, though one that is complicated by the fact that the bargainers have conflicting preferences as to which division they coordinate on. And therefore salient divisions, conventions, or prevailing conceptions of fairness may lead the bargainers to focus their expectations on one particular outcome, and the costs associated with a failure to coordinate may deter them from deviating from what is expected. If two people are bargaining over the division of a sum of money, all these factors may lead them to coordinate their expectations around an agreement that divides the money equally.[6]

This answer to the puzzle implies that there are two possible explanations for a failure to reach immediate agreement. One is that the bargainers have failed to coordinate on a particular division of the money. Unfortunately it is not clear what they should do in this case. The other possible explanation is that they agree on how the gains should be divided but they disagree on how to measure them. This explanation is consistent with the suggestion that delay in reaching agreement is the result of a lack of relevant information.

The other solution to the puzzle posed by the existence of multiple Nash equilibria has two parts. One is to note that the definition of rational behavior given by the Nash equilibrium is incomplete, since in many situations it is consistent with behavior that is patently not rational. For example, suppose one of our bargainers thought he might gain if he threatened to detonate a bomb killing both bargainers if the other did not agree to his terms. If the other bargainer rejected his demand then the one who had made the threat would not want to carry it out, since the only consequence of carrying it out would be that he was killed along with the other bargainer. In other words, once the other bargainer refused his demand, carrying out the threat would no longer be part of a Nash equilibrium. A tighter definition of rational behavior would rule out equilibria that contained such incredible threats, and such a definition provides one part of a possible solution to the puzzle of too many Nash equilibria in bargaining situations.

The other part of the solution is to require that the process by which offers and counteroffers are made be modeled explicitly and any agreement then be the result of a (suitably refined) equilibrium combination of strategies in such a negotiation game. In modeling the bargaining process it is plausible that negotiators will prefer agreements that come sooner to

---

6. Note, however, that since the bargainers have conflicting preferences as to what division they should coordinate on, any convention that determined that might be the source of significant conflict. (Compare the example of the choice of language mentioned in the preceding chapter.)

agreements that come later, and even if a demand by one bargainer is accepted by the other an exchange of offers will require a finite amount of time. Ariel Rubinstein (1982) was the first to show that with these assumptions there is a unique combination of strategies that satisfy the requirement of sequential rationality just mentioned.[7]

Because both bargainers prefer present agreements to future ones, Rubinstein's model implies that they should reach agreement immediately. Thus explanations of delay focus on the possibility that some of the information required by the bargaining solution is missing. In Rubinstein's model an obvious candidate for this role is the discount rates of the two bargainers. Since each bargainer presumably knows her own discount rate, the problem must be that this information is not common knowledge. And since each bargainer has an incentive to misrepresent it, this problem cannot be overcome simply by having each bargainer reveal it to the other. Thus the only way each can acquire information about the other's discount rate is through observing what offers each makes and rejects in the course of the bargaining process, which provides a formal justification for the idea that the bargaining process allows for the revelation of information.[8]

If we are to use this reasoning as a way of explaining strikes, we would have to distinguish between prestrike exchanges of offers and exchanges of offers once the strike has begun. Any exchange of offers prior to a strike takes place while the firm is operating and therefore while labor and management are benefiting from some existing division of its revenues. If one is satisfied with that division but the other is not, then the fact that the satisfied party discounts future benefits provides it with no motivation to agree to any change in the status quo. It is rather the expected outcome of bargaining in the context of a strike that might motivate the satisfied party to agree to make some concession.

In bargaining theory the set of possible agreements is commonly called the bargaining frontier, and the outcome that would occur in the absence of agreement is called the disagreement outcome. Thus in prestrike negotiations labor or management threatens to revert temporarily to the disagreement outcome in order to renegotiate the terms of the wage bargain. However, if they share enough information about the consequences of doing so then this will not be necessary.

In prewar crisis bargaining, the disagreement outcome is war. In the

---

7. See the discussion of Rubinstein's argument in the next chapter.

8. Rubinstein's answer to the bargaining problem depends not just on a refinement of Nash's definition of rational behavior but also on Rubinstein's specific assumptions about how bargainers are expected to negotiate with each other. While these assumptions are not implausible, they are not the only plausible assumptions one might make. For a survey of the literature on this subject, see Kennan and Wilson 1993.

next chapter we will see that this analysis of bargaining in the context of strikes has important implications for understanding the occurrence of war. But for war to occur there must be organizations that expect to benefit from the use of force. Thus we must first consider what bargaining theory tells us about the benefits from organizing and from using force.

Bargaining and Organization

With complete information the outcome of Rubinstein's bargaining game is not an equal division of the money. Rather, the bargainer who gets to make the first offer can take advantage of the fact that her adversary discounts future benefits and demand a larger share. Thus Rubinstein's analysis seems appropriate for situations in which there is no commonly accepted norm concerning how the money is to be divided, but each is simply out to get as much as she can from the other. Because of Rubinstein's assumptions about how the bargaining process proceeds, each bargainer is able, in effect, to deliver a little ultimatum to the other: accept my demand now or pay the price of waiting until I consider yours later. The longer the other bargainer has to wait, the bigger the premium the one making the first offer can extract.[9]

In the limit one bargainer might be able to confront the other with a choice between accepting her demand or getting nothing at all. A bargainer able to deliver such an ultimatum (or take-it-or-leave-it offer) could successfully demand all (or nearly all) the money.[10]

Take-it-or-leave-it demands are usually not credible because they imply that the person making the demand would prefer no agreement at all to an agreement on any other terms, which is normally not true. However, such demands may be credible if one individual has many alternative bargaining partners. Then if one potential partner rejects a demand there are others to replace him. That is how an organization increases the bargaining power of workers: it prevents management from making many take-it-or-leave-it offers to individual workers.

But if a bargain struck between management and a labor union benefits all workers, then individual workers may have no incentive to contribute to the support of the union, since if others contribute a person who does not will benefit anyway and if others do not contribute one person's contribution would be ineffective. Thus workers may face what is

---

9. The Rubinstein bargaining model is discussed further in the next chapter.
10. If what is at stake is not the division of a commonly known sum of money but, for example, the price for which something will be sold, a seller able to make a take-it-or-leave-it offer may demand more than the other is willing to pay and there will be no bargaining process through which he can learn that he was mistaken. In that case it is possible that no mutually beneficial agreement will be reached.

known as a collective action problem in capturing the potential gains from bargaining with management. If so, their bargaining power will be less than it would otherwise be.[11]

Bargaining and the Use of Force

If the delay between offers in the bargaining process modeled by Rubinstein is small enough, then the Rubinstein solution will deviate only slightly from the equal division that a norm of fairness might prescribe. However, a requirement that the bargainers receive equal benefits from agreement can have surprising implications. Suppose, for example, that the sum to be divided is one hundred dollars and that some benefactor has offered to pay a bonus of fifty dollars to one of the bargainers if agreement is reached. Then if the money is divided equally one bargainer will receive fifty dollars and the other one hundred dollars, and the gains from agreement will therefore be unequal. If the bargainers are to benefit equally, therefore, the bargainer whose gains will be supplemented must get only twenty-five dollars of the money to be divided and the other must get seventy-five dollars.

Moreover, if, instead of supplementing one bargainer's gains, someone is expected to take some action that will cost him fifty dollars if no agreement is reached, the effect is exactly the same: that person will gain from the agreement both the share of the money he receives and the fifty dollars he would have lost if no agreement had occurred. Thus if the two bargainers' gains are to be equal, he must receive only twenty-five dollars of the money to be divided. This example illustrates the fact that there are two normative issues raised by bargaining: how the gains from agreement should be divided and what disagreement outcome should be taken as the baseline from which the gains are measured. When we consider that the person who is expected to deprive one of the bargainers of fifty dollars in the event of no agreement may be the other bargainer, it also helps us understand one of the uses of force.

While there may be people who derive utility directly from harming others, most harm is done because it is a way of achieving some other benefit. For example, if someone occupies a piece of land that I want, I may kill him in order to take it. Instead of killing him, however, I could allow him to continue to work the land and threaten to kill or harm him if he refused to give me any food he produces above what is required to keep him alive.

---

11. Note that the incentives that give rise to the collective action problem resemble those in the Prisoner's Dilemma game. The seminal work on the collective action problem is Olson 1965. See also Hardin 1982.

If all incentives to use force were like the first, then violent conflicts would all be like conflicts between animal predators and their prey, and its point would always be simply to separate people from things of value that they control. Often, however, the point of violence for human predators is, as in the second example, to influence the behavior of the victim, which would be true even if all I wanted was to persuade him to give up what he had. But then it is unclear why harm would actually be done to him or his property. The literature on bargaining provides a possible answer to that question.

Seen in that context, force is a way by which individuals can manipulate the disagreement outcome in a bargaining situation in order to gain something at the expense of others. However, as in any bargaining situation, both would have an interest in avoiding its actual use. I might, for example, threaten to beat the man unless he agreed to share his harvests with me. But beating him prevents him from working. We will both gain, therefore, if I stop beating him and he begins working. Thus a situation in which the man is continually beaten and does no work is the disagreement outcome in a bargaining situation in which he and I negotiate the terms on which he will work for me, and beating him may be a way of revealing information about the relative gains from agreement.[12]

Given some expectation as to how the gains from agreement are to be divided, I have an interest in maximizing the other person's gains by minimizing the expected value to him of disagreement. However, some threatened consequences of disagreement may not be credible. For example, I might threaten to kill the person I want to work for me if he refuses to comply, but if he refused and I killed him I could never benefit from his work. Thus threatening to beat him is more credible than threatening to kill him.

However, if there are many alternative workers, anyone that I kill might be replaced by another. This is another example of how the existence of many alternative bargaining partners can make take-it-or-leave-it demands more credible and therefore strengthen a person's bargaining power.

Like a firm dealing with many individual consumers, an organized group can make take-it-or-leave-it demands of many individuals, and thus the potential gains from the forcible redistribution of possessions or the forcible exploitation of the labor of others provides a motivation for the organized use of force. Indeed, such organizations are sometimes spoken of as though they were firms selling a product for profit and sharing the proceeds among their members. The "product" of such an organization is protection, and what it "sells" is protection against itself.

---

12. For a discussion of bargaining between master and slave, see Berlin 1998. See also Morgan 1999.

Like business firms, such organizations create the potential for three types of conflict: conflicts with their "customers," conflicts with competing "firms," and conflicts within the organization over the division of its revenues. Bargaining with the use of force can occur in all these contexts.

Members of an organization of economic predators have conflicting interests in dividing the gains from predation, and since the gains from any redistribution can be shared among the members of any group that objects to the current distribution, the leader of every organization of economic predators has to be concerned about the emergence of a competing coordinator among his followers. A combination of punishment of individual dissidents with attempts to inhibit free communication among them can make opposition seem risky and preserve the lion's share of the gains for the leader.

"Customers" could increase their bargaining power if they were organized, since then the exploiters could not make take-it-or-leave-it demands of individuals. However, if any agreements they reach would benefit exploited individuals whether they resisted or not, then, unlike competitors to the leader from within the organization but like workers without a union, they might have to overcome a collective action problem if they are to organize.

Thus the incentives faced by the "customers" of such an organization may resemble the Prisoner's Dilemma, while the incentives faced by potential members of a protection organization resemble the Stag Hunt—they have an incentive to coordinate their expectations on a cooperative outcome. Indeed, both the name *Stag Hunt* and the supporting story from Rousseau are singularly appropriate, since the skills humans developed for hunting and herding large animals may well have facilitated the hunting and capture of other humans. Thus the differential incentives faced by economic predators and their victims would seem to favor predation.

However, there are three important limits to the gains from economic predation. One is that economic predators do not produce anything and are therefore dependent on their prey to produce the goods that will support them both. Of course, the potential prey may not produce enough to make predation more attractive than doing something productive. With increasing productivity, however, predation becomes profitable, but the predator becomes dependent on the prey for his own well-being.

The second potential limit on predation is that if one group of predators can organize then so can another, and therefore the gains from predation invite competition from other predators. This provides another, secondary, way that force becomes a means to an end, since one organized group of predators can use force to eliminate another and gain exclusive access to its "customers." It can do that by destroying the competing organization's instruments of coercion, disrupting it so that it can no longer function as an organized group, or threatening to punish its members if they do not agree to go out of business. But as we saw in the previous chapter, one of the insights of the raison d'état literature is that recurring conflicts among predators can increase the bargaining power of their prey and thus over time reduce the gains from predation.

This, then, is one possible answer to the question we started with, of why one group would gain from forcibly disarming another.[13] However, forceful contests between competing predators are risky and costly, and thus the leaders of two competing organizations may both prefer to reach an agreement rather than fight a contest in which each tries to eliminate the other. Thus bargaining is also relevant to understanding violent contests between predators.[14]

There are two types of agreement they might reach to avoid competing with each other: they can merge and share the revenues from extortion, or they can divide the "market" between them. In principle there are many ways they might agree to divide the "market," but dividing their "customers" geographically is obviously the most efficient way of organizing coercion, and the most efficient division of territory is into contiguous blocks.

Thus an understanding of bargaining over these two types of agreement seems directly relevant to understanding the development of the European state system. A set of agreements among economic predators to divide the world among them might be called a world of independent states, and one of the central questions raised by the literature on the European state system is why such a set of agreements could not be permanent or, if not permanent, at least renegotiated without the actual use of force.

The third important limit to economic predation is that it is possible for its actual or potential victims to overcome the collective action problem that they face and engage in forceful bargaining with the predators. The Prisoner's Dilemma and Stag Hunt games are helpful metaphors in thinking about how this might be possible. However, we must avoid being seduced into thinking that they might be models of any actual situation, which would involve many people with many choices and in which uncertainty about what people's preferences actually are would likely play an important role.

The reason for thinking that the victims of economic predation might

---

13. Note the irony of this discussion in the context of structural Realism: Jervis (1978) argued that substituting the Stag Hunt for the Prisoner's Dilemma provided a possible solution to the security dilemma and therefore might prevent war. But because the incentives of economic predators resemble those of the Stag Hunt rather than the Prisoner's Dilemma, predation is profitable and violent conflicts among predators can be worth their costs.

14. The implications of this point will be explored in the next chapter.

face a situation analogous to the Prisoner's Dilemma is that resistance is likely to be both dangerous and costly, anything that weakens the predator would benefit all his victims whether they cooperate in opposing him or not, and individuals acting alone could not expect to accomplish anything. People who cooperate in replacing the predator, however, could expect to benefit from doing so in a way they otherwise would not. That is perhaps why economic predators often have more to fear from within their own ranks than from the population they exploit.

Of course, competing predators can come from within the exploited population as well as from within the established predator's own ranks, and therefore one way of organizing resistance to an established ruler is to organize competing exploiters from among the exploited. If such a group is successful, however, the result may be either long-lasting violent competition among predators or the creation of an even more effective predator organization to replace the original one. In the first case, the gains from predation will be limited while the violence lasts, but the exploited will suffer nonetheless, and therefore life will be "solitary, poor, nasty, brutish, and short." In the second case the gains from predation will be increased rather than diminished. But neither case is fundamentally different from the examples already discussed.

To see why people who merely wanted to resist predation might not actually face a collective action problem, let us look again at the sources of the "dilemma" in the Prisoner's Dilemma. They are twofold: the preferences of the actors and the constraints under which they must choose.

Consider first why the preferences of the actors might be different. One possibility is that if enough other people cooperate, then the actions of individuals might not be entirely without effect. If so, then individuals might prefer to cooperate in resistance, if they were sufficiently confident that others would cooperate as well. Then their preferences would resemble the preferences in the Stag Hunt game rather than the Prisoner's Dilemma.

Now consider the constraints on the choices of the prisoners in the Prisoner's Dilemma: they must independently choose between only two alternatives and do so only once. If their choices are repeated, or if they have more choices and do not choose independently, then even if their preferences remain the same they may no longer have a single dominant choice, and coordination on a mutually beneficial outcome may be possible.

For example, just as people who expect to do business repeatedly with each other have an incentive in any particular transaction not to cheat, so people who live in the same village may have an incentive to support a villager who is being treated in a way they consider unfair, if they want support from others when they are treated unfairly. Moreover, everyone engaged in long-term relations with others has at his disposal ways of rewarding costly cooperation or punishing failures to cooperate that are significant for the persons being rewarded or punished but that cost the person administering them little or nothing. These include honor and esteem for the cooperator and dishonor and social isolation for the non-cooperator.[15]

The effect of all these possibilities is to convert a collective action problem into a coordination problem. However, there are still important differences between the coordination problem faced by predators and the coordination problem faced by those who merely want to resist predation. It will not always, or perhaps often, be true that the actions of individuals who cooperate in resistance will have a significant impact on the outcome, but individuals who cooperate in predation can always be given a share of the gains. Moreover, if resistance requires the cooperation of people who are part of an existing stable group of some sort, then any such groups that exist may be too small to resist a powerful organization of predators effectively or lack the means of mobilizing whatever conventions or social norms they have developed to enable resistance. Predators, however, can make use of soldiers of fortune, who can be readily attracted by the expected gains from predation.[16]

Moreover, the mechanisms that can enable resistance to predation can also be used to facilitate it. Every effective military organization knows how to make use of the mechanisms just described to make soldiers willing to risk their lives in combat, many successful predators have avoided conflicts within their ranks by using their own families as the core of their organizations, and many predatory organizations try to attract support and avoid resistance by claiming to serve collective interests or to be enforcers of valued group norms. All these devices not only make predatory organizations more effective but also make predation more profitable for their leaders, since the less leaders have to use the gains from predation to compensate their followers, the more of the gains they can keep for themselves. This helps explain why it is possible to debate whether the Crusades during the Middle Ages were motivated by religion or predation,

---

15. Since cooperation is important for human survival, there is reason to believe that humans have evolved psychological mechanisms that facilitate it. One of these may be an inborn inclination to punish noncooperation or violations of social norms (Bowles and Gintis 2004). For some experimental evidence in support of this possibility, see Fehr and Gächter 2002. For a discussion of the collective action problem from an evolutionary perspective, see Wilson 2002.

16. For a discussion of how rebels can overcome the collective action problem, see Lichbach 1995. See also McAdam, Tarrow, and Tilly 2001. For a discussion of coordination mechanisms, see Chwe 2001.

there is often disagreement about whether armed groups are bandits or revolutionaries, and there can now be disagreement about whether "greed or grievance" motivates civil wars in various parts of the world (Berdal and Malone 2000).

The Protection Business

In hunter-gatherer societies, the gains from economic predation are small, while the survival of the group requires cooperation among its members. Thus acts of predation by members of the society against other members are mainly carried out by individuals, and since the group is small they can be punished in informal ways. Moreover, the gains from collective predation by one such society against another are also likely to be small, and therefore conflicts among them are likely to be the result of acts of individual predation by members of one group against members of another. This may lead to collective retaliation and counter-retaliation, but such feuds eventually die out and are not a threat to the independence of the groups (Boehm 1987).

With the development first of settled agricultural communities and then of trade among them, however, the gains from organized predation increase. It can take three forms: raiding (or banditry), in which organized groups attack settled communities or traders and carry off their harvests or other goods; the capture of valuable agricultural land or trading routes by one group from another; and long-term exploitation, in which an organized group of warriors acquires control over settled communities and subsists off their produce.[17]

As already noted, groups engaged in economic predation are sometimes said to be in the protection business. This is not always just a bad joke. And in the case of settled predators, this expression conveys an important insight.[18]

The relation between settled economic predators and the people they exploit is similar to the relation between a parasite and its host or between a farmer or rancher and the domesticated animals that support him, in

---

17. This is the main theme of McNeill 1982. McNeill calls economic predators "macroparasites," that is, "men who, by specializing in violence, are able to secure a living without themselves producing the food and other commodities they consume" (1982, vii).

18. Because groups of economic predators may have an interest in protecting the people they prey upon, they are now sometimes called "mafias." The idea is developed in Tilly 1985. For an analysis of the Sicilian mafia that argues that it really is in the protection business, see Gambetta 1993. For a recent study of the so-called Russian mafia by one of Gambetta's students, see Varese 2001. These ideas are developed further in Volkov 2000 and 2002. The seminal work on states as organizations in the protection business is Lane 1958. Lane's idea is the main theme of Glete 2002. See also Levi 1988.

that settled economic predators have an interest in the productivity of the people who support them and in protecting them from other predators. This is why the "protection" that is "sold" by such predators can be the genuine article:

> the king is . . . the owner of the country. Like the owner of a house, when the wiring is wrong, he fixes it.[19]

Thus even an economic predator, if he is engaged in the long-term exploitation of a settled community, would have an interest in providing some of the core services we associate with governments. But the terms of trade between protector and protected can vary enormously. At one extreme a protector may be a pure predator, the wealthiest person in the territory that he controls, and provide few benefits for anyone else. At the other extreme he may be hired by the people he protects, many of whom enjoy greater wealth and job security than he does (Grossman 2000). The extent of the services offered by a protector, and the terms on which they are provided, will be influenced by the relative bargaining power between the protector and his customers. And this will be influenced in turn by the amount of competition the protector faces and the ability of the people he protects to organize themselves in bargaining with him.

Consider, for example, the famous Japanese film by Akira Kurosawa called, in English, *The Seven Samurai*. In this film, peasants in a Japanese village are plagued by roving bandits who regularly steal their harvest, and they pool their resources to hire samurai warriors to protect them. They find seven rootless samurai warriors who agree to help and who succeed in defeating the bandits. In this story the exploiters are roving bandits, the villagers are able to organize because they are a small community, and the samurai warriors are rootless and unorganized. The story would end differently if the bandits were strong enough to establish control over multiple villages, which would be unable to coordinate resistance against them, or if the surviving samurai warriors remained in the village after the battle that ends the film and extorted much greater payments from the villagers. The last possibility exemplifies the fact that even groups that manage to organize themselves in defense of exploitation by others are exposed to the danger of being exploited by the people they have empowered to defend them.

Since the people a predator exploits provide the means of protection against competing predators, the possibility of competition from other predators may increase an established predator's interest in their produc-

---

19. A statement by an Italian monarchist, quoted in Banfield 1958, 27. For an analytical treatment of this point, see Olson 1993, who calls settled economic predators "stationary bandits."

tivity. And the fact that the people he exploits are not dumb animals but are capable of resisting efforts to mobilize them against competing predators may increase his interest in their well-being. Moreover, these two possibilities can reinforce each other, since (1) an effective means of resisting an established predator is to support a competitor, (2) competitors may have an interest in facilitating resistance to an established predator, and (3) measures that a predator takes to increase the productivity of his prey may also increase the ability of his prey to organize themselves to resist him. All these things may be true of both competing predators from within the territory controlled by an established predator and those outside it.

The Social Contract

A state is usually defined as an organization that has several properties, among which are (1) an organized ruling group (the government) that (2) can successfully use the threat of force to compel individuals (3) within a well-defined territory (4) to surrender economic resources (taxes), which are used to support not only the ruling group but also its (5) regulation of the population it controls and (6) defense of its control from other organized groups, both within the territory it controls and outside it. How are we to explain the development of organizations with these properties?[20]

Max Weber wrote:

> "Every state is founded on force," said Trotsky at Brest-Litovsk. That is indeed right. If no social institutions existed which knew the use of violence, then the concept of "state" would be eliminated, and a condition would emerge that could be designated as "anarchy," in the specific sense of this word. (1946, 78)[21]

It is clear that in this passage Weber has in mind not just any use of force or violence but the organized use of violence. To understand the development of states, then, we must explain the development of organizations capable of engaging in killing and destruction and then show why they would be interested in creating something that would have the properties ascribed to states. A plausible explanation can be found in the incentives

---

20. See, for example, the definitions of a state by Weber (1946) and Finer (1997, 1–94). Unfortunately, much of the literature on the rise of the state familiar to students of international politics focuses on the development of the European state in the context of feudalism. But human organizations with the defining properties of a state have long existed and have developed in many places. In addition to Finer, see Johnson and Earle 1987 for a survey of the anthropological literature.
21. Note that in this passage Weber equates anarchy with the *absence* of violence.

for economic predation, and defense against it, created by the development of settled agricultural communities and trade among them (North 1981).

But neither economic predators nor people who organize to defend themselves against them have an interest in violence for its own sake, any more than a man who holds up a liquor store wants to shoot the person behind the counter. What they want is to be able to profit from an agreement whose terms are determined by the threat of violence. It is the provisions of these agreements that determine the peculiar features that distinguish any particular organization that has the properties listed previously from all the others.

Any particular state, therefore, can, like a business firm, be understood as a network of contracts (Aoki, Gustafsson, and Williamson 1990). One set of contracts regulates the internal functioning of the ruling group (the government), another regulates the relation between the government and the population whose behavior it tries to control, and a third regulates the relation between a government of one territorial area and the governments of other territorial areas (Glete 2002, 1–41). Unlike the contracts that organize a business firm, however, the disagreement outcome in negotiating the contracts that define a state is determined by contests in violence. Moreover, these contracts are never entirely independent of each other, and the enforcement of all of them is problematic.

Weber famously defined a state as

a human community that (successfully) claims the *monopoly of the legitimate use of physical force* within a given territory. (1946, 78; emphasis in original)

It is the contractual basis for the functioning of a state that explains the role of legitimacy in its organization.

The idea of a fair bargain can be a way of thinking about the properties of an ideal or just state, and an actual state that did not satisfy those properties might be considered illegitimate because it was unjust. But even the relation between master and slave is subject to bargaining, and so also are unjust states governed by tacit or explicit agreements. Even though the bargaining power of slaves may be insufficient to compel the abandonment of slavery, it can be enough to punish a master who has deviated from rules governing his behavior that were the product of earlier bargaining between them, and such rules, however vague or implicit, might be said to define what is and what is not legitimate behavior for a master or for a ruler.

Just as the terms of any contract reflect the relative bargaining power of the people who sign it, so standards of legitimacy understood in this way reflect the relative bargaining power of the component parts of a state. A change in relative bargaining power will therefore make it possible to renegotiate the contract. But, as in the relation between labor and management, one of the determinants of relative bargaining power is the relative ability of the participants to organize, which is affected in turn by their ability to coordinate their actions. Thus the mere availability of the idea of a radically different type of contract, if it becomes common knowledge, can change the relative bargaining power of ruler and ruled, since such an idea can facilitate the organization of resistance to the government defined by the current contract. The relation between "realistic" standards of legitimacy and "utopian" ones is therefore complex, and the way people talk about government can undermine it (Mannheim 1936).

Anarchy and Hierarchy Reconsidered

Kenneth Waltz wrote:

> The parts of domestic political systems stand in relations of super- and subordination. Some are entitled to command; others are required to obey. Domestic systems are centralized and hierarchic. The parts of international-political systems stand in relations of coordination. Formally, each is the equal of all the others. None is entitled to command; none is required to obey. International systems are decentralized and anarchic. The ordering principles of the two structures are distinctly different, indeed, contrary to each other. (1979, 88)

The distinction described in this passage is the foundation of what came to be known as "structural Realism." But it should now be clear that it rests on a confusion, a confusion that is fostered by the words that Waltz uses to describe the distinction he wants to make. The opposite of a centralized system is not anarchy but a decentralized one. *Anarchy* is *an-* plus *-archy*. It refers to the absence of a leader or ruler, which structural Realists equate with the absence of any institutional structure.[22]

Thus this passage conflates two different distinctions. One is between a centralized and a decentralized institutional structure, and the other is

---

22. Strictly speaking, the opposite of anarchy is not hierarchy but "archy," a word that does not exist by itself in English but must be qualified by some prefix that describes what sort of "archy" it is (e.g., monarchy or oligarchy).

between relations among people that are governed by an institutional structure and those that are not.[23] Structural Realism therefore begs the question of whether peace requires some sort of *-archy* or could be achieved instead by a decentralized institutional structure.[24]

This confusion has been compounded by the confusion between the absence of government and Hobbes's state of nature. If a world without governments is a world without states as commonly defined, then people who live in a world of hunter-gatherer societies might be said to be in the state of nature, but it would not be the state of nature described by Hobbes.[25] Hobbes's state of nature was a world of competing economic predators, any of whom could become the nucleus around which what Hobbes called a commonwealth could be constructed and some of whom did. And there is nothing in what Hobbes wrote that implies that a world of commonwealths must have the properties that Hobbes attributed to what he called the state of nature.

Like Hobbes, many students of international politics do not distinguish between individual acts of predation and predation by organized groups. This failure helps support the view that the difference between government and anarchy is that under government there is someone to enforce contracts and property rights and in anarchy there is not, a view that makes plausible the use of the Prisoner's Dilemma game as a way of describing anarchy or the state of nature. A settled economic predator with sufficient interest in the productivity of his subjects may be interested in resolving conflicts among them and defining and enforcing their property rights, but there is no enforcer of the contract (implicit or explicit) that governs the relations between the predator and his subjects, any more than there is an enforcer of any contracts he might have made with economic predators in other territories that delineate which territories they each control. In both cases, as in bargaining between master and slave, any partic-

---

23. To appreciate the difference, think about the distinction between having a commonly known "rule of the road" and not having one. A failure to appreciate this distinction is what distinguishes structural Realism from what is commonly called the "English school" of writers about international politics. For a representative example of the English school, see Bull 1977. For a recent discussion of the English school, see Keene 2002.

24. Hans Morgenthau, it should be noted, distinguished clearly between a system without any institutional order and a system with a decentralized institutional structure and argued that the fundamental property of modern international politics was not the absence of effective international norms or law but its decentralized institutional structure (1948, part 6). See also the discussion of this issue by Martin Wight, a founding member of the English school, in Wight 2002, chaps. 9 and 10.

25. See the analysis of the anthropological and archaeological data in Kelly 2000. It was perhaps in part the European experience of hunter-gatherer societies in the New World that motivated Rousseau's criticisms of Hobbes (Meek 1976).

ular agreement is enforced only by threats to repeat the forceful bargaining that produced it.

Because a ruler commands an organization, and violators of his edicts do not, a ruler will be able to confront violators with take-it-or-leave-it demands. Even if there are many violators, all of whom meet with a violent response, this violence will not count as warfare, because it will not consist of a military contest between organized groups. It is the ruler's monopoly of the *organized* use of force that explains his ability to enforce property rights without war, but his monopoly of the organized use of force exists only because the members of his organization cooperate in applying it, and any resistance to it is not organized. Thus the superior force of the state is not the cause of the reliability of agreements that are accepted in lieu of violence but its result, and when the agreements that support it unravel then so does the state. A potential cause of such unraveling is an attempt by the state to enforce too much.

Waltz's distinction between hierarchy and anarchy derives additional plausibility from the fact that the history of international politics is usually told as the history of warfare between or among independent states. This fosters the view that states exist independently of other states and some way needs to be found to prevent them from fighting each other. But every war ends in a peace settlement of some sort, and the states that participate in any given war were all products of some prior peace settlement. As Robert Randle said:

> It is . . . wars and their settlements that have structured the state system of the modern era: they have provided the matrix for interstate relations, including the context of subsequent wars and their settlements. . . . Peace settlements . . . created the modern state system; they have characterized the relations of states and the international law of those relations; and it is through them, in part, that the modern state became what it is. (1973, 506)

Thus sovereignty does not reflect an absence of agreements but is itself the result of agreement. Indeed, Finer lists, as one of the defining properties of a state, the fact that it is

> recognized by other similarly constituted states as independent in its action on its territorially defined . . . population, that is, on its subjects. This recognition constitutes what we would today call its international "sovereignty." (1997, 2–3)

There is no external enforcer of the agreements constituting a state's sovereignty, but neither is there an external enforcer of any of the other agreements that constitute a state.

A history of modern international politics told as the history of peace settlements would be a history that revealed the institutional development of the European state system, which was eventually extended to encompass the globe.[26] It would show that both the interstate system and the states that make it up are constantly being renegotiated and that the modern state is as much the product of agreements among states as it is of agreements between governments and the populations they govern. When states use force to renegotiate a previous peace settlement they appear to be the source of the problem, but when a new agreement is negotiated they reemerge as part of the solution. And no valid argument has been given that shows that they could not be part of a long-lasting peace settlement.

Constructivists, in criticizing structural Realism, emphasize the fact that the state is a social construction whose origins lie as much in the international system as in the societies they govern. However, the alternative they offer to simply taking states as given, as structural Realism does, is an analogy with the process by which individuals acquire their identities through socialization. But individuals do not negotiate their identities by the use of force. States are the product of a process by which groups of individuals with well-defined identities use violence to bargain over the institutional structures that will regulate conflicts among them. And one of the issues to be bargained over may be the nature of the culture that they will subsequently be part of.

The Global Constitution

As we have seen, Waltz characterized the interstate system as "decentralized." If this does not mean simply the absence of an institutional structure, as the word *anarchy* implies, what does it mean?

In thinking about the answer to this question, we must distinguish between a world of states with an uncontested institutional structure and a world in which the structure is contested. This is something we are accustomed to doing in talking about the internal structures of states. The institutional structure of the U.S. government once was the subject of a violent contest, but there seems little prospect of that happening again in the immediate future. Thus the institutional structure of the U.S. now conveys a great deal of useful information about how life in the United States is conducted. This could not be said of contemporary Colombia, however, or Afghanistan or the Balkans. We can imagine possible institutional structures for the people who live within those areas and think about what sort of institutions, if any, might prove to be acceptable to everyone within them who might be in a position to use violence to contest them. If we are

---

26. See, for example, Holsti 1991; Osiander 1994; and Ikenberry 2001.

to think usefully about the possibility of a peaceful global order we must
do the same for the state system itself.

A global order that consists of a state system, rather than a world government, would have an institutional structure that did not include an
organization at the global level with the defining properties of a state listed
previously. Thus there would be no global organization that could use
threats of force to tax individuals in the constituent states. And, therefore,
since the states themselves would constitute the institutional structure of
the global order, the state system would be defined by the three sets of
agreements, listed earlier, that defined the constituent states.[27]

But if a world of sovereign states is simply a world without a global
government, then agreements defining the external sovereignty of states
might include provisions that regulate the other two sets of contracts that
define the constituent states. And, indeed, this has always been true. Wars
were fought in the eighteenth century to determine the ruling family of one
or another member of the European state system; the nature of the government of France was one of the issues determined by the settlement that
ended the wars of Napoleon; and the nature of the states that will govern
the Balkans, as well as their territorial boundaries, is still being negotiated
between the members of NATO and the people who live in that area.[28]

If a state is unable to control individual or small-group acts of predation within its territory, it will be unable to prevent people who inhabit its
territory from engaging in acts of predation on the territory of other states,
and therefore a minimal condition for the external sovereignty of states is
that they be able to exercise internal sovereignty. Thus over time the state
system invented by the Europeans has come to resemble the scheme for
regulating conflicts between or among ethnic groups described by Fearon
and Laitin in their study of ethnic conflict: governments are responsible
for preventing individuals inhabiting their territory from engaging in acts
of predation against people who inhabit the territory of other governments, a division of responsibility that diminishes the number of occasions
for violent conflicts between or among states (Fearon and Laitin 1996).
The current so-called war on terrorism is based on this principle, but it is

---

27. See the recent discussion of the global constitutional order in Bobbitt 2002, especially
book II.
28. Contrast this discussion with Krasner's (1999) discussion of sovereignty. Krasner claims
that, "According to the Westphalian model relations between rulers and ruled ought not to
be subject to any external actors" (73). The many exceptions to this supposed norm lead
Krasner to characterize the "norm" of sovereignty as "organized hypocrisy." Note that it is
important to distinguish among (1) any conditions that are attached to the interstate agreements defining states' sovereignty, (2) interventions to enforce those conditions (e.g., the
enforcement of basic human rights), and (3) the use of force to renegotiate those conditions.

merely the latest installment of a long story.[29] Fearon and Laitin list a number of properties of ethnic groups that may give them a comparative advantage over other groups in controlling acts of predation by their members. A similar claim might be made for states in comparison with other possible enforcement agencies.

Peace and the State

The difference between the existence of a monopoly of the legitimate use of force within states and the absence of such a monopoly among them is what Waltz really had in mind when he distinguished between hierarchy and anarchy. And a side effect of the existence of multiple states, of course, is that they can use their ability to support organized military forces to engage in violent conflicts with each other, which they frequently do. Since war requires the organized use of force, one might think that a world of states would necessarily make war within states impossible, while war among them could not be ruled out. This is why structural Realism has seemed plausible to so many people.

But a monopoly of the legitimate use of force can be lost, and therefore wars within states are not impossible. And the mere possibility of war among states does not imply that it will occur with any significant probability. Thus the inference from the institutional structure of a state system to the incidence of war within it is not valid.

It is true that, for war to occur within states whose institutional structure is not already contested, an organizational problem has to be solved that need not necessarily be solved for war to occur between states. If war is to occur within the territory of an existing state that enjoys a monopoly of the legitimate use of force, then the state's military forces must be divided and/or a new military force must be created to oppose the one previously controlled by the government.[30] States with a monopoly of the legitimate use of force within their territories, however, may maintain armies ready and able to fight each other on short notice.[31]

These differences imply that there might be an institutional impediment to war within some states that does not exist between some states.[32] However, there are other, less obvious implications of these differences

---

29. Much of the story is told in Thomson 1994.
30. For a description of this process in conjunction with the U.S. Civil War, see Bensel 1990.
31. There may, however, be a need to organize an alliance if a war is to be fought among states.
32. But not all states. Canada, for example, would have some organizational problems to solve before it would be prepared to fight a war against the United States.

whose effects are contrary to this obvious one. It is possible, for example, for groups of individuals within states who contemplate violence to coordinate their expectations sufficiently that they each expect to profit from using force, yet they lack an organization that could commit them all to an agreement that they might all prefer to the expected consequences of using force. In that case peace within the territory of an established state might be harder to achieve than peace between states.

Consider, for example, the Los Angeles riot in the aftermath of the acquittal of the Los Angeles policemen who had been videotaped beating a black man, Rodney King. Shared outrage at the verdict in that trial caused many blacks to congregate around the same traffic intersection, and their observation that the police chose to withdraw from the scene rather than try to control the crowd told them that individuals who decided to use force would not face either effective opposition or especially dire consequences. Thus each was free to vent his or her rage against white people, or appropriate property from the many stores in the area, until a large enough military force was organized to oppose them. But if the leaders of this military force contemplated negotiations with the rioters there would be no one to negotiate with, and therefore quelling the riot required sufficient use of force to demonstrate to all the individuals involved that the balance of power between them and the police had been reversed.

Spontaneous demonstrations such as this one can have immediate revolutionary consequences if they occur in the capital of a centralized state (e.g., Paris), and if the public authorities are unable to alter the expectations that support them they can lead to recurring violence over the long run.[33] However, if no single organization develops that can negotiate an agreement and then persuade the dissidents to accept it, then a negotiated settlement of such conflicts may be impossible. For example, in attempting to negotiate a settlement between rebels in Kosovo and the government of Serbia prior to the military conflict over Kosovo, the U.S. government had difficulty in finding someone who could reliably speak for the rebels. And one of the main incentives for the government of Israel to agree to the creation of a Palestinian state seems to be the possibility that an agreement negotiated with such a state might reduce decentralized violence by Palestinians against the citizens of Israel.[34]

---

33. As a former adviser to a Chinese leader has been quoted as saying, "There are so many people with grievances. They'll wait for some public signal, and then they'll come together when they know others will do the same thing" (Ziegler 1997, 20).

34. For an argument that a lasting peace between Israel and the Palestinians requires one state and not two, see Said 1999.

What Next?

Thus not only can states with a monopoly of the legitimate use of force within their territories make war with other states; they can make peace with them as well, which they also do. This is something that organizations without a monopoly of the legitimate use of force are unable to do. The institutional structure of a state system does not tell us why the peace that states make among themselves could not be as lasting as the peace some states, but not all, have made within their territories.

Moreover, precisely because of the institutional impediment to the renewal of conflict that a government would entail, the members of warring groups may have less confidence in the terms of a peace settlement that creates a common government than one that provides for separate states with separate military forces. Thus even if there is a subsequent conflict between or among the resulting states, the extent of the violence may be less than if an agreement had not been reached, and the existence of separate states may not be its cause but rather may reflect prior expectations that conflict was likely.

To understand the recurrence of war in a system of states, we must therefore understand why states that could make peace with each other make war instead. Moreover, every war takes place in a world that was created by some prior peace settlement and will end with another one. So to understand the recurrence of war, we must explain why peace settlements do not last. To do that we must look more closely at the relation between bargaining and war.[35]

---

35. For two seminal articles on this subject, see Fearon 1995b and Powell 1996. Much of what I have to say in the following chapters is based on ideas developed in those articles.

CHAPTER 4

Bargaining and War

Kenneth Waltz's "third image" of the causes of war (1959), which was the foundation for what came to be known as "structural Realism" or "Neo-realism," was inspired, as we have seen, by Jean-Jacques Rousseau's description of a world of predatory rulers. But it is unclear from what Rousseau wrote why a world of predatory rulers had to be as conflictual as it was, since, as I pointed out in the previous chapter, competing predators would appear to have an incentive to reach agreements to share the benefits of rule among themselves.

Kant, like Rousseau, thought it was obvious that a world of predatory rulers would be a world in which war was frequent, but, bad as this was, he believed it was nonetheless better than the alternative, since a lasting peace among predatory rulers would have prevented achievement of the justice and prosperity that he expected would be the eventual consequence of recurring wars. Once justice and prosperity had been achieved, he thought, peace might be possible. But like Rousseau and nearly all other writers on this subject, he had little to say about why war occurs at all.

Thus if we are to evaluate these ideas we must think about why wars occur, and we should begin by thinking about wars among predatory rulers. To do that, we must write down what seem to be the relevant properties of such a world and see if they have any clear-cut implications for the occurrence of wars.

Warring Predators

As we saw in the previous chapter, a contest in forcible disarmament is not the only form that a contest in killing and destruction might take, but it is the obvious place to begin in thinking about wars among competing economic predators. There are two reasons why one economic predator might expect to gain from forcibly disarming another: if one controls valuable territory, then the other might expect to gain from capturing it; and if both are trying to exploit the same producers, then either could increase his gains by eliminating the other.

A contest in forcible disarmament might lead to the disarmament of either side, and the probability with which either outcome might occur would be a function of the military capabilities of both sides. Thus such a contest resembles in some ways an athletic contest—though it would be more accurate to say that many athletic contests and other games were designed to resemble military contests. This helps account for much commonsense reasoning about war, which is based on the idea that wars are contests that either side might win or lose, with a probability that is determined by their relative power or military capabilities.

However, the analogy between contests in forcible disarmament and athletic contests might lead one to ask whether wars can have only two outcomes, since athletic contests can end in ties, and it is often said of a war that it ended in a stalemate. But athletic contests end in ties because the rules by which they are conducted specify when the game ends and the score might be tied at that point. When people want to avoid ties, then the game is continued until one side or the other wins. There are no rules that specify when a war should end, and therefore if a contest in forcible disarmament ends before either side has been disarmed it is because the combatants chose to end it—which they might have done because they saw no immediate prospect of either defeating the other.

Thus the problem with much commonsense reasoning about war is not that it assumes that wars have only two outcomes but that it overlooks the fact that such contests can be interrupted if the combatants choose to stop fighting, and therefore it assumes that after war begins states no longer face a choice between fighting and not fighting. But if rulers can decide to stop fighting or continue, they can also make any decision to stop fighting conditional on the acceptance of an agreement of some sort. Economic predators, for example, could agree on a redivision of the valuable territory that they are fighting over, instead of continuing to fight until one or the other had been disarmed. And, indeed, many wars have ended in just this way. But this is something they could have done without fighting at all, and therefore the fundamental problem in explaining the occurrence of war is to explain why the participants had to fight before reaching an agreement that settles whatever is in dispute between them.[1]

This implies in turn that, even if there are only two ways that a contest in forcible disarmament can end, there can be many possible outcomes of a war, since a war can be ended by an agreement, and there are many possible agreements that might be reached. In a contest between economic predators, for example, the territory they control could in principle be divided in indefinitely many ways. And therefore, if we are to explain why states fight on the basis of their expectations about the likely consequences

---

1. This is the main theme of Blainey 1988.

of fighting, we must take into account their expectations not only about the likely outcome of a contest in forcible disarmament but also about the outcome of the bargaining process that might accompany it.

The first major writer to point this out and attempt to determine its implications was a Prussian military officer, Carl von Clausewitz, who lived from 1780 to 1831 (Clausewitz 1976). Like Hobbes, Clausewitz wrote in an arresting style that lends itself to quotations taken out of context. In addition, he never finished his great treatise, *On War,* and it was published by his wife after his death. As a result, he has been misunderstood almost as often as he has been quoted. Moreover, while his analysis was surprisingly modern and sophisticated, we can now see that at the heart of it is what is commonly called the bargaining problem, whose full complexity has only become apparent as a result of the analytical techniques developed by game theorists.

Clausewitz wrote, "War is . . . an act of force to compel our enemy to do our will" (1976, 75). From this it followed, he claimed, that "the aim of warfare is to disarm the enemy," since "[i]f the enemy is to be coerced you must put him in a situation that is even more unpleasant than the sacrifice you call on him to make," and "[t]he worst of all conditions in which a belligerent can find himself is to be utterly defenseless" (77). "Force," he wrote,

> is thus the *means* of war; to impose our will on the enemy is its object. To secure that object we must render the enemy powerless; and that, in theory, is the true aim of warfare. (75; emphasis in original)

But the enemy can be expected to resist this outcome, and this resistance must be countered if he is to be disarmed. "Each side, therefore, compels its opponent to follow suit; a reciprocal action is started which must lead, in theory, to extremes" (77).

Statements such as these have led some people to interpret Clausewitz as an apostle of total war. But such an interpretation overlooks the qualifying phrase *in theory* that appears in these quotations. In practice, Clausewitz wrote, war does not usually look like that at all.

In practice, Clausewitz wrote, "war is simply a continuation of political intercourse, with the addition of other means," a statement that is often quoted but, in light of such statements as the ones quoted previously, often interpreted as mere cynicism. However, Clausewitz meant this statement to be taken literally:

> We deliberately use the phrase "with the addition of other means" because we . . . want to make clear that war in itself does not sus-

pend political intercourse or change it into something entirely different. (1976, 605)

Thus at the heart of Clausewitz's discussion of war in practice, or, as he sometimes called it, "real war," is the fact that war is typically accompanied by the same bargaining process that preceded it and that will continue after it ends.[2] And the reason this is possible is that, as Clausewitz put it, "war does not consist of a single short blow," and therefore negotiations with the enemy need not await his complete defeat (79).

One implication of this fact, Clausewitz wrote, is that "real war" may actually consist not of a contest in forcible disarmament that is interrupted by a negotiated settlement but of a contest in killing and destruction in which the adversaries do not even try to disarm each other. Rulers may instead simply fight over a particular piece of territory or even engage in military operations whose object "is neither to conquer the enemy country nor to destroy its army, but simply *to cause general damage*" (Clausewitz 1976, 93; emphasis in original). "What is more," he wrote,

> a review of actual cases shows a whole category of wars in which the very idea of *defeating the enemy* is unreal: those in which the enemy is substantially the stronger power. (91; emphasis in original)

Thus Clausewitz claimed that a ruler could be optimistic about the outcome of war, even though he was not optimistic about defeating the enemy in a contest in forcible disarmament—a possibility that is overlooked entirely by most commonsense reasoning about war.

"Warfare thus eludes the strict theoretical requirement that extremes of force be applied," Clausewitz wrote, and "[t]he probabilities of real life replace the extreme and the absolute required by theory."

> Once the extreme is no longer feared or aimed at, it becomes a matter of judgment what degree of effort should be made; and this can only be based on the phenomena of the real world and the *laws of probability*. . . . reality supplies the data from which we can deduce the unknown that lies ahead.
>
> From the enemy's character, from his institutions, the state of his affairs and his general situation, each side, using the *laws of probability*, forms an estimate of its opponent's likely course and acts accordingly. (80; emphasis in original)

---

2. Clausewitz sometimes calls war in theory "absolute war," and he sometimes refers to "real wars" as wars with "limited aims" (1976, book 8).

However, while "[t]heory must concede all this,"

> it has the duty to give priority to the absolute form of war and to make that form a general point of reference, so that he who wants to learn from theory becomes accustomed to keeping that point in view constantly, to measuring all his hopes and fears by it, and to approximating it *when he can* or *when he must.*
>
> A principle that underlies our thoughts and actions will undoubtedly lend them a certain tone and character, though the immediate causes of our action may have different origins, just as the tone a painter gives to his canvas is determined by the color of the underpainting. (581; emphasis in original)

What Clausewitz seems to be saying is that, while states that are fighting may not actually try to disarm each other, they must bear in mind the fact that they could, and absolute war, even though it never occurs, must be the "measure of all their hopes and fears."

But "[i]f theory can effectively do this today," he wrote,

> it is because of our recent wars. Without the cautionary examples of the destructive power of war unleashed [by Napoleon], theory would preach to deaf ears. No one would have believed possible what has now been experienced by all. (581)

It is striking to compare this statement with Thomas Schelling's comment about the limited nature of the Korean War: "It is a strange spectacle, and indeed what makes it plausible is only that it actually occurred" (1960, 130). The expectations of Clausewitz's readers were conditioned by experience of the limited wars of the eighteenth century. The expectations of Schelling's readers were conditioned by experience of the total wars of the twentieth century. But Clausewitz and Schelling agree that, as Schelling put it, "[w]ar is always a bargaining process" (142), that the nature of wars is determined by states' choices rather than the technology that is available, and that to explain why they choose to fight the wars they fight one must understand the bargaining process that wars are part of.

But this means that there are two fundamental puzzles about war and not just one: we must explain not only why states must fight before reaching an agreement, when they could have reached an agreement without fighting, but also why they chose to agree to fight only a limited war, when the outcome of a contest in disarmament would have been different.

To someone familiar with the modern literature on bargaining, Clausewitz's solution to both puzzles practically leaps off the page. It has two parts. Here is the first:

if one side cannot completely disarm the other, the desire for peace on either side will rise and fall with the probability of further successes and the amount of effort these would require. If such incentives were of equal strength on both sides, the two would resolve their political disputes by meeting half way. If the incentive grows on one side, it should diminish on the other. Peace will result so long as their sum total is sufficient—though the side that feels the lesser urge for peace will naturally get the better bargain. (Clausewitz 1976, 92)

Translated into modern terminology, this says that a contest in disarmament (absolute war) is the disagreement outcome in any bargaining over the terms of a settlement that might substitute for war. Thus the more optimistic a ruler is about the outcome of absolute war, the better the terms he will demand and expect in any agreement he might accept instead, and vice versa; and if the demands of the two adversaries are compatible, an agreement can be reached without fighting.

Here is the second part of Clausewitz's solution to these puzzles:

When we attack the enemy, it is one thing if we mean our first operation to be followed by others until all resistance has been broken; it is quite another if our aim is only to obtain a single victory, in order to make the enemy insecure, to impress our greater strength upon him, and to give him doubts about his future. If that is the extent of our aim, we will employ no more strength than is absolutely necessary. (92)

This second statement says that if military operations are not designed to disarm the enemy, their purpose is to influence his expectations about what the outcome of absolute war would be, were it to be fought. Thus the function of "real wars" is to reveal information about the adversaries' military capabilities.[3]

Taken together, these two ideas raise two important questions. The first is whether, if rulers' expectations about the outcome of absolute war are sufficiently consistent, they would always be able to reach an agreement without fighting.[4] The second is whether, even if this is not true, they might nonetheless only need to fight wars that are not very costly or even, perhaps, engage in other types of conflicts that, while inefficient, are nonetheless much less costly than military conflicts would be—interruptions of trade, for example.

---

3. This is the central theme of Blainey 1988. The idea is developed in Wagner 2000.
4. This is the main claim made by Geoffrey Blainey (1988).

Whatever the answers to those questions may prove to be, Clausewitz's two ideas clearly imply that the belief that the increasing costliness of war might in itself be sufficient to make war obsolete is unwarranted: the costliness of absolute war might make an agreement to avoid it desirable, but rulers can nonetheless choose to fight wars that they expect to be less costly instead. That is why the belief that World War I had demonstrated that war was too costly to be repeated was misguided and may even have contributed to the occurrence of World War II.

Let's Make a Deal

Clausewitz's analysis of war gives us further reason to take seriously Kenneth Waltz's analogy between wars and strikes.[5] It implies that, to understand what happens on the battlefield and its consequences, we must understand not only the military contest but also the bargaining process that accompanies it. This poses a very complicated set of problems, and thus we should not be surprised if formal models prove to be necessary in thinking about it.

Let us begin by asking whether we should expect predatory rulers with consistent expectations about the outcome of a military contest to be willing to reach a peaceful agreement dividing valuable territory between them rather than fight over it. A contest in forcible disarmament (Clausewitz's absolute war) resembles a costly lottery, since there is some probability that either side might win. Winning such a contest would imply control over all of the territory in dispute. By agreeing to divide it up rather than fight, however, rulers could avoid both the costs and the risks associated with a military contest. Thus the choice between a war and a negotiated settlement involves a choice between a sure thing and an uncertain prospect.

Such a choice is represented in figure 5. Arrayed along the vertical axis are all the probabilities of winning the contest, from zero to one. Arrayed along the horizontal axis are all the possible fractions of the territory in dispute that a ruler might receive, from zero to one. The lines in the figure represent possible points of indifference for some particular ruler between getting some fraction of the territory for certain and fighting a contest for all of it with some specific probability of winning. The straight line, for example, represents the preferences of a ruler who is always indifferent between getting some fraction q of the territory and fighting a contest in which he expected to get all of it with a probability p of the same size. The curved line, on the other hand, represents the preferences of a ruler who, if

---

5. See the discussion at the beginning of the previous chapter.

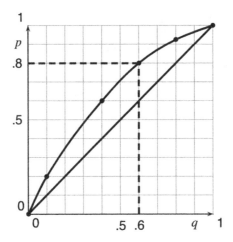

Fig. 5.   Choice between a lottery and a sure thing

confronted with some probability p of winning all the territory, would accept a lesser fraction q for certain instead. (In the figure, for example, this ruler would accept 60 percent of the territory as equivalent to the value of a contest for all of it that he had a probability of winning of .8.)

We have seen that Clausewitz was not bothered by the idea that expectations about the outcome of war could be represented by probabilities. Nonetheless, it is important to be clear about what these probabilities represent. The modern answer is that they are personal or subjective probabilities, which means they represent the odds at which a ruler would be prepared to bet on the outcome of a war. Thus they represent points of indifference between the gamble associated with war and a hypothetical lottery with known probabilities leading to the same outcomes, and therefore they are really just preferences. That does not imply that they are arbitrary, however. Rather, they incorporate all the information that a decision maker believes to be relevant to determining the outcome, in the same way that a person who bets on the outcome of a sporting event tries to take into account everything that he or she knows about the contestants and believes to be relevant.

Thus figure 5 is just a way of summarizing the preferences of someone choosing between a sure thing and a lottery: the probabilities represent points of indifference between the actual lottery and some hypothetical lottery with known probabilities, and the lines in the figure represent points of indifference between this lottery and possible divisions of the prize. Moreover, there is no right answer to the question of what either should be. The two lines in the figure merely represent two possible sets of preferences—there are indefinitely many possible lines like the one that is bowed upward in figure 5 and indefinitely many that might sag downward as well. S-shaped curves, or curves with more complex shapes, are also possible. (You might ask yourself what your points of indifference would be, if the quantity at stake were a sum of money and the probabilities were actual gambles.) Moreover, nothing I have said so far requires that any decision maker actually thinks in these terms at all: a decision maker need not map out how he would respond to all the possible choices he might confront in order to choose between some particular contest and some particular proposed compromise. Thus figure 5 helps us organize our thinking but does not necessarily represent the way a decision maker organizes his.[6]

While there may be many divisions of disputed territory that an individual ruler would prefer to fighting a contest for all of it, if a contest is to be avoided both rulers have to accept the same settlement, and making a settlement more attractive for one requires making it less attractive for the other, as figure 6 illustrates. Now each point on the horizontal axis represents a possible division of the territory in dispute, between a fraction that goes to the ruler on the left (q) and the remaining fraction that goes to the ruler on the right ($1 - q$). The left vertical axis represents the left ruler's probability of winning the military contest (p), and the right vertical axis represents the right ruler's probability of winning ($1 - p$). The curve starting at the left-hand side of the horizontal axis is the indifference curve from figure 5, and the other curve is the corresponding indifference curve for the other ruler. In figure 6, it is assumed that the probability that the ruler on the left will win is .8. The question we are interested in is whether there must be some division of the territory along the horizontal axis that both will prefer to fighting over all of it.[7]

---

6. Figure 5 illustrates the fact that we can use a divisible good to measure what a gamble is worth to someone, or a gamble to measure what the good is worth, but there is nothing that measures both independently of each other. If we use the gambles on the vertical axis to measure the value of various quantities of the good on the horizontal axis, then the probabilities on the vertical axis are von Neumann-Morgenstern utilities, which are the basis for contemporary expected utility theory. (The justification for the idea that people would want to maximize their expected utility is that, if the value of the outcome of every choice is measured by the probability of winning the same gamble, then maximizing expected utility is equivalent to maximizing the probability of winning that gamble.) Thus there is little connection between "utility" as defined by expected utility theory and the classical concept of utility, which presupposes a way of measuring levels of personal well-being. For a useful introduction to expected utility theory, see Raiffa 1968.

7. For an influential discussion of this question, see Fearon 1995b. For some criticisms of Fearon's answer, see O'Neill 2001.

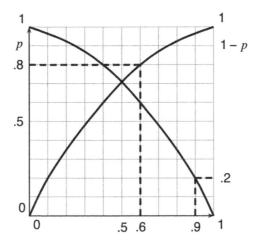

Fig. 6. Choice between a contest and a bargain

As figure 6 is drawn, there are many such divisions: the ruler on the left will prefer any division giving him more than 60 percent of the territory, and the ruler on the right will prefer any division giving him more than 10 percent. Thus any division giving the ruler on the left between 60 percent and 90 percent of the territory will be preferred by both rulers to fighting a contest for all of it. Moreover, it is easy to see from figure 6 that this will be true regardless of how likely it is that the ruler on the left will win: reducing p will shift the range of possible agreements to the left along the horizontal axis (as Clausewitz claimed it would), but it will always exist.[8]

The reason this is true is that the lines of indifference between contests and bargains represented in figure 6 are bowed upward, which means that, for every probability of winning, both rulers would accept a smaller fraction of the territory in dispute as a substitute for fighting a contest for all of it. If instead each would accept only a fraction equal to the probability of winning, there would be no agreement both would prefer to fighting and only one agreement they both would be willing to accept: one in which $q = p$ and $1 - q = 1 - p$. And if both curves sagged downward, there would be no agreement they both would accept as an alternative to fighting. Thus

---

8. This is why Wittman (1979) argued that the balance of power affects only the terms of a negotiated settlement that might be accepted in lieu of war but not whether war occurs or not. However, as we will see, figure 6 leaves unclear why war occurs at all, and therefore Wittman's reasoning was incomplete.

the answer to the question we started with is that there may be agreements both rulers would prefer to fighting, but there need not be.[9]

There are, however, reasons to believe that often there will be such agreements. One reason is that in choosing between sure things and gambles people often do have preferences that resemble the ones in figure 6. (Ask yourself the following question: If you had a lottery ticket that gave you a 50 percent chance at winning $1,000,000, would you refuse to sell it if the most you could get for it was $500,000?) And the other reason is that a war is not just a gamble; it is a very costly contest.[10] Thus it may well often be true that a ruler confronted with the prospect of a costly and risky contest for valuable territory would be willing to accept a division of the territory giving him a fraction of it that is smaller than his probability of winning all of it.[11]

A reason for thinking that this might not be true of both rulers is that, if the issue is a possible redistribution of territory that is already distributed between them, then any compromise agreement would entail one side's surrendering some territory to the other. If, for example, the ruler on the left controlled 50 percent of the territory in dispute but could defeat the other with a probability of .8, then he would prefer war to the status quo, and to avoid war the ruler on the right would have to appease him by surrendering some of his territory.[12] Often people seem to be willing to accept

---

9. By convention, indifference curves bowed upward like the ones in figure 6 are said to represent aversion to risk, curves that sag downward are said to represent risk acceptance, and indifference curves that are straight like the one in figure 5 are said to portray risk neutrality. Because the probabilities in these figures are also von Neumann-Morgenstern utilities, such curves are sometimes also said to represent diminishing marginal utility, increasing marginal utility, and linear utilities, respectively. All these terms are very misleading. These curves merely reflect an individual's points of indifference between gambles and sure things, and since such indifference points will be influenced by both the risk involved and the values an individual places on the objects in question, there is no way to know what actually determines them. It is best to think of them as simply reflecting an individual's preferences, like any other indifference curve.

10. Only the probabilities of winning are represented explicitly in figure 6, but not the expected costs of fighting. The expected costs would nonetheless affect the shapes of the indifference curves.

11. If this were not true, it would be hard to explain why wars are often ended by negotiated settlements before either side has been completely disarmed.

12. This example illustrates a flaw in commonsense reasoning about war that is more fundamental than the fact that it overlooks the possibility of negotiated settlements: even if a compromise is not possible, whether a ruler prefers war to the status quo or not depends not just on how optimistic he is about the outcome of war but on the status quo distribution as well. Even with a probability of winning of .8, the ruler on the left will prefer the status quo to war as long as he already controls at least 60 percent of the territory. Since compromises that are preferred to war may not always exist, this is something that we must bear in mind.

greater risks to avoid what they consider to be losses than they would accept to achieve possible gains of the same size, so the ruler on the right might have an indifference curve that sagged downward rather than the one attributed to him in figure 6.[13]

However, war is not just risky; it is also costly. Moreover, there is good reason to expect that the indifference curve of the ruler on the left would be bowed upward. Thus there might still be compromise settlements that both would prefer to fighting.

What have we learned from all this? When force is used not to disarm an adversary but to harm people or destroy their property (or, as Clausewitz said, "to cause general damage"), it is obvious that its purpose must be to compel an agreement that both the perpetrator and the victim would prefer to a continuation of the conflict, and therefore contests in punishment must be part of a bargaining process. A contest in disarmament, however, is a contest to determine how much punishment two adversaries can subsequently inflict on each other: the winner of such a contest can use force to punish the other without organized resistance.[14] As Clausewitz wrote:

> War is nothing but a duel on a larger scale. Countless duels go to make up a war, but a picture of the whole can be formed by imagining a pair of wrestlers. Each tries through physical force to compel the other to do his will; his *immediate* aim is to *throw* his opponent in order to make him incapable of further resistance. (1976, 75; emphasis in original)[15]

Thus every contest in disarmament leads to, and is motivated by, a subsequent contest in punishment, in which the winner of the contest in disarmament has an extreme bargaining advantage over the loser. Clausewitz claimed, however, that bargaining did not have to await the outcome of

---

13. Risk acceptance might also be caused by domestic political incentives—for an interesting discussion of this possibility in the context of World War I, see Goemans 2000. Evidence that aversion to losses makes people risk acceptant is emphasized by the experimental psychologists who developed prospect theory (Kahneman and Tversky 1979). However, the gamble associated with war involves not just a probable loss but a probability of a large gain combined with a larger probability of a large loss. The evidence that people are risk acceptant in those circumstances is not so clear. For a discussion of some of the pitfalls to avoid in thinking about attitudes toward risk, see O'Neill 2001.

14. In debates about the use of nuclear weapons during the cold war, a distinction was made between the countervalue and counterforce uses of weapons. Countervalue military contests are contests in punishment, and counterforce contests are contests in forcible disarmament. The first war in the Persian Gulf was an example of a counterforce contest. The ongoing conflict between Israel and the Palestinians is an example of a countervalue contest.

15. Here Clausewitz is talking about what he elsewhere calls "absolute war," not "real war."

the contest in disarmament but could precede it or accompany it. It should now be clear that, in the case of warring economic predators at any rate, there is good reason to take this claim seriously. To explain why *any* war occurs, therefore, one must explain why the adversaries could not have reached an agreement without fighting.

Bargaining and Fighting

It might appear that, if there is a range of divisions of disputed territory that two rulers both prefer to fighting over all of it, they will be able to agree on one of them rather than fight. However, when strikes occur it is obvious that there is a range of wage bargains that both labor and management prefer to shutting down the firm, or the industry, and yet strikes sometimes occur anyway. Thus while we have learned that there might often, perhaps even always, be compromise settlements that predatory rulers would prefer to fighting over disputed territory, that does not imply that they will in fact be able to agree on one without fighting.

In the case of strikes, as in any bargaining situation, the problem is that, while there are many agreements that both sides prefer to shutting down the firm, they have conflicting preferences about which of those agreements should be chosen, and strikes are a means of resolving that disagreement. But it is surprisingly difficult to explain exactly how a strike does that, why strikes are sometimes resorted to and sometimes not, or why some are so much longer and more costly than others. Explaining why wars occur is even more difficult.

As we saw in the previous chapter, attempts by economists to explain costly delays in reaching mutually beneficial agreements in situations resembling strikes have focused on the construction of explicit models of haggling (i.e., exchanges of offers and counteroffers that precede agreement). But there are several ways in which the bargaining process associated with war is more complicated than the one economists have focused on.

First, the essence of any bargaining process is the combination of a common interest in avoiding disagreement with conflicting interests as to the terms of an agreement. In the sort of bargaining situations exemplified by strikes, the disagreement outcome (a failure ever to agree) is fixed and is just an extension of the situation that exists while haggling occurs (in the case of strikes, the firm or industry is shut down). In the case of wars, the disagreement outcome (war) is not fixed but is the product of decisions made by the antagonists. Moreover, if Clausewitz is right, the disagreement outcome (absolute war) need not be the same as the war that is fought while the antagonists exchange offers and counteroffers (real war).

Second, the recent literature on bargaining by economists has focused on the role played by private information about the preferences of the bargainers, which they have a strategic incentive to misrepresent. In explaining wars, however, Clausewitz (implicitly) and Blainey (more explicitly) emphasize the role of conflicting beliefs about military capabilities, something that seems irrelevant to understanding strikes (though unregulated strikes, of course, have often been violent).

And third, the literature on bargaining typically assumes that the bargainers can be confident of getting any agreement they might accept. But the emphasis by structural Realists on the anarchic nature of international politics and the influential role the Prisoner's Dilemma game has played in shaping many people's beliefs about its implications make such an assumption problematic in any explanation of the occurrence of war. Indeed, some structural Realists would say that the fundamental cause of war is that agreements between or among states are unenforceable.[16] In an intellectual environment that has been largely shaped by debates about structural Realism, one might almost say, paraphrasing the remarks by Clausewitz and Schelling about limited war quoted earlier, that were it not for Clausewitz it might be hard to get some people to take the subject of this chapter seriously.

If we are to follow the lead of the recent literature in economics about bargaining, we must deal with each of these complications. The obvious place to begin is to think about what Clausewitz called "absolute war," or a contest in disarmament. Even if Clausewitz is right in thinking that such wars rarely occur, this is the war that will take place if no agreement is possible, and therefore this is the war that the probabilities in figure 6 refer to. The nature of such a war will be determined by the strategies chosen by each side, but it seems safe to assume that each will choose what it believes to be the optimal strategy for disarming the other, given the expected strategy of its opponent, and therefore the properties of such a war can be assumed to be independent of the bargaining process.

Even so, there is no reason to think that all contests in disarmament are alike. But if we are to model the haggling process associated with absolute war, we must construct a model of haggling while fighting, and the nature of this process will be affected by how the war is fought. One of the disconcerting results of the economics literature on bargaining is that many conclusions about bargaining are dependent on seemingly minor properties of the process by which offers and counteroffers are exchanged. If that process is affected by how contests in disarmament are fought, we must be cautious about the generality of any conclusions we might reach that are based on assumptions about how a war is to be fought.

---

16. See, for example, Jervis 1978.

Because of the central role that Ariel Rubinstein's work on bargaining has played in the economics literature on the subject, a natural place to begin is to see if it could be applied to an analysis of bargaining that might take place during a contest in forcible disarmament.[17] Rubinstein's model is based on two plausible assumptions: (1) bargainers alternate in making offers and counteroffers to each other, with the process ending when one bargainer accepts another's offer; and (2) they prefer agreements reached sooner to agreements reached later. One reason for the latter assumption might be that they discount future benefits, and another might be that delaying agreement would entail some risk that they would not be able to reach an agreement at all. Both seem potentially relevant to thinking about war.

Rubinstein showed that in a bargaining game that incorporates these assumptions there is only one Nash equilibrium that remains an equilibrium at every stage of the bargaining process.[18] While a rigorous proof of this proposition is difficult, it is not so difficult to acquire an intuitive understanding of why it is true. Suppose the bargainers are negotiating over the division of a sum of money, and consider the possibility that an equal division might be an equilibrium. If this is an equilibrium at every stage of the bargaining process, then even if an equal division is not the opening offer, the other bargainer would counter with it and expect it to be accepted. But he could not get it until his turn came to make an offer, and therefore he should be willing to accept less than that now in order to avoid having to wait. Thus the assumption that an equal division is a subgame perfect equilibrium leads to a contradiction. To avoid such a contradiction, each bargainer must be indifferent between accepting what the other proposes immediately and getting his own demand one period later. There is only one division that satisfies this requirement, and it is the Rubinstein solution to the bargaining problem.

The importance of the requirement that an equilibrium continue to be an equilibrium at every stage of the bargaining process can be seen most clearly by thinking about prestrike negotiations. In such negotiations a bargainer who is dissatisfied with the most the other side is willing to offer can hope to do better only by shutting down the firm. But that would be costly for both sides, and at every stage thereafter either could make the other choose between accepting an offer or paying the cost of extending

---

17. For an exposition of Rubinstein's work, see his own account in Osborne and Rubinstein 1990. See also Muthoo 1999. For a nontechnical discussion of the economics literature on bargaining, see Muthoo 2000.
18. Game theorists call a Nash equilibrium with this property a "subgame perfect" equilibrium. As noted in the previous chapter, there are indefinitely many Nash equilibria in such a bargaining game, a fact that seemed for many years to imply that the concept of an equilibrium alone was not strong enough to imply anything about the bargaining problem.

the strike. The symmetry of their positions might suggest an equal division of the gains from agreement, but a bargainer who has the chance to make the first offer gains a slight advantage from the fact that the other would be willing to accept a bit less in order to avoid initiating a strike—an advantage that would alternate between them at every stage of the strike were one to take place.[19]

This reasoning implies that, if the amount of money to be divided and the extent to which each bargainer discounts future benefits are both commonly known, the bargainers should be able to reach an agreement without a strike: they already know everything they need to know to reach an agreement, and they also know that a strike would be costly but would not change anything. But if one believed that a strike would change what the other believed about one of these values, he might expect to get a more favorable agreement by striking. This, then, is a possible explanation of the fact that sometimes bargainers are able to reach agreement quickly and sometimes they are not. To complete this explanation, however, we would need to show how a strike could affect their beliefs.

Before considering that question, let us see whether this reasoning could be extended to a contest in forcible disarmament.

Fighting while Bargaining

Wars are unpleasant, which is reason enough to believe that warring rulers would prefer to reach agreements sooner rather than later. But unlike strikes, a contest in forcible disarmament can end before the combatants decide to end it: one or the other side might be defeated and therefore be unable to continue fighting. Part of the uncertainty associated with war is uncertainty about how long that will take, and therefore any delay in reaching agreement might entail not only the unpleasantness of further fighting but also some risk, however small, that the contest might reach a decisive conclusion before an agreement could be reached. A ruler who rejects an offer in hopes of getting a better one later, therefore, faces a risk that the war will be over before his demand can be accepted.[20] This is an additional reason for preferring to avoid postponing an agreement.

Of course, if the war ends there is a chance that a ruler might win, but there is also a chance that he might lose—it is that uncertainty that creates the possibility of an agreement in the first place. Postponing agreement is therefore a compound gamble: there is some chance that the war will end decisively before one's own demand can be accepted, and if it does there is

---

19. If the time between offers is small, this advantage will be small and the division will deviate only slightly from equality.
20. Think of the possibility that Saddam Hussein was holding out for a better deal at the onset of the second war in the Persian Gulf in 2003.

some chance that one might be defeated. Even so, exchanging offers while fighting occurs on the battlefield will often be feasible.

Thus there is reason to think that Rubinstein's analysis of bargaining is relevant to a contest in forcible disarmament (Clausewitz's "absolute war"). Note that Rubinstein's model implies that there is an advantage to being the bargainer who makes the first offer. In bargaining over the forcible redistribution of territory, it is obvious who that would be: the ruler who is dissatisfied with the current distribution would have to initiate a contest in forcible disarmament to change it, and therefore the satisfied ruler would have the advantage of making the first offer.[21]

But Rubinstein's analysis implies that, if both the information in figure 6 and each ruler's points of indifference between agreements now and agreements later are commonly known to both rulers, they should be able to reach an agreement without fighting. One has only to state that condition to see how difficult it is to satisfy it. But if Clausewitz and Blainey are right, a failure to satisfy it does not imply that they must fight an all-out contest in disarmament until one or the other is incapable of fighting further. Rather, war itself might reveal the information they need to reach an agreement, in which case war would be, as Clausewitz famously said, "simply a continuation of political intercourse, with the addition of other means." What we need to consider is how these "other means" could make an agreement possible if it were not possible at the outset.

One obvious possibility is that what happens on the battlefield reveals information about the combatants' relative military capabilities. In thinking about the significance of this fact, however, we must be careful to distinguish between two possible effects of battlefield outcomes on the expectations of the two rulers.

One is that they might become less uncertain about the ultimate outcome of the contest: as the contest progresses, it may seem more and more likely to both of them that one or the other will eventually win (as the outcome of a football game may seem less uncertain at the end of the third quarter than it did at the outset). But our discussion implies that this is irrelevant to the question of whether they could reach an agreement or not. As they become less uncertain of the outcome, the probabilities in figure 6 deviate more and more from equality. But as we saw, changing the probabilities has no effect on their interest in reaching agreement; it merely changes the terms of any agreement they might reach. Thus as the contest progresses one or the other might be willing to accept more and more unfavorable terms as it seems more and more likely that he will eventually lose, but the ability of the two rulers to reach an agreement

---

21. A model of absolute war with these properties is presented in Wagner 2000.

without fighting would not be affected by that fact, and anticipation of it prior to war is no more relevant than the fact that one might eventually win, since that information is already contained in the probabilities represented in figure 6.

What is important instead is that the rulers' expectations might become more *consistent*. If we label the two rulers i and j and call the probability with which each might win p_i and p_j, respectively, then consistency of their expectations requires that $p_j = 1 - p_i$, as is the case in figure 6. If this is not true, and the difference between p_i and p_j is great enough, then there may be no agreement they both prefer to fighting. One can readily see from figure 6, for example, that if they both expect to win with a probability of .8, then each would have to be given at least 60 percent of the territory if he were to choose not to fight, which is impossible.

But even if their expectations are not inconsistent enough to rule out the possibility of any mutually acceptable agreement, they may nonetheless be inconsistent enough to motivate fighting. For any inconsistency implies that each would expect experience on the battlefield to make the other less optimistic about winning and therefore willing to accept a less favorable agreement than he would be willing to accept prior to fighting. Thus while an agreement might have been possible prior to war, one ruler might expect to be able to get a better one by fighting, *while the other believed that to be unlikely.*[22] This has a very important counterintuitive implication, which is that the possibility of ending a war with a negotiated settlement *might actually make war more likely than it otherwise would be.*

To see why this is true, look again at figure 6 and imagine that the expectations of the two rulers are somewhat inconsistent but not inconsistent enough to eliminate a range of possible divisions of the territory on the horizontal axis. Then if the status quo is within that range and it is not possible to reach an agreement after fighting begins, both rulers will prefer the status quo to fighting, and therefore neither would choose to fight. If, however, fighting does not rule out the possibility of subsequent agreement, then a ruler might expect that fighting for a while would reveal his true military strength and therefore lead to an agreement with more favorable terms.[23]

On the other hand, if the rulers' initial expectations are so inconsistent that no agreement is possible prior to fighting, then the possibility of a negotiated settlement after fighting begins means that any war that occurs may be less costly than it otherwise would be, since it can be ended by mutual agreement if their expectations become consistent enough in the

22. If they both believed this to be true, their expectations at the outset would have been consistent, and therefore they would be able to reach an agreement without fighting.
23. Similarly, if strikes always led to the dissolution of the firm and never to agreements, one would expect fewer strikes to occur.

course of fighting. Thus the availability of negotiated settlements may make peace more or less likely, depending on the circumstances.

Before exploring the implications of this point, let us look more closely at exactly how battlefield outcomes might lead rulers to revise their expectations and what else, if anything, they might reveal.

Learning from Fighting

Learning from battlefield outcomes is based on inductive reasoning, an example of which was discussed at the very beginning of chapter 1: if one believes that it is more likely that an anonymous dog in the dog pound would resemble a Labrador retriever if it were a Labrador retriever than if it were not, then the fact that it resembles a Labrador retriever increases one's confidence in the hypothesis that it is one. If, on the other hand, it has characteristics that it would be expected to have if it were a pit bull, then one will be skeptical of the claim that it really is a Labrador retriever.

Similarly, it is plausible to think that military leaders begin a war with an idea of how it will be fought, which leads them to think that certain battlefield outcomes are more likely than others. If these expectations are borne out, then their confidence in them will increase, but if not they will decrease.

As noted in chapter 1, this reasoning can be justified by the axioms of probability theory. One's expectations prior to receiving new information are represented in a "prior" probability distribution (like, e.g., the ones in figure 6), and new information leads to a revised, or "posterior," probability estimate, which is a conditional probability: the probability that one's hypothesis is correct, given that the event in question occurred. For this to be possible, two other conditional probability estimates are required: the probability that the new event would have occurred if one's hypothesis was correct and the probability that it might have occurred if one's hypothesis was incorrect. The formula that allows one to compute a posterior probability from this information is called Bayes's rule, and the process is called Bayesian updating. Bayes's rule implies the relation between prior and posterior probabilities just described.[24]

Note that all these probabilities are based on some understanding of how the war will unfold and not just on knowledge of the number of some objects in a larger universe (like the number of aces in a deck of cards). But, like scientific theories, this understanding will be based on both creative guessing and deductive reasoning. Thus learning can consist not merely of Bayesian updating but also of the discovery of possibilities that

---

24. An account of all this in the context of scientific reasoning can be found in Howson and Urbach 1993. People often make mistakes in such reasoning, which is an important example of how human decisions may not be a "reflective equilibrium."

one had not thought of. For example, in the second war in the Persian Gulf the advance of U.S. forces in Iraq apparently was initially more difficult than expected because the Iraqis decided to use irregular forces to attack the extended supply lines of U.S. troops as they advanced toward Baghdad. But newspaper accounts indicate that this was an Iraqi strategy that U.S. military planners had not anticipated. It is important also to note that there were disagreements among military commentators about how much revision this unexpected development required in initial U.S. expectations about the eventual outcome of the war.

In discussing how Rubinstein's bargaining model might be extended to an analysis of bargaining while fighting, I implicitly assumed that the military contest proceeded continuously in the background while rulers exchanged offers and counteroffers and that victory or defeat could come at any time. However, while that might be true of the final stages of a military contest, this discussion of learning from battlefield outcomes calls attention to the fact that many wars are made up of discrete battles, and battles early in the contest do not entail much risk of total defeat. Such battles can have two effects: (1) they can change the probability that one side or the other will eventually win, and (2) as just noted, they can convey information about what those probabilities are.

But if a battle is fought with the second effect in mind, then bargaining will be delayed until its outcome has been observed. Moreover, this would continue to be true until both sides thought that no more favorable information could be conveyed by further fighting. This perhaps helps explain why, even though there may have been prewar attempts to reach a negotiated settlement that failed, once a war begins peace negotiations typically do not occur throughout military conflicts but are resumed only toward their end. As Paul Pillar wrote in an important study of peace negotiations, "the opening of peace negotiations usually must await a common perception of the trend of military events" (1983, 199). Thus while an exchange of offers and counteroffers could occur throughout a military contest, it usually does not.

Moreover, while battles can both change the balance of military capabilities and convey information about it, it is possible for battles to be fought whose only function is to convey information. Such battles can occur even in the midst of a contest in disarmament. Consider, for example, General von Falkenhayn's discussion of the German military position at the end of 1915, during World War I, which includes the following passage describing plans for the battle of Verdun:

> the strain on France has almost reached the breaking point. . . . If we succeeded in opening the eyes of her people to the fact that in a military sense they have nothing more to hope for, that breaking point would be reached. . . . To achieve that object the uncer-

tain method of a mass break-through, in any case beyond our means, is unnecessary. We can probably do enough for our purposes with limited resources. (Falkenhayn 1920, 249)[25]

But it is clearly also possible that battles might convey information about relative military capabilities even though they are not part of a military contest that would eventually lead to the complete disarmament of one side or the other. This appears to be what Clausewitz had in mind when he wrote that in "real wars" states might not try seriously to disarm each other at all.

The possibility of revealing information without actually attempting to defeat one's adversary implies, as Clausewitz suggested, that the contest I originally described might not occur at all, even though expectations about its outcome would motivate any agreement that might be reached. Thus the wars that we see are not necessarily good guides for constructing a model of a war that would be fought if the aim were only the complete disarmament of the enemy. And even if such a contest began, peace negotiations might take place in the context of a cease-fire agreement, which could be accepted because both sides thought there was no further information to be revealed by fighting. This reinforces my earlier comment about the difficulty of constructing a truly general model of bargaining and war.[26]

Revealing Private Information

The preceding discussion of bargaining while fighting is very different from the literature about bargaining that has been developed by economists. To understand why, we must look again at figure 6. There are two elements of figure 6 that will influence the terms of an agreement that the two rulers might accept as an alternative to war. One is their probabilities of winning the contest, and the other is the shapes of their indifference curves. We have just seen that if they have inconsistent estimates of their probabilities of winning and believe that fighting could change them, they could have a motive to fight for a while in order to improve the terms of a deal. We must now consider whether the same might be true of their indifference curves.

Part of the answer to that question is the same as the one just given about the probability of winning: battles also convey information about the costs that a contest in disarmament would entail.[27] As already noted,

---

25. I owe this example to Hein Goemans.

26. There are now a number of different models of bargaining while fighting. For summaries of recent work on the subject, see Powell 2002 and Reiter 2003.

27. This perhaps helps explain why the point of military operations might be, as Clausewitz said, "neither to conquer the enemy country nor to destroy its army, but simply *to cause general damage.*"

while the costs of fighting are not explicitly represented in figure 6, they will influence the shapes of the indifference curves that are portrayed there. And therefore battlefield outcomes can influence not only the probabilities on the vertical axes but also the points of indifference between probabilities and territorial divisions.

However, two rulers with the same expectations of the consequences of fighting a contest in disarmament, including expectations about its costs, might nonetheless have different points of indifference between territorial divisions and probabilities of winning. Moreover, by misrepresenting his preferences a ruler could improve the terms of the agreement. The question we must consider, then, is whether fighting would also be a way of revealing information about the true preferences of the two bargainers. That is the question that has been the main focus of the literature on bargaining developed by economists.[28]

A technique for constructing game theoretic models of this problem was developed by John Harsanyi, for which he received a Nobel prize in economics (Harsanyi 1967–68). It is based on the idea that, while a player of a game might not be certain about the preferences of another player, he might nonetheless have an idea of what range of possible preferences he might have and be able to assign each of them a probability. If the second player knows that the first has only probable knowledge of his preferences, then whatever the second player's preferences actually are, his choices would be influenced by his knowledge of the first player's uncertainty. Thus one might imagine that the uncertain player confronts one of many possible players, each of whose choices would be determined by his true preferences, and those choices might therefore reveal information about what that player's preferences actually are. Each of the possible sets of preferences that a player might have is commonly said to determine his "type."

Clearly, learning from the choices made by someone who has an incentive to mislead you is a far more complex problem than learning about an adversary's military capabilities by observing battlefield outcomes. Battlefield outcomes cannot be faked, and therefore the probability with which they were expected to occur is only a function of one's prior understanding of how the war would be fought, how weapons would work, how well trained and motivated the military forces were, and so forth. The probability with which an adversary would be expected to make

---

28. For a survey, see Kennan and Wilson 1993. Note, however, that in bargaining in the context of war the preferences of more people than the ones conducting the bargaining are relevant. Information about the reactions of domestic political actors, or the decisions of potential allies, is not revealed by learning about the preferences of the people conducting the bargaining but can be garnered by observing the course of the war just like information about military capabilities.

a choice one can observe, however, will be a function both of whatever his true preferences happen to be and the effect he expects his choices will have on one's own expectations. If he is also known to be uncertain about one's own true preferences, then the problem is even more complex and there are often multiple equilibrium combinations of choices.

Many game theorists would claim that I have exaggerated the difference between learning about preferences and learning about relative military capabilities. The reason for this claim is that, if two people with common prior probabilities always update them in accordance with Bayes's rule, then their probabilities will remain the same. Any differences in their probabilities must therefore be the result of their having been exposed to different information, and therefore if I learn that another person's probability estimate is different from my own I should infer that he knows something I do not know and change my estimate accordingly. Thus, in the situation represented in figure 6, both inconsistent probability estimates and inconsistent beliefs about each other's true indifference curves would be the result of private information that the two rulers had an incentive to conceal, and both could therefore be revealed by the choices they made during any bargaining that accompanied fighting.[29]

Clearly one's enemy may have an incentive both to feign confidence in his military capabilities that he does not really have and to conceal some of them so that one cannot take countermeasures against them. And therefore knowledge that he is unexpectedly confident of winning a military contest ought to make one wonder if he knows something one does not know. That does not imply, however, that his bargaining behavior is a perfect substitute for battlefield outcomes as a source of information as to his true military capabilities, since even if one had access to all the information he had one might disagree with the inferences he drew from it. This is not only because one might doubt his competence as a military strategist but also because, like science, learning about war is only partly a matter of Bayesian updating. A military contest is like a very costly experiment that tests competing theories about how the war will unfold, and just as scientists with different theoretical commitments frequently disagree about what they think experiments will reveal, so equally well-informed military strategists may disagree about what battlefield outcomes to expect.[30]

---

29. See, for example, the discussion of this question in Fearon 1995b.

30. This is an example of an issue one would be unlikely to think of if one had not subjected one's thinking to the discipline of a formal model. For a discussion of the relevant theory, see Geanakoplos 1989 and 1992. For an interesting discussion of war as a way of testing competing theories, see Smith and Stam 2004. For accounts of competing bets and heated disputes between scientists backing different hypotheses, see Glanz 1998 and 1999. See also the discussion from a Bayesian perspective of the strength of scientists' beliefs in the truth of their ideas in Press and Tanur 2001.

A plausible reading of Pillar's book on peace negotiations is that statesmen rely primarily on battlefield outcomes for information about military capabilities and then reveal any remaining private information during the bargaining process that accompanies peace negotiations (Pillar 1983). However, while Pillar interprets war termination as a bargaining process, his book was written before models of bargaining with incomplete information were available and therefore does not actually investigate this question. There are many historical studies that criticize statesmen's failure to learn rapidly enough from battlefield outcomes (e.g., Iklé 1991) but few careful studies of exactly how they do it. This is an important research frontier in the study of war.[31]

The theory of games with incomplete information had a big impact on the literature about deterrence during the cold war, where the issue was how political leaders could reveal prior to war whether they were really willing to carry out deterrent threats if they were challenged. Much of that literature assumed that bargaining ended when war began and therefore whatever war had been threatened would occur if a defender who was not bluffing was challenged.[32] This overlooks the fact that, as Clausewitz said, "war in itself does not suspend political intercourse or change it into something entirely different." However, the cold war literature on limited war is consistent with Clausewitz's idea that the function of limited war is to reveal information about absolute war, which might mean that absolute war never occurs.[33]

Bargaining, War, and Alliances

Like most discussions of both war and bargaining, the analysis so far has been couched in terms of a contest between only two predatory rulers. But wars can involve more than two states. We must therefore consider what effect adding more rulers would have.

With more rulers, alliances become possible. Alliances can affect not only the conduct of war but also the bargaining process that might accompany it. In thinking about these added complications, I will follow the same analytical strategy employed earlier and consider first what effect they would have on a contest in disarmament (Clausewitz's absolute war)

31. For a pioneering study of how German and French leaders responded to the same course of events on the battlefield during World War I, see Goemans 2000.
32. This assumption is reflected in Fearon's (1995b) pioneering article on this subject.
33. For example, one of the main themes of the recent history of the Korean War by William Stueck (1995) is that the Korean War can usefully be considered to have been a substitute for World War III.

and then introduce the possibility of bargaining over the terms of a nego-tiated settlement that might be accepted as an alternative to such a contest.

The idea of subjective or personal probabilities seemed sufficient as a way of capturing the uncertainty associated with a contest in disarmament between two rulers, since they contained all the information that was important in making a choice between fighting such a contest and accept-ing a division of the territory in dispute instead. However, in thinking about contests among varying configurations of allies it will be necessary to think about the effect of shifts in alliances on the probability with which one side or the other would be expected to win. Shifts in alliances would lead to realignments of the military forces that would fight each other, and it is the distribution of those military forces that would determine the degree of confidence that a ruler would have about his ability to disarm his adversary. So if we are to think about the effect of alliances we must say something about the effect of any particular distribution of military forces on the probability of winning or losing.

As I pointed out earlier, personal probabilities are both subjective and nonarbitrary: they reflect the choice that a person would make between the uncertain prospect he actually confronts and a lottery with the same out-comes and known probabilities, but these choices would obviously be based on everything that person knew that he thought might affect which outcome occurred. Thus there are two potential sources of disagreement about the effect of any particular distribution of capabilities on the expected outcome of war: there might be disagreement about what capa-bilities were relevant or how they should be measured and disagreement about what any particular distribution of capabilities implied about the probability of winning or losing.

While any assumptions we make about these issues will be arbitrary, we must make some assumptions if we are to think about the relation between alliances and war. I will therefore make assumptions that reflect the way these issues are often discussed, while bearing in mind that they are arbitrary. If such assumptions lead to conclusions that differ from claims commonly made by writers on the subject, they can provide the basis for a counterexample to those claims. But before leaping to any conclusion as to what the right answer to the question really is, we would need to consider whether different assumptions would lead to different conclusions.

To get the analysis started, then, I will assume (1) that military capa-bilities can be measured at least to the extent that one can determine the ratios between them (so that one can say, for example, that one side has twice the military capabilities of the other) and (2) that the ratio between the probabilities with which each side might win a military contest is the same as the ratio between their military capabilities (so that, e.g., if one side is twice as strong as the other, it is twice as likely to win a contest in disarmament between them).[34]

Thus, if we label the military resources of state i as r_i and the probability that one state will disarm another p, in a two-state contest

$$\frac{p_i}{1 - p_i} = \frac{r_i}{r_j} .$$

This implies that

$$p_i = \frac{r_i}{r_i + r_j} .$$

And therefore the probability of victory of each state can be equated with the percentage of total military resources that it controls.

To make things as easy as possible, let us assume there are only three predatory rulers who might participate in a contest in disarmament. If one attacks another, the third could either join in or not. If it were to join the fight we must consider how that would affect the probabilities associated with the outcomes. One possibility is that, if two rulers both fight the third, then the third state faces the sum of the military resources of the other two, and therefore the probability that this lone state k will win will be

$$\frac{r_k}{r_i + r_j + r_k} .$$

The probability that the other two will be victorious will, of course, be the complementary probability, which implies that, if two of three equally powerful states fight together, they will be twice as likely to defeat the third as each would be separately.

But what happens if the two rulers who fought together succeed in disarming the third? Many writers assume, implicitly or explicitly, that they will then divide the territory of the defeated ruler between them. But if they could do that, one might wonder why there could not have been an agreement dividing the disputed territory among all three rulers at the outset. Much of the literature assumes that this is not possible.[35] But this begs the question raised by Clausewitz's analysis of war, which is why states cannot reach negotiated settlements without fighting. It makes more sense to ask

34. For references to the literature about contests that conform to these assumptions, see Skaperdas 1998.
35. See, for example, the important recent contributions to the literature by Schweller (1998) and Powell (1999, chap. 5), both of which explicitly make this assumption.

first how a contest in disarmament would be fought and then to consider what negotiated settlements might be feasible as an alternative to it.

If an absolute war is a contest in disarmament fought until one state has rendered its adversary incapable of further resistance, and the point of such a contest is to enable a predatory ruler to capture all the territory in dispute, then if there are three rulers an absolute war would be a contest in disarmament fought until every state but one had been disarmed and one ruler therefore controlled all the territory. If two rulers fought a third and disarmed him, therefore, then the contest would not be over until they had fought each other.

The probability that state i will eventually disarm the others if it begins as state j's ally is the probability that states i and j will win the first stage of the contest times the probability that state i will defeat state j in the second stage. In the following analysis I will initially assume that defeat entails the destruction of the third state's military capabilities—for reasons that will become clear, the possibility that the defeated state has military resources that can be transferred to the victors after its armed forces have been destroyed will be examined separately in the next chapter. If defeat entails the destruction of a state's military capabilities, then the relative power of the two victorious allies will be unchanged by the defeat of the third state.[36] The probability that state i will eventually disarm the others if it begins as state j's ally is therefore

$$\frac{r_i + r_j}{r_i + r_j + r_k} \left(\frac{r_i}{r_i + r_j} \right),$$

which reduces to

$$\frac{r_i}{r_i + r_j + r_k}.$$

Thus with these assumptions each ruler faces the same probability of defeating the other two whether it fights alone or fights with an ally in the first round of the contest. Each would therefore be better off sitting out the first round and then challenging the winner, since no matter what the distribution of military resources, the probability with which any state will win a contest against either of the other two will be greater than the probability with which it would win a contest against the other two combined.

---

36. It is possible that fighting the first round might weaken the allied states, but so long as neither expects to be affected proportionately more than the other this would not affect their prewar expectations.

But the other two would then prefer to join together to fight such a state rather than fight each other first, and that is therefore how we should expect this contest to be fought.[37]

It is instructive to compare this conclusion with Kenneth Waltz's famous claim that the potential danger posed by a powerful ally would lead weak states to ally with each other to "balance" the power of stronger ones rather than to "bandwagon" with stronger states against weaker ones. As we saw in our discussion of Waltz's claim in chapter 1, the argument Waltz gave for it is incomplete. A state forced to choose between a stronger and a weaker ally confronts a complex tradeoff: if it joins the stronger side it will confront a more powerful adversary after victory, but if it joins the weaker side victory will be less likely.[38]

In the little model of absolute war just discussed, these two factors exactly cancel each other out, and therefore states should be indifferent between the two possibilities. Moreover, if powerful allies can be expected to bear a larger proportion of the costs of war than weaker ones, then a state would actually prefer a more powerful ally.[39] This example illustrates once again how easy it is to overlook the implications of even simple assumptions.

Nonetheless, the implications of these assumptions seem very counterintuitive. Before accepting the implications at face value, we need to consider whether there is something wrong with the assumptions.

The conclusions we arrived at are the result of the way military resources are assumed to accumulate as compared to probabilities: military resources are added together to produce greater strength, whereas probabilities are multiplied. That is why, if all three rulers have equal resources, a ruler who fights both the other two together faces the sum of their resources and therefore has a one-third probability of winning, whereas if he fights them separately he has a fifty percent chance of winning each contest, but the accumulation of risk implies that he has a probability of beating both of them separately of only .25.[40]

If alliances combined military capabilities in a way that was not sim-

---

37. If the states all have the same military capabilities, for example, then in a contest in which two first fought the third each would have a probability of winning of one-third, whereas a state that sat out the first round would have a probability of defeating the survivor of .5. But then each of the other two would have a probability of defeating both the others of only .25, and they could therefore do better by joining together to fight the third before fighting each other.
38. For Waltz's argument, see the discussion in chapter 1. See also the discussion of it in Powell 1999, chap. 5.
39. This is one of the assumptions in Powell's analysis of this question (1999, 162).
40. Moreover, a state that combines its military forces with its allies' forces increases the probability of winning the first round of the contest but exposes itself to the risk that it might be defeated along with its ally.

ply additive, that is, if there were economies of scale in alliances, fighting an alliance would be more risky. Using the notation in Powell 1999, let g be a parameter that describes the possible effect of economies of scale in alliances. Then the probability that state i will win a military contest if it initially allies with state j will be

$$\frac{r_i}{r_i + r_j}\left[\frac{g\,(r_i + r_j)}{g\,(r_i + r_j) + r_k}\right],$$

which reduces to

$$\frac{gr_i}{g\,(r_i + r_j) + r_k}.$$

If $g > 1$ and $r_j > r_k$, then the value of this expression would be increased if state i allied with state k instead of state j, and now Waltz's claim would be supported.[41]

However, even if there are economies of scale in alliances, they might not be great enough to outweigh the advantage of waiting out the first round of the contest and just fighting the winner. Moreover, it is also possible for coalition warfare to be inefficient, so there might be diseconomies of scale in an alliance. If so, a weak state would actually prefer to fight alone.[42] Thus there are many possible combinations of factors that might, in any given situation, lead a state to prefer balancing to bandwagoning, to have the opposite preference, or to be indifferent between them, and therefore, contrary to Waltz, no general statement can be made as to what states will do.

In talking about absolute war in a two-state setting, I pointed out that, while the optimum way of conducting such a war posed a complicated strategic problem in its own right (since each state's strategy depended on the expected strategy of the other side), there was good reason to think that the solution to that problem was independent of any bargaining that might take place between the two adversaries. Expectations about the outcome of that contest could then be taken as the disagreement outcome in bargaining over the terms of a negotiated settlement.

This discussion of a three-way contest in disarmament implies that, as one might expect, expectations about its outcome depend not just on the military capabilities of the adversaries and the strategies they employ but also on information about the effect of alliances and perhaps also about which alliances will form. Nonetheless, the solution to the problem of how

41. On this point see also Skaperdas 1998.
42. For a possible example, see the statements of British policymakers about defending France in the period before World War II quoted in Schweller 1998, 150.

to fight a three-way contest in disarmament is also independent of any bargaining that might occur, and, given the other requisite information, expectations about its outcome can also be represented as a set of probabilities that express how optimistic each state would be about eventually emerging as the sole winner of such a contest. Moreover, if all states are equally matched they would each be far less optimistic about winning such a contest than if there were only two states.

In the simple case we first looked at, for example, if all states have the same military capabilities they would each expect to win a contest in disarmament among them with a probability of one-third, and therefore each might be willing to accept less than one-third of the territory in dispute rather than fight for all of it. This is because, while two of them could, with a much higher probability, capture all the territory, they would still have to fight each other for control over it. Of course, they might anticipate being able peacefully to agree about how to divide it, but if so there seems to be no reason all three states could not do the same. That is the question we must now examine.

Unfortunately, the analysis of n-person bargaining is much less developed than the analysis of two-person bargaining. Moreover, it is even more difficult to construct a model of bargaining while fighting when there are more than two states than when there are just two. Perhaps the best we can do is construct a plausible scenario and identify this as an important question for future research.

Suppose, then, that a contest in disarmament among three states begins with a contest between two of them against the third. If the two allied states win, then the second stage of this contest will be a two-state contest like the one examined previously. With complete information the two victorious states will therefore agree to a division of the territory without fighting.

Now suppose that bargaining during the first stage of the contest takes place as follows: one ruler proposes a division of territory to the other two. Each in turn can accept the offer or propose another. If both accept then the conflict ends and the division is implemented. If a ruler whose turn it is to respond proposes another division then the contest continues, and if no one has been defeated by the next period the other two respond to that proposal. The contest continues in this way until one side has been disarmed or all the participants accept a division of the territory.

This is a scenario that resembles the Rubinstein two-person bargaining game. There is a three-person version of Rubinstein's game that has been discussed in the literature, in which there is a subgame perfect equilibrium set of offers similar to the ones that characterize the two-person bargaining game. As in the two-person case, therefore, with complete information one might expect that agreement would be immediate and therefore the military contest would not occur.[43] However, if expectations about the contest were not consistent, then there might be an incentive to fight more limited wars to reveal information about what to expect should an absolute war be fought. Thus the relation between bargaining and war in a world of three states appears to be qualitatively similar to the relation when there are just two.

There is one striking difference between a three-state world and the two-state case discussed earlier, however, which is that in the three-state case a war of all against all is the disagreement outcome in any bargaining that may occur even if the only wars that occur are bilateral wars. This is because a war between state i and state j that reveals information about state j's military capabilities has implications for the terms of a negotiated settlement involving a possible war among all three states. Thus the outcome of a war between states i and j could lead to a revision of the territory held by state k, even though state k did not participate in the conflict. In this situation everything concerns everybody, whether they all participate in a military conflict or not.

Bargaining, War, and the Balance of Power

We saw in chapter 2 that in Western political thought the concept of a state system dates back at least to fifteenth-century Italy and that what Kenneth Waltz called "balance-of-power theory" has long been an important element of thinking about it.[44] One controversy about state systems concerns how to explain the ability of states to maintain their independence. Another concerns the effect of systems of independent states on human welfare. The most important issue in the latter context is the frequency of warfare, though the Prisoner's Dilemma game has led many people to doubt the ability of independent states to cooperate in the pursuit of any common interest. What Waltz called balance-of-power theory includes controversies about how to explain both the ability of states to maintain their independence (often called the stability of state systems) and variations in the frequency of warfare among them.

Sometimes in these controversies the balance of power refers to the

---

43. For a discussion of this game, see Osborne and Rubinstein 1990, 63–65. In the three-person game, any convention about how goods should be divided can be supported by strategies that reward someone who rejects a deviant offer by giving him all the gains from bargaining in the following period, and therefore subgame perfection does not guarantee uniqueness in the three-person game. But it is not clear in this context where such a convention might come from. However, for the purposes of this discussion it does not matter what the outcome of this bargaining game is expected to be, so long as, with complete information, there is an equilibrium outcome.

44. For general surveys of writings on this subject, see Claude 1962 and Sheehan 1996.

distribution of military capabilities among individual states, and sometimes it refers to the distribution of capabilities between alliances. Common sense suggests (wrongly) that war between two states is least likely
when their military capabilities are equal. Often it is assumed implicitly
that if states are to maintain their independence, then weak states must
"balance" against the power of strong ones. Common sense might also
suggest that balancing would serve to reduce the likelihood of war when
there are more than two states, though many writers have denied this.

It seems likely that the availability of negotiated settlements as an
alternative to war will have an impact on both the frequency of war and
system stability. We have seen that negotiated settlements that everyone
prefers to war may not always exist, and in the next chapter we will see that
the necessity that agreements be self-enforcing may reduce further the
number of agreements that are feasible. Nonetheless, it is obvious that
states often do accept such agreements and that Clausewitz was right in
claiming that the possibility that they might be accepted has a profound
impact on both the likelihood of war and how it is conducted. Before looking at factors that may restrict the availability of negotiated settlements,
therefore, let us consider what effect their availability might have on controversies about the balance of power and its significance.

The Distribution of Power and the Likelihood of War

Common sense suggests that war between two states is least likely when
their military capabilities are equal, but commonsense reasoning fails to
take into account the effect of fighting on the bargaining that accompanies
it. Donald Wittman (1979) argued that, since the distribution of military
capabilities would affect the terms of any agreement they might accept but
not whether they both would prefer an agreement to war, the balance of
power should have no effect on the likelihood of war. Geoffrey Blainey
(1988) claimed, however, that states would be more likely to agree on the
terms of an agreement if their capabilities were unequal than if they were
equal. As we have just seen, the fact that a mutually acceptable agreement
exists does not mean that states will not fight, so Blainey might be right.
However, the argument that he gave for his claim was both incomplete
and confused, so we must decide for ourselves whether there is any reason
to believe that it is true.

Blainey's fundamental claim was that "[w]ars usually begin when two
nations disagree on their relative strength, and wars usually cease when the
fighting nations agree on their relative strength" (1988, 293). The reason
he gave for this claim was that disagreements about relative strength lead
to disagreements about relative bargaining power (115–19). As we have
seen, there is good reason to take this claim seriously.

The reason Blainey thought that war was more likely when power was distributed equally than when it was not was that he thought states were most likely to disagree about their relative strength when they were equal (108–24). One has only to state this claim to see a serious problem with it: if states disagree about their relative strength, how can one say whether they are equal or not?

The only reason Blainey gave for believing this proposition was true was that warring states find it easier to reach agreement after fighting than before fighting began—otherwise the war would not have occurred. But when a war ends, Blainey claimed, one state has revealed that it is stronger than the other. From this he concluded that peace was most likely when there was a "clear preponderance of power" (113).

Not only is this not a valid argument, but its plausibility rests on a confusion between *uncertainty* and *inconsistent expectations.* As we saw, as a war progresses states may become less uncertain about how it will end, but this implies nothing about whether the two states' expectations are consistent—indeed, if they are both maximally uncertain their expectations *must* be consistent, since they would both assign equal probabilities to winning and losing.[45] Since it is the consistency of their expectations that is important in reaching agreement, states that are maximally uncertain about the outcome of war may have no difficulty in agreeing on the terms of a negotiated settlement they would both prefer to fighting, if a negotiated settlement is possible at all. This would be compatible with another intuition that is common in the literature, which is that negotiated settlements are most likely in wars that are stalemated.[46]

Nonetheless, it is possible to construct an argument in support of the proposition that equality of power can make war more likely. But doing so reveals that the proposition is not always true.

As we have seen, the balance of power between or among states can be thought of in two ways: as a distribution of subjective probabilities assigned to the possible outcomes of a contest in disarmament between or among those states and as a measure of the distribution of the military capabilities among them on which such probability estimates would be based (e.g., size of armed forces, nature and number of weapons systems, size of population, quantity of industrial production, and so forth). How-

---

45. However, the consistency of their expectations might not be common knowledge, so it would still be possible for one ruler to feign confidence he did not really have.

46. I suggested earlier that a stalemate is best thought of in terms of expectations about the length of a military contest rather than which side is more likely ultimately to win. Nonetheless, one reason a war might be expected to last a long time is that the two sides are thought to be evenly matched. The importance of a "mutually hurting stalemate" in producing negotiated settlements of civil wars has been emphasized by William Zartman. See his essay in Licklider 1993 and the discussion of that thesis in other essays in that volume.

ever, some of the factors that might be expected to influence the outcome
of a contest in disarmament are more easily identified and observed than
others. In addition to the factors just mentioned, for example, the training,
morale, and fighting spirit of a state's armed forces, as well as the nature of
the strategies that will be employed in fighting, are also important. Thus
some of the factors that determine the probability with which a state will
win a military contest are more easily observed than others.

It is plausible to think that the more evenly matched two states are
with respect to the military capabilities that can be observed and measured, the greater the significance of the factors that cannot be so easily
observed. Just as the quality of the coaching may determine the outcome
of a professional football game but have little effect on the outcome of a
football game between a professional and a high school team, so the outcome of a war between two equally powerful states may be determined by
which side has the better generals, but not even the best general could
enable Guatemala to disarm the United States. And it is easy to see how
each of two rulers could believe in his own military genius even though it
was common knowledge that their military forces were evenly matched.
This provides a possible justification for Blainey's claim and also solves
the problem of how one could say that two states were evenly matched
even though they disagreed about their relative military capabilities.

However, we have seen that, if rulers are to reach a negotiated settlement, they must have consistent beliefs not only about their probabilities
of winning a military contest but also about the cost of doing so. And it is
clearly possible for rulers who agree that one is much more likely to be able
to disarm the other nonetheless to disagree about the cost the stronger
state would have to pay. The U.S. war in Vietnam may be an example of
this: it was perhaps the great disparity in military power between the
United States and North Vietnam that made political leaders in the United
States underestimate the ability of North Vietnam to impose costs on the
United States, and the ability of North Vietnam to force a revision of that
estimate led to a settlement of the contest that was far less favorable to the
United States than the one it had expected at the outset.[47]

Of course, inconsistent expectations about a contest in disarmament
are not sufficient for fighting to occur. A ruler must also be optimistic
enough about his ability to alter the expectations of his opponent at an
acceptable cost to make it worth his while to try. Thus "real war," like
"absolute war," is a costly contest with an uncertain outcome. But the
probabilities assigned to the possible outcomes of real war need have little
relation to the probabilities assigned to the outcomes of absolute war.

---

47. The bargaining process that accompanied the termination of the war in Vietnam is examined at length by Paul Pillar (1983) in the book referred to previously. Pillar interprets the war
in Vietnam as primarily a contest in the imposition of costs.

Even if a ruler hopes to alter the enemy's beliefs about his own relative military strength, the aim may not be to show that he is stronger than the enemy but merely to show that he is not as weak as the enemy thought. And it is possible that the point of the contest will not be to affect the enemy's estimate of the probability of winning the contest at all but to influence his estimate of the costs that winning would entail. Thus it is possible to hope to gain a bargaining advantage by losing battles, which helps explain why Clausewitz claimed that weak states could hope to gain by fighting stronger ones and why military forces might be used not to disarm one's adversary but merely "to cause general damage."

We saw that what is true of two-state contests seems likely also to be true of multistate contests. Thus Wittman was right in claiming that there is no general connection between the distribution of military capabilities between or among states and the likelihood of war.[48]

The Distribution of Power and the Independence of States

As already noted, the phrase *balance of power* is sometimes used to refer to the distribution of military capabilities among individual states and sometimes to the distribution between warring alliances. When it refers to individual states, it often has meant not that the individual states were equally powerful but that no individual state was powerful enough to defeat all the others combined. As we saw, that was how Saint-Pierre used the term.[49] Similarly, Friedrich Gentz wrote early in the nineteenth century that "if the states system of Europe is to exist and be maintained by common exertions, no one of its members must ever become so powerful as to be able to coerce all the rest put together" (quoted in Gulick 1955, 34).

If this condition is satisfied, weak states could perhaps preserve their independence by joining together to oppose strong ones. And if they do, then the power of strong states will be balanced by the power of an opposing coalition. This is how the distribution of power among individual states, "balancing" (to use Waltz's influential terminology), and the distribution of power between opposing coalitions are related.

As the seventeenth-century tract by the Duke de Rohan discussed in chapter 2 illustrates, the history of Europe can plausibly be told as a history of states forming balancing coalitions to oppose attempts by power-

---

48. Note that this discussion has been based on the assumption discussed previously that states rely primarily on battlefield outcomes in revising their expectations about their relative military capabilities. The question of the relation between the distribution of power and the likelihood of war is much more complex if one assumes that each side knows its own true capabilities but misrepresents them and that that information is revealed in the course of making offers and counteroffers.

49. See the discussion in chapter 2.

ful states to establish hegemony over them: first Spain, then France under Louis XIV and Napoleon, then Germany under the kaiser and Hitler, and then the USSR after World War II. Moreover, the tendency for such balances to form could be offered as an explanation of the fact that none of those attempts was successful.

However, those would-be hegemons had allies. Moreover, while no European state succeeded in eliminating all the others, balancing did not protect the independence of states in the ancient Chinese Warring States System, the Greek city-state system, or the subsequent Hellenistic one.[50] And, in spite of what Waltz claimed about balance-of-power theory, no one has offered a valid argument for the proposition that weak states should always be expected to ally with each other against strong ones.

In addition, it is not even clear why balancing would protect the independence of states. It might do so if the equality of power between coalitions prevented war from occurring, since if no war occurred no state could be defeated. But the frequency of war in the European state system seems to rule out that possibility. Moreover, we have already seen that the idea that equality of power between antagonists makes war less likely than it otherwise would be is itself based on invalid reasoning. But if wars between evenly matched antagonists occur, then one would expect that at least some of the time the potential hegemon would win. And even if it lost, one must ask why it would not be eliminated by the members of the victorious coalition.[51]

In Europe, balance of power thinking can be traced back at least as far as the Renaissance, when warring princes competed for control of northern Italy, and it flourished in the eighteenth century. That was a time when, as Rousseau's writings illustrate, international politics could plausibly be said to have consisted of struggles among predatory rulers for control over valuable territory. In those circumstances, as we have seen, everyone is in conflict with everyone else, even if they might ally temporarily, but compromises are possible because territory is divisible. This implies a different relation between the balance of power and the ability of states to maintain their independence.

There are two ways in which states might lose their independence: they might be disarmed in a military contest, or they might agree to give up their independence in a negotiated settlement. But these are in reality not two ways but one, since disarming a state only weakens its bargaining power but does not determine what will happen to it. Thus whether any

---

50. For a comparison of the history of Europe with the history of China that focuses on this question, see Hui 1999 and 2000.
51. This last question is perhaps why some authors have claimed that balancing is something that only satisfied states would engage in. However, as we saw, Waltz explicitly denied that this was true.

particular distribution of military capabilities among states leads to a loss of independence for one of them depends on both the preferences of their leaders and their bargaining power.

If rulers are warriors trying to maximize their ability to profit from the labor of others and there are economies of scale in predation, then they might all be better off if they joined forces, and therefore any conflict between them would only be about the terms on which they would give up their independence. All three states might therefore disappear even though they were all militarily equal. Thus in Europe many of the "little monarchs" that Hobbes wrote about disappeared into the armed forces of big ones.[52] Fustel de Coulanges claimed that the conquest of the ancient world by Rome was facilitated by the fact that aristocratic leaders in many city-states thought that submission to Rome would protect them from popular forces at home (1956, 373–74). And the recent conquest of much of Afghanistan by the organization known as the Taliban was made possible in part by the fact that leaders of opposing groups expected to profit from submitting to it (Rashid 2000, 35).[53]

If giving up their political independence is very costly for the leaders of states, however, then only relatively weak states would have to agree to do it. Thus equality of power among individual states will lead to system stability, but system stability will not require "balancing."

Waltz made an influential distinction between "internal" and "external" balancing, which seems to imply that they are just two ways of doing the same thing (1979, 118). But according to Waltz, internal balancing consists of "moves to increase economic capability, to increase military strength, to develop clever strategies." Since the distribution of such capabilities among all states will influence the distribution of any goods to be divided, all states can be expected to be interested in strengthening their own capabilities relative to others'. If no state has a natural advantage over all the others, the result of such competitive efforts might well be that states are and remain relatively evenly matched, just as one team need not dominate the National Football League forever even if there were no rules whose purpose is to avoid the creation of "dynasties."

If so, and if the leaders of all states also place a high value on remaining independent, then this will lead to agreements among them that pre-

---

52. See, for example, Henry Kamen's (2003) recent account of how the Habsburg family used the scanty resources of the Spanish monarchy to organize predators from all over Europe to share in the benefits of a global empire. For an analysis of the organization created by entrepreneurial Spanish monarchs, see Glete 2002, 67–139.

53. Formal models of interstate war usually assume that the size of the object in dispute is fixed and an actor that loses its independence loses everything. But this clearly need not be true. Waltz himself said that "the system won't work if all states lose interest in preserving themselves. It will, however, continue to work if some states do, while others do not, choose to lose their political identities, say, through amalgamation" (1979, 118).

serve their independence, even though wars may be necessary to reveal the true distribution of power. But this does not imply that states have engaged in "external balancing," if that consists of joining with weak states against stronger ones or forgoing the opportunity to absorb defeated states when it arises.

It is not surprising to discover that this is Clausewitz's own explanation of the ability of European states to maintain their independence. The reason "even gifted commanders and monarchs . . . had to be content with moderate success," he wrote, "lies with the balance of power in Europe." Political relations among European states, he said,

> had become so sensitive a nexus that no cannon could be fired in Europe without every government feeling its interest affected. Hence a new Alexander needed more than his own sharp sword: he required a pen as well. Even so, his conquests rarely amounted to much. (Clausewitz 1976, 590)

And the reason conquests rarely amounted to much was that the military resources available to states were limited and commonly known:

> Their means of waging war came to consist of the money in their coffers and of such idle vagabonds as they could lay their hands on either at home or abroad. In consequence the means they had available were fairly well defined, and each could gauge the other side's potential in terms both of numbers and of time. War was thus deprived of its most dangerous feature—its tendency toward the extreme, and of the whole chain of unknown possibilities which would follow. . . .
>
> The conduct of war thus became a true game, in which the cards were dealt by time and by accident. In its effect it was a somewhat stronger form of diplomacy . . . in which battles and sieges were the principal notes exchanged. Even the most ambitious ruler had no greater aims than to gain a number of advantages that could be exploited at the peace conference. (589–90)

The French Revolution and Napoleon removed the limits on France's military resources, Clausewitz wrote, and made them more difficult to measure. However, the other states of Europe were able to recover from their surprise before it was too late, and therefore even "the terrible Bonaparte" was unsuccessful. Nonetheless, we should note, France did not lose its independence.

Note that there are two elements to Clausewitz's explanation of interstate conflict in Europe prior to Napoleon: the fact that the military resources available to states were limited and the fact that they were commonly known, or, as he put it, that "each could gauge the other side's potential":

> The enemy's cash resources, his treasury and his credit, were all approximately known; so was the size of his fighting forces. No great expansion was feasible at the outbreak of war. (590)

One possible interpretation of what he wrote is that it was the limits that were important:

> Knowing the limits of the enemy's strength, men knew they were reasonably safe from total ruin; and being aware of their own limitations, they were compelled to restrict their own aims in turn. (590)

One might infer from these comments that states were able to maintain their independence because no one had the ability to threaten it.

However, Clausewitz denied this:

> Even a royal commander had to use his army with a minimum of risk. If the army was pulverized, he could not raise another, and behind the army there was nothing. That enjoined the greatest prudence in all operations. Only if a decisive advantage seemed possible could the precious instrument be used, and to bring things to that point was a feat of the highest generalship. (590)

Thus absolute war even in the eighteenth century was risky, and what enabled states to minimize the risk of complete defeat was the fact that their capabilities were commonly known, which enabled them to fight limited rather than absolute wars. Our discussion of the relation between bargaining and war helps explain why this might be true.

By removing many of the limits on the capabilities of eighteenth-century states (which, as Clausewitz said, "in a sense consist only in man's ignorance of what is possible"), the military revolution that the political revolution in France made possible made it more difficult for states to have a common understanding of what their relative capabilities were. As a result, in the wars with Napoleon,

> There seemed no end to the resources mobilized; all limits disappeared in the vigor and enthusiasm shown by governments and their subjects. . . . The sole aim of war was to overthrow the oppo-

nent. Not until he was prostrate was it considered possible to pause and try to reconcile the opposing interests.

"Will this always be the case in the future?" he asked. "From now on will every war in Europe be waged with the full resources of the state, and therefore have to be fought only over major issues that affect the people?" Clausewitz declared himself unable to answer this question (593).

The French Revolution compelled the predatory rulers of Prussia, Austria, and Russia to make war "a concern of the people," as Clausewitz put it, which is consistent with Kant's claims about the effect of recurring wars on the constitution of states (592). Kant's answer to Clausewitz's question about what the effect of this change would be was optimistic. The nineteenth century seemed to support such optimism, but the twentieth century did not. In deciding whether Kant may be right in the longer run, we must bear in mind the distinction Clausewitz made between the magnitude of states' capabilities and their ability to estimate them consistently.[54]

Bargaining and the Recurrence of War

Before discussing the effect of the recurrence of war, let us consider what we have learned about how to explain it. Blainey's explanation for the recurrence of war during the eighteenth century was that those wars were indecisive and indecisive wars tend to produce short periods of peace. The reason the Napoleonic wars led to a lasting peace, he claimed, was that they were decisive (Blainey 1988, 112–13).

Blainey thought that indecisive wars produced short periods of peace because peace required "a clear ladder of international power," which indecisive wars did not establish (1988, 109). As we saw, his justification for that proposition was that wars end when one state shows that it is clearly stronger than the other. But if eighteenth-century wars were indecisive they must have ended even though no state had done that. Thus eighteenth-century wars are not explained by Blainey's thesis; they are counterexamples to it. Blainey claimed Clausewitz's support for his idea, but, as we have just seen, Clausewitz's explanation of the limited nature of eighteenth-century wars was that statesmen found it *easy* to arrive at a mutual understanding of their military capabilities, and his explanation

---

54. For a discussion of Clausewitz's own ideas on the relation between war and the development of the European state and his involvement in the reform movement in Prussia stimulated by the wars with Napoleon, see Paret 1985.

for the "decisive" nature of the Napoleonic wars was that this ability was upset by the French Revolution.[55]

The analysis of the relation between bargaining and war offered previously implies that two conditions must be satisfied for a ruler to try to overturn a prior peace settlement by going to war: (1) there must be some change that leads him to think that his bargaining power has increased by more than another ruler (or rulers) believe, and (2) he must place a higher value on a military contest that might reveal his true military capabilities than on the terms of the existing settlement. What Clausewitz said about eighteenth-century warfare implies that rulers considered it a safe and inexpensive way of revealing small changes in their relative bargaining power and that this was the result of the fact that they had a good common understanding both of their relative military capabilities and their reluctance to take large risks. Thus they all felt free to challenge prior agreements "as soon as a change of circumstances shall have given fresh strength to the claimants," as Saint-Pierre said.[56] Since rulers in the eighteenth century were engaged in constant attempts to engineer changes in their circumstances, relatively frequent but limited wars were to be expected.

How things might have been different after Napoleon's wars is not so clear. But Clausewitz's discussion of the recurrence of war in the eighteenth century reinforces the importance of our earlier observation that the ability to bargain while fighting, while it may reduce the severity of war, may also increase its frequency.

What Next?

Throughout this discussion I have assumed that land is valued by rulers only for its contribution to their wealth or the wealth of their extended families or their followers. But land can be a source of military capabilities as well, and therefore the redistribution of land might lead to the redistribution of military capabilities and thus a change in the expected value of a military contest. This, of course, was true of Europe in the eighteenth century, and it is what the literature on the balance of power has always assumed.[57] Thus our analysis of warfare among predatory rulers is seriously incomplete.

---

55. For an interesting argument that it is the length of wars and not their decisiveness that determines how much information they reveal, see Smith and Stam 2002.
56. See the discussion of Saint-Pierre's ideas in chapter 2.
57. This can be confirmed by even a cursory reading of any standard work on this subject, for example, Gulick 1955.

Moreover, I noted earlier that in thinking about the relation between bargaining and war one could not, as most of the literature on bargaining does, ignore the question of how agreements are to be enforced. Yet so far I have ignored it. When there is a connection between the object in dispute and the relative bargaining power of the adversaries, this problem is especially complex. I will try to correct both these deficiencies in the next chapter.

CHAPTER 5

Enforcing Agreements

As we have seen, Hobbes's statement that "covenants, without the sword, are but words, and of no strength to secure a man at all," along with the Prisoner's Dilemma game, have helped make plausible the view that the central difference between international politics and domestic politics (or between "anarchy" and "hierarchy," to use Kenneth Waltz's terminology) is that within states contracts are enforceable and among states they are not. But this view rests on two confusions. One is a confusion about the relation between the enforceability of contracts and conflict over their terms, and the other is a confusion about enforcement.

The confusion about the relation between enforceability and conflict is illustrated by the comparison discussed in the previous chapter between wars and strikes. The fact that agreements that end strikes are enforceable does not prevent strikes but rather encourages them, since it increases their value. Similarly, we saw that wars might be more frequent if negotiated settlements are possible than if they are not.[1]

Of course, if a contract signed after a strike could never be altered, then no further strikes would be possible. But it would probably be harder to reach agreement on the terms of a permanent contract than one with a limited duration and harder to enforce it were it to be signed. A more promising way to deal with the cost of strikes is to try to reduce the inefficiency of bargaining over the terms of a contract or to agree on an alternative way of resolving conflicts, such as compulsory arbitration.

---

1. This is a point that is insufficiently appreciated by writers who argue that interstate norms and international law are more efficacious than is commonly appreciated by Realists and infer that they are therefore more likely to prevent interstate wars than Realists believe (see, e.g., Kratochwil 1989). Hans Morgenthau wrote that "during the four hundred years of its existence international law has in most instances been scrupulously observed" (1948, 211). A willingness to fight over the rules that are to govern the international order may be the result of a belief in their efficacy, and the "anarchic" nature of the international order is in part the result of attempts by states to avoid conflicts by limiting the extent to which they will be constrained by that order. (On this point, see the section of Waltz's book *Theory of International Politics* called "The Virtues of Anarchy" [1979, 111–14].) And a rule that says effective control over a well-defined tract of territory is sufficient to elicit recognition as a sovereign state by other rulers greatly increases the value of capturing that territory by forceful means.

Thus a better way of characterizing the difference between domestic and international politics might be that within states there is agreement on procedures for resolving conflicts that are more efficient than the unrestrained bargaining that takes place among them. The important question, then, is how costly interstate bargaining must be and whether its costs could be reduced.

The confusion about enforcement derives from the idea, expressed in Hobbes's famous statement just quoted, that enforcement of agreements (including agreements to abide by procedures for resolving conflicts) always requires confronting violators with superior force. As we saw in chapter 3, such reasoning rests on a confusion between the government's role in enforcing agreements among individuals and the enforcement of the agreements that define the state itself. One such set of agreements defines the organization of the government, another its relation to its subjects, and a third the boundary between its territory and the territory of other states, and they are all subject to renegotiation by the use of force. There is no external enforcer of any of them, and therefore what enforces them all is a comparison of the benefits they provide with expectations about the consequences of trying to renegotiate them. A more economical way of saying the same thing is that all these agreements must be self-enforcing.

In evaluating any such agreement, therefore, whether hypothetical or actual, a party to it must consider not only its provisions but also how long it could be expected to last and what the consequences might be of an attempt to renegotiate it. Even if one did not expect to gain from future renegotiation oneself, someone else's attempt to renegotiate it would at least be costly and could perhaps lead to another agreement with different terms.

Since force can be used to negotiate the terms of all these agreements, the terms of any agreement that is accepted will reflect both how people are organized for the use of force and the distribution of instruments of violence among them. Changes in either of these conditions can therefore provide the opportunity for renegotiation. Such changes can be caused by exogenous factors, which might be expected or unexpected; they can be the result of efforts made by parties to the agreements to change them; and they can even be a consequence of the agreement itself.

Unexpected exogenous changes can lead to unexpected forceful renegotiation, but if they are totally unexpected they can have no effect on whether agreements can be reached or their terms. Changes that are anticipated with some probability, however, whether exogenous or not, make the negotiation of mutually beneficial agreements even more difficult than the analysis of forceful bargaining in the previous chapter implies.

We will see that it is the possibility of changes in the distribution of bargaining power that makes the security dilemma seem plausible as an explanation of war. However, the problems caused by expectations of such changes are neither a necessary consequence of the absence of government nor always eliminated by the creation of one.[2]

The Struggle for Power

We saw in the previous chapter that contests in forcible disarmament are contests to determine the relative bargaining power of the antagonists in subsequent forceful bargaining. Complete disarmament (which Clausewitz compared to pinning a wrestler to the mat) not only eliminates the defeated state's ability to threaten the victor's military forces but also enables the victor's military forces to replace the enemy's police and make take-it-or-leave-it demands of individual members of its government or other residents of its territory.

However, destroying the enemy's army may not eliminate entirely his capacity for organized resistance, perhaps through guerrilla warfare, or his ability to bargain collectively over the terms of a peace settlement. Thus the consequences of victory in a contest in disarmament are not uniform, and inconsistent expectations about what they will be are an additional possible impediment to a negotiated settlement.

In the previous chapter I assumed that victory in a contest in disarmament enabled the victor to appropriate the valuable territory of the loser. Using this assumption I showed that Clausewitz was right in suggesting that there will often be divisions of the prize that the antagonists will prefer to fighting over all of it, and any division that is agreed to will be influenced by the distribution of military capabilities between or among them at the time the agreement is made, whether this happens prior to fighting or after fighting has begun.

But contests in disarmament can be preceded by contests in armament. Like contests in disarmament, contests in armament can be inefficient. However, the source of this inefficiency is often misunderstood. Moreover, Kant's ideas suggest that such contests can have beneficial effects that are easy to overlook.

One obvious form such a contest might take is what is commonly called an arms race. Arms races might be inefficient because their result can be that the adversaries' relative military capabilities remain the same but they both spend more on arms. If so, they would both be better off if they could agree to reduce their military forces in a way that did not alter

2. The following discussion owes a great deal to Fearon 1994 and 1995b. For a general theoretical analysis of the effect of expected future changes in bargaining power on the ability of adversaries to avoid conflict, see Powell 2004.

their relative military capabilities. However, if one complied with such an agreement and the other did not, then the one that did not would gain a military advantage. As we saw in chapter 1, this might appear to imply that arms races exemplify the inefficiency explained by the Prisoner's Dilemma game and therefore that the explanation for them is the absence of any means of enforcing an arms limitation agreement.

But this inference is wrong, because it overlooks the possibility that one state's maintenance of an arms limitation agreement can be made conditional on the other's behavior, in which case violating the agreement would be self-defeating since it would lead to the rearmament of the other side. That is why arms limitation agreements are accompanied by arrangements for detecting cheating. Of course, the costs associated with such arrangements, and whatever residual arms capability is necessary to provide a base for rearmament if necessary, are themselves inefficient, but the magnitude of the inefficiency is far less than the inefficiency that an unrestricted arms race would entail.

However, such an agreement is possible only if states can agree on some level of armaments that they want to maintain. But if any distribution of military capabilities determines the terms of an agreement that might be accepted as an alternative to a contest in forcible disarmament, then it will not be possible to agree on some distribution of military capabilities without agreement on the terms of a political settlement that both would prefer to war—in the situation analyzed in the previous chapter, that would be an agreement on the distribution of territory. Thus just as states may fight if they have inconsistent expectations about the terms of an agreement that would be accepted after fighting, so may they engage in an arms race if they have inconsistent expectations about the terms of an agreement that would be accepted after a competition in armament.

But in that case an arms race resembles a limited war: it is a contest conducted prior to a contest in forcible disarmament, whose outcome will determine expectations about that contest. And like a limited war, an arms race may reveal enough information about the states' relative bargaining power that a more costly and dangerous conflict can be avoided—recall Clausewitz's observation that it was lack of information about the level of armaments that Napoleon could mobilize that accounted for the length and the cost of the wars that were fought in the aftermath of the French Revolution. Like any bargaining, therefore, such an arms race would be inefficient. But like limited war, its inefficiency would be far less than the inefficiency associated with a contest in forcible disarmament.

Moreover, just as states may engage in arms races, so may they also engage in competition in creating the resources from which armaments are derived. But these are bureaucracies, modern economies, tax systems, and the ability to persuade the bulk of one's male population to fight. As we saw in chapter 2, it was this competition that drove much of the process of state building in Europe.[3] Rousseau was of two minds about whether on balance the effects of this competition were good or bad. Kant thought that in the long run they would be good, but during Hitler's and Stalin's time this might have seemed naive. The end of the cold war and the liberalization of China made many people take Kant's ideas more seriously.

During the winter, the future looks bleak, but during the spring optimism revives. To know what to expect, we must know what explains the cycle of the seasons. Unfortunately, we do not know what to expect from the struggle for power. But its explanation is neither that men are endowed with "a perpetual and restless desire of power after power, that ceaseth only in death," nor that "covenants, without the sword, are but words, and of no strength to secure a man at all." Three other explanations are possible: (1) the participants all remain too optimistic about how they will fare if the contest is continued to agree on the terms of an agreement that might end it; (2) it is not possible to coordinate the actions of everyone whose cooperation would be necessary to end it; and (3) an agreement to end it would not be self-enforcing.

Whatever the explanation, this competition is one important source of the recurring changes in bargaining power that make more difficult the construction of other stable, self-enforcing agreements. One of its possible consequences is the creation of incentives for states to attack their adversaries before they are attacked by them.

Incentives to Attack First

One of the recurring controversies about arms races is whether they make war more likely. I have just pointed out one way an arms race could make war less likely, though in any given case this effect might be concealed by the fact that it ended in war: it may have failed to reveal enough information about the adversaries' relative bargaining power to make an agreement possible without fighting. However, an arms race could also make war more likely, if it leads to a military advantage from attacking before one's adversary does.

In any arms race one side or the other may achieve a temporary advantage. But the one that does may not want to attack immediately to capitalize on it, since it may be optimistic that the arms race will eventually reveal enough information about the two sides' military capabilities and interests to lead to a negotiated settlement on favorable terms. If it believes that its adversary has a long-term advantage in the struggle for power,

---

3. For a recent survey, see Glete 2002.

however, it may have an incentive to attack before its own temporary advantage disappears. And whatever the distribution of military capabilities, it is possible that there is an advantage to being the one that attacks first. The first situation may lead to a preventive war, and the second to a preemptive one. I will discuss preemptive wars first. Throughout the discussion I will continue to assume that the competitors are predatory rulers competing over the distribution of valuable territory.

Preemptive Wars

The possibility of a preemptive war became a preoccupation during the cold war, when many people worried that an incentive to attack first could lead to a nuclear war even though neither side wanted to fight one. Many discussions of this possibility are based on the assumption that a state can only choose between attacking another state and not attacking. In those circumstances, a state that chooses not to attack exposes itself to the possibility of an attack by the other state. If it believes the other is about to attack, its choice is then not between war and the status quo but between two different wars: a war in which the other state attacks first and a war that begins with its own attack. Thus if a state mistakenly believes that a nuclear war is inevitable but prefers one in which it attacks first, it appears that two states could fight a nuclear war even though neither in fact preferred such a war to the status quo. Such a war might be called "unwanted" or even "inadvertent," though it would have been intentional.[4]

But this reasoning ignores the possibility of a negotiated settlement as an alternative to war. If a negotiated settlement is possible, the effect of incentives to attack first becomes more complicated.

In discussing the balance of power in the previous chapter, I pointed out that it can be thought of in two ways—as the distribution of military capabilities or potential or as the probability with which each side in a military contest could be expected to disarm the other—and I assumed that only the former was relevant to estimating the latter. But if there is an advantage to being the first to attack, then the probability of victory depends not just on the distribution of military capabilities but also on who attacks first.

---

4. One must be careful with words like *accidental* or *inadvertent* when applied to wars. Weapons can be fired or detonated accidentally (with very costly consequences if they are nuclear weapons), or airplanes can accidentally fly over another state's airspace, but it is not obvious how a military contest could occur by chance. However, an accident could cause a war that might be called inadvertent or unintended if it caused a state with an incentive to attack first to believe that its enemy was about to attack. For a recent discussion and citations to the literature, see Powell 2003.

We saw in the previous chapter that any state dissatisfied with the existing distribution of territory would have to attack the other state if it wanted to compel a redistribution of it, and therefore the probabilities of success that determine the range of possible settlements would have to take that into account. If there is an advantage to attacking first, then each side's probability of success would have to be its probability of disarming the other, conditional on its being the first to attack. In that case the probabilities in figure 6 need not add up to one, and so the effect is similar to the effect of inconsistent expectations discussed in the previous chapter. The result could be to narrow the range of possible agreements (if there is an advantage to attacking) or to expand it (if there is a disadvantage to being the attacker). But even if there is an advantage to attacking, this need not eliminate the range of possible agreements entirely. And if it does not, then the advantage to attacking first will already have been taken into account in determining the existing distribution of territory.

Thus if an advantage to attacking first is to lead to an attempt to change the status quo, the advantage must have increased. But a state confident of having the advantage of attacking first might still prefer a compromise settlement to fighting. And therefore if the effect of attacking first is common knowledge, and a state chooses to attack rather than to demand a concession, this cannot be just because there is an advantage to attacking first but must be because there is an advantage to a *surprise* attack. In that case it could not demand a concession without revealing its intention to attack, and the other state could not commit itself not to take advantage of that information. And therefore the state optimistic about capturing the advantage of attacking first might attack and then demand a concession, after it had secured its advantage.[5]

If it did, however, the resulting war would be no more unwanted or inadvertent than any other war, since the attacking state would expect to gain a bargaining advantage by attacking. It would, however, have been inefficient if the victim had been prepared to offer a concession that the attacker preferred to fighting.

Moreover, if the only information that is required to reach an agreement is information about which side owns the advantage of attacking first, then it should be possible to reach an agreement soon after fighting starts, and therefore wars fought solely because of first strike advantages should be short. Indeed, this is one possible explanation of some of the "limited aims" wars that Clausewitz wrote about, since the advantage of attacking first might consist of the ability to capture a piece of lightly defended territory before the enemy is able to respond. Ownership of this

5. An incentive to attack by surprise is therefore similar to incentives to conceal other components of a state's military capabilities, in order to prevent the enemy from taking countermeasures against them.

territory could then be confirmed in a peace agreement, or it could be traded for some other gain instead.[6]

The preemptive war scenario assumes not just that a state sees an advantage to attacking without warning but also that its potential victim mistakenly anticipates an attack and decides to try to attack before the first state is able to. But if the incentive to attack without warning is the result of being able to catch the victim unawares before he is able to mount a proper defense, the potential victim might not want to preempt an attack but prefer instead to defend himself against it, thereby nullifying the advantage of a surprise attack. For preemption to be considered, the optimal military response to an expected surprise attack must instead be a surprise attack of one's own, which is not implied merely by the existence of an advantage from attacking first.

Moreover, this scenario overlooks the possibility that the second state might offer a concession instead. A state that had the advantage of a surprise attack would have to give it up if it demanded a concession from the victim. But a state that expected to be the victim of such an attack might prefer to concede the advantage of attacking first to its adversary, since if it attacked instead it could not be certain of forestalling the enemy's attack, and even if it did it would still have to face the cost and risk of fighting. If so, then the result might be an unnecessary concession, but not a war that neither wanted to fight.

Note that this is especially likely to be true if the war to be fought were a nuclear war, and therefore it is actually easier to construct a scenario leading to an inadvertent conventional war than a nuclear one.[7]

Note also that, if neither state is optimistic about the outcome of a competition for the advantage of a surprise attack, it may be possible to agree on measures that would reduce or eliminate it.

Preventive Wars

A preemptive war would be the result of a state's attempt to prevent an adversary from acquiring the bargaining advantage that a surprise attack would give it. A preventive war would be the result of a state's attempt to

---

6. World War I is sometimes explained as the result of Germany's incentive to attack first to avoid fighting Russia and France simultaneously. But such an explanation fails to explain why the war did not end as soon as it was clear what advantage Germany had gained by attacking first. For a discussion of why World War I lasted as long as it did, see Goemans 2000. Of course, the fact that the war did not last long would be small consolation if it were a nuclear war.

7. In the case of nuclear war, one must also explain why there would be an advantage to attacking first and show how a state could come to be confident that another was about to attack if it were common knowledge that the only reason either would ever attack was to preempt an expected attack by the other side.

prevent an adversary from acquiring the advantage that an expected future increase in its military capabilities would give it.[8]

Like preemptive wars, preventive wars are often discussed as though states faced a simple choice between attacking now and waiting to fight a less desirable war later. If so, then the difference between them is that in a preemptive war the disadvantage to waiting is that the enemy gets to attack first and its attack is imminent, while in a preventive war the disadvantage to waiting is that the enemy will grow stronger with time but the attack will come later. Once again, however, the problem is more complicated if one considers the possibility of a negotiated settlement as an alternative to fighting.

We saw that, if a negotiated settlement is possible, the alternative to a preemptive attack is a preemptive concession. The alternative to a preventive war, however, is acceptance of the possibility of having to make a concession in the future. But a concession will be required only if (1) the adversary's military capabilities increase as expected, (2) it is not possible to compensate for that increase by actions to increase one's own capabilities, and (3) the adversary's preferences will enable it to translate its new relative military capabilities into sufficient bargaining power to compel a concession.[9] These conditions might imply that the cost of the future concession should be discounted heavily.

If the only barrier to agreement without fighting is knowledge of which side will have the advantage of attacking first, a preemptive war, we saw, might be expected to be short. The aim of a preventive war, however, would not be to compel an immediate agreement that reflected the current distribution of military capabilities but to forestall a future agreement when the distribution of military capabilities would be less favorable. But that might imply that the initiator of a preventive war, if the war went well, could not cash in his success by accepting an early negotiated settlement but would have to proceed until he had weakened his adversary to the point that he no longer feared its future military capabilities—though he might quickly accept a negotiated settlement if he soon became pessimistic about how the war would end. A successful preventive war might therefore be expected to be far longer and more costly than a preemptive one.[10]

Thus the possibility of a preemptive war entails a choice between a

---

8. Note that the expected future increase in the enemy's military capabilities might consist of a future advantage from attacking first, a fact that makes it even easier to confuse the two problems. For an influential early discussion of preventive war, see Levy 1987. A more recent discussion is in Fearon 1995b. Preventive war is the main theme of Copeland 2000.

9. Recall the discussion in the previous chapter of the determinants of bargaining power when the alternative to agreement is a contest in disarmament.

10. This would not be true if the attacker only wanted to destroy a part of the enemy's military capabilities, for example, a nascent nuclear weapons capability.

war that could be expected to be short (though one in which one might not be certain of having the advantage of attacking first) and an immediate concession, while a preventive war entails a choice between a longer and more costly war and the uncertain prospect of a possible future concession. The explanation of both is the inability of states to commit themselves not to exploit a future change in their relative military capabilities, and the effect of both is to reduce the range of agreements that are feasible as alternatives to war, but not necessarily to eliminate it. It seems plausible that in a world of conventional weapons, at any rate, fluctuations in relative military capabilities will lead more often to contemplation of preventive than preemptive wars; but the conditions that must be satisfied for a preventive war to be chosen imply that they will often be rejected.[11]

The Security Dilemma Reconsidered

While any war is inefficient if the negotiated settlement that ends it would have been preferred by both combatants to fighting, many people came to believe that Herz's security dilemma implied that wars could occur even though both sides actually preferred the prewar status quo. We saw that that is not true. However, it can be true of both preemptive and preventive wars (though it need not be): the state whose attack is preempted might actually not have intended to attack, and the state whose increase in power is prevented might never have challenged the status quo.[12]

The absence of government alone does not imply that either preemptive or preventive wars will occur, so they cannot be explained solely by "anarchy." But might governments nonetheless prevent them, so that the absence of government is at least a necessary part of the explanation for their occurrence?

The belief that governments can reliably prevent such conflicts is another example of the confusion between the role of governments in regulating conflicts among the people they govern and the role of governments as parties to conflicts with the people they govern. The organizational advantage that governments have over potential domestic opponents or that political leaders have over potential dissidents within the government implies that leaders of opposition groups will often have an incentive to launch a coup d'état or a rebellion before the government

---

11. Bismarck famously said that "preventive war is like suicide from fear of death" (quoted in Levy 1987, 103). Of course, people do commit suicide from fear of death.
12. See the discussion of the security dilemma in chapter 1. Note that for both states to prefer the status quo to war, it is only necessary that, given the existing distribution of military capabilities, both would prefer the existing distribution of territory to the expected outcome of trying to change it. Thus even predatory rulers competing for valuable territory might both be satisfied with the status quo.

is able to act against them or acquires the power to do so. And for that reason, many acts of political repression are designed to preempt or prevent dissent rather than to respond to it. Incentives to attack first can add to the inefficiency of forceful bargaining wherever it occurs, and it occurs not only among governments but also within them and between governments and the people they govern.[13]

Since the end of the cold war, some scholars have used the security dilemma to explain the civil wars in the Balkans and the attempted genocide in Rwanda. In doing so there has been a tendency to equate the security dilemma with an incentive to wage a preventive war. And since everyone assumes that the security dilemma is caused by anarchy, there is also a tendency to assume that if the cause of civil war is a security dilemma it must be because the government collapsed and plunged everyone into anarchy.[14] But the security dilemma does not imply the occurrence of preventive wars, and governments can lead to preventive civil wars that would not have occurred had the antagonists been separate states with separate military forces—hence the possibility of resolving domestic conflicts by partition.

Offense and Defense Reconsidered

To defend something is to "make or keep [it] safe from danger, attack, or harm" (*American Heritage Dictionary*). Thus the aim of the defense is to maintain the status quo, and the aim of the offense is to change it. In the context of contests in disarmament, if force is not used the status quo will be unchanged, so the offense must be the initiator of the use of force. And if the use of force is to have any effect, the initiator must engage the military forces of the enemy, wherever they are. And therefore, given an equal distribution of military capabilities, to say that the offense has an advantage could mean either that the initiator of the contest is more likely to win a contest in disarmament than the side that awaits an attack or that the side that fights on its home ground is more likely to lose.[15]

The fact that incentives to attack first can make a connection between the security dilemma and war seem plausible is perhaps one reason why many people have found persuasive Robert Jervis's (1978) claim that the severity of the security dilemma depends on whether the offense or the defense has an advantage in military contests, since saying that the offense has an advantage over the defense clearly implies that, other things being

---

13. See Fearon's (1994) discussion of ethnic war in the Balkans and Weingast's (1998) discussion of the U.S. Civil War. See also the discussion in Lake 2003.
14. See the essays collected in Walter and Snyder 1999, especially Snyder and Jervis 1999.
15. See Clausewitz's discussion of the distinction between offense and defense in Clausewitz 1976, 357–59.

equal, the attacker has an advantage in contests in disarmament.[16] However, we saw that, while the existence of an advantage to being the attacker may reduce the range of feasible agreements, it need not eliminate it. And if it did eliminate it, then *it could not be true that both states preferred the status quo to war.* Moreover, if there is a range of agreements that both states prefer to war, then the fact that the attacker has an advantage will lead to war only if (1) there is also an advantage to attacking without warning and (2) the defender is successfully surprised or the defender's optimal response to an expected attack is a surprise attack of its own.

The connection between the offense-defense balance and preventive war is less direct. However, if the offense has an advantage, then a state would find it more difficult to counter an expected future increase in its adversary's military capabilities than it otherwise would be and would be more optimistic about disarming its adversary if it attacked before the increase occurred. And therefore, while it is not necessary that attackers have an advantage for preventive wars to occur, they might be more likely if that were true.

But even if offensive advantages make preemptive and preventive wars more likely than they otherwise would be, it does not follow that they make wars more likely. We saw in the previous chapter that wars might be frequent even if the probability of success in a contest in disarmament was completely unaffected by whether a state attacked first or not, since it is not necessary to disarm one's adversary in order to use military force to change the status quo—force can be used to extract a concession instead. And, as we learned from Clausewitz, the less likely it is that a state will be disarmed in a war, the more attractive war becomes as a form of coercive diplomacy. In those circumstances what determines the frequency of war is not the offense-defense balance but the frequency of changes in relative military capabilities great enough to support an attempt to renegotiate the agreement that ended the previous war.[17]

Bargaining over the Distribution of Power

So far I have assumed that what is at issue is the distribution of valuable territory among predatory rulers and argued that the distribution of mili-

---

16. See the discussion in chapter 1. It is also easy to be misled and think that if the offense has an advantage over the defense then the offense is likely to be successful, which need not be true.

17. Note that Clausewitz claimed that "defense is the stronger form of waging war" but did not think that was inconsistent with the frequency of wars in the eighteenth century (1976, 359).

tary capabilities, by influencing the distribution of bargaining power, determines the distribution of valuable territory.

But this overlooks one of the most important facts about interstate conflicts: the distribution of territory can affect the distribution of military capabilities. Territory can affect military capabilities in two ways: its location or topography can directly affect the ability of states to deploy military forces against each other, and population and economic resources located within it can be converted into military capabilities. Thus an agreement about the distribution of territory between states might influence the subsequent distribution of military capabilities between them and therefore change the relative bargaining power on the basis of which the agreement was reached. A concession of territory by state A to state B, therefore, could enable state B to demand a further concession at a later point, and so on, until state A had ceased to exist. Since no state could commit itself not to take advantage of such an increase in its future bargaining power, it would appear that no agreement could be self-enforcing and therefore none was possible.

It would be wrong to leap to the conclusion that every possible agreement that states might accept instead of fighting has this property. Nonetheless, many obviously do, and it clearly implies a major constraint on their ability to reach agreements without fighting. It is what makes describing a struggle for territory as just a struggle for power seem plausible, and, as we will see, it helps explain much that has been written about the balance of power. In spite of that fact, it has not received much analytical attention.[18] Let us see if we can figure out what its implications might be.

One obvious implication is that territory with this property becomes even more valuable, since it not only has value in itself but also makes the forceful acquisition of additional valuable territory more likely. And territory that has no economic value might become valuable because of its strategic significance.

The problem, however, is not that territory might be valuable enough to be worth fighting for, since we have already assumed that to be true. Even if territory were just the same thing as military power, for example, then, in figure 6, p would always equal q and only rulers whose risk acceptance was great enough to outweigh the expected costs of an absolute war would ever want to fight for more. And if rulers are risk averse, there

---

18. One of the few discussions is in Fearon 1995c. For a contemporary example of the problem, think of the claim made by some Israelis that trading land for peace with the Palestinians would be self-defeating, since giving the Palestinians land would enable them to demand more.

might be a wide band of territorial distributions around q that would be preferred by both sides to a military contest for all of it.

The problem is rather that an agreement that changed the relation between the distribution of territory and the distribution of power would not be self-enforcing. Since, as we saw, the opportunity to coerce a territorial concession by fighting makes war more likely than it otherwise would be, the fact that states could not be expected to make a concession to avoid an absolute war might actually make war less frequent, not more. But this increased stability in the distribution of territory would have a price: if the disparity between the distribution of territory and the distribution of power were great enough that one state or another would prefer a contest for all of it to the existing distribution, the contest could not be prevented by a negotiated settlement.

However, such an agreement would not even be considered unless there were an initial disparity between the distribution of power and the distribution of territory, which would imply that the two cannot simply be equated with each other. One reason such a disparity might exist is that states differ in their ability or willingness to convert the economic resources available in the territory they control into military capabilities.[19] And since territory that a state concedes to an adversary as an alternative to war might not immediately increase its adversary's military capabilities, the state making the concession might hope to compensate for it by increasing the resources it mobilized from its remaining territory in the meantime. If so, then making the concession might be preferable to fighting.[20]

This is what came to be known as "appeasement" in the period preceding World War II. One of the main arguments against appeasement is that concessions strengthen one's adversary, enabling him to demand more later. But a possible rebuttal is that appeasement buys time that can be used to increase one's own military capabilities.[21]

Moreover, even if appeasement is rejected and war occurs, the result-

---

19. Another obvious possible reason for such a disparity is that not all territory has equal military value.

20. James Fearon (1995c) has shown that if states discount the future then there are conditions under which states would prefer to make such a concession even if they did not expect to be able to compensate for it by increasing their own military forces. Note also that since preventive war is the result of an expected future increase in a state's military capabilities, the connection between territory and power could make it possible for a state faced with the prospect of a preventive war to avoid it by conceding in the present some of the resources from which its military capabilities are derived.

21. Thus appeasement of Hitler by Britain prior to World War II has been defended as allowing Britain time to rearm. Another, independent, argument against appeasement is that it may cause the adversary to make incorrect inferences about one's preferences, leading him to expect more concessions later even if the distribution of military capabilities is unchanged.

ing war need not be Clausewitz's absolute war. If territory changed hands as the war progressed or if the defender's success led the attacker to be less optimistic about the ultimate outcome, then at some point the distribution of territory might fall once again within the zone of agreement in figure 6, and the two sides could then agree to accept the status quo rather than continue fighting. This, then, is another possible explanation for the "limited aims wars" that Clausewitz wrote about.

But if the alternative to appeasement is not absolute war but limited war, then a state contemplating appeasement confronts a choice between the loss of territory for certain and a limited contest whose outcome might be that it retains the territory it would have conceded. This clearly makes the rejection of appeasement more attractive, and therefore, once again, reducing the expected severity of war makes its occurrence more likely.

Balance of Power Theory Reconsidered

We saw in the last chapter that the relation between absolute war and negotiated settlements among three states is qualitatively similar to the relation when there are just two: given rulers' preferences between divisions of disputed territory and a costly contest for all of it, the distribution of military capabilities among all three states will determine what division they will all accept (if any) as an alternative to fighting. As we just saw, a connection between the distribution of territory and the distribution of power between two states makes peaceful agreement on a division of the territory more difficult. But its effects are somewhat different when there are more than two states.

If negotiated settlements are not possible, then two states fighting a third must anticipate a subsequent war between them if they succeed in disarming their enemy. If negotiated settlements are possible, however, then two allies negotiating with a third will anticipate a negotiated settlement with each other if they disarm their enemy, which is a more attractive prospect. An agreement leaving them each with half the territory, for example, would be more attractive than the prospect of a subsequent military contest that gave each a 50 percent chance of winning all of it. Thus an absolute war in which two states allied together to disarm the third and then divided its territory between them would be more attractive than an absolute war in which the victorious allies had to fight each other after defeating their enemy.

As I noted in the previous chapter, this is the scenario that is assumed implicitly or explicitly by most writers on the balance of power. It poses the problem of the stability of state systems in its starkest form, since if no state is more powerful than all the others combined, there will always be some coalition of states that is more powerful than an individual state, and if they could always agree on the division of their victims' territory after defeating it, then it is not clear how any interstate system could be stable.[22]

As we saw, one possible answer is that a negotiated settlement among all three states is possible, which might lead to a territorial concession by the third state but not to the elimination of any of them. But a connection between the distribution of territory and the distribution of power would make such negotiated settlements problematic, because they might not be self-enforcing.

However, while this may inhibit agreements among all three states, it need not inhibit an agreement between two victorious allies about how to dispose of the territory of the third state if they disarm it. This is because the two allies would not be redistributing territory they already possessed (which would lead to a change in their relative power) but redistributing territory that belonged to the third state (whose power would be irrelevant if it is eliminated). Thus they could divide the territory of the defeated state in such a way that the prewar distribution of power between them was not altered.

This possibility is illustrated in the following description of predation in Renaissance Italy by Garrett Mattingly:

> Historians have been able to discover one general principle in six-teenth-century diplomacy related to the idea of national interest, the principle of the balance of power. There are, indeed, episodes in the period 1494 to 1559 when it looks as if that principle was really being applied, especially when it was a question of the com-bination of two or more strong states against a weak one. Here the principle requires such a partition of the victim's territories as not to change decisively the strength of any victor in relation to his partners. . . . But since it really means little more than that the biggest dog gets the meatiest bone, and others help themselves in the order of size, it is hard to be sure that the sixteenth century appreciated the full beauty of a balanced system. (1964, 140–41)

The eighteenth-century principle of "reciprocal compensation" can be explained in the same way. According to Gulick, this principle required that "aggrandizement by one power entitled other powers to an equal compensation or, negatively, that the relinquishing of a claim by one power must be followed by a comparable abandonment of a claim by another" (1955, 70–71).[23]

But, as the quotation from Mattingly illustrates, it is easier to satisfy

---

22. This is why William Riker claimed that writers on the balance of power were wrong and state systems were inherently unstable (1962, 160–187).
23. See also Schroeder 1994, 6–7.

this principle in negotiations among victorious allies than in negotiations between them and their victim. This, then, is a possible justification for the common assumption that three states could not reach a negotiated settlement as an alternative to war but two states could do so after defeating the third.[24] And it seems to imply that our discussion of the relation between bargaining and war among three states exaggerates the ability of states to maintain their independence. Both temporary appeasement of the aggressors by their victim and limited wars between them would still be possible, but if appeasement is followed by more appeasement then it cannot protect states' independence, and if the gains from limited wars are cumulative then states may eventually be eliminated. Perhaps we should take another look at why writers on the balance of power thought this would not happen.

As we saw, the idea that weak states could band together to defend themselves from stronger ones is not a good reason, since they will not necessarily do it, and even if they did, wars might nonetheless lead to the elimination of states.[25] But some writers on the balance of power claim not only that weaker states join together to "balance" stronger ones but also that they design peace settlements to restore a "balance" if they are victorious. Gulick's well-known book on the balance of power, for example, is not just about the formation of a coalition to counter Napoleon's France but also about the attempt to craft a peace settlement that would restore a balance of power after France was defeated, and Gulick claimed that the "necessity of preserving the components of the system may be taken as a corollary of the balance of power" (1955, 73).

This would imply that the independence of states is protected not by balancing but by the unwillingness of states to eliminate other states even if they are able to do so. But why would states forgo the opportunity to exploit a military victory to the fullest?

It might appear that they would behave in this way only if their sole interest were in protecting the territory they already controlled.[26] However, in their survey of interstate conflict during the eighteenth century, McKay and Scott say that

> Rulers and statesmen strove ceaselessly to increase the power, and
> therefore the wealth, of their state. State power was everywhere

---

24. For an alternative interpretation, see the discussion in Powell 1999, 160. Powell's explanation of this behavior is that it just reflects the relative bargaining power of the victorious allies. And it is true, of course, that an unconstrained division of the defeated state's territory between the victorious allies would reflect their relative bargaining power and therefore their relative military capabilities. But this just provides further reason for thinking that the victorious allies would find it easy to agree on a self-enforcing division of the victim's territory.
25. For a recent extended analysis, see Powell 1999, chap. 5.
26. This is what Schweller claims (1994, 1998).

measured in terms of territorial extent and population, which in turn determined revenue and the size of the army. . . . Additional territory was everywhere the aim of policy. (1983, 211)

If a lack of interest in territorial expansion is required for states to be reluctant to deprive other states of their independence, then it is hard to see why they would have been reluctant to do it in the eighteenth century.

A possible answer is that an agreement between two states to divide the territory of a third state between them is not as self-enforcing as I have made it out to be. The distribution of military capabilities, as we have seen, might be a function of the distribution of territory, but it cannot be equated with the distribution of territory, and therefore the relative power of two victorious states might change even if it is not changed by the distribution of the third state's territory between them. And if it does, then the postwar territorial distribution may no longer be stable.

Moreover, redistributing the third state's territory will make both of the victorious allies more optimistic about capturing all the territory than they were before the war. For example, if they were all initially equal, the probability with which each could expect to capture all the territory might be one-third. If two then join together to eliminate the third and divide its territory in such a way as to leave them still equal, then the probability with which each might expect to capture all the territory will have increased to one-half. Any further increase in the capabilities of one of them will leave it far more optimistic about complete victory than it was initially.

Thus when there are more than two states, one state cannot expand without giving some other state the opportunity to become more powerful. As we saw in chapter 1, this was the basis for Kenneth Waltz's claim that even expansionist states could not simply try to maximize their power. He claimed that this implied that states would form balancing coalitions, but we saw that this was not necessarily true. However, if agreements between victorious allies are not self-enforcing, it may imply that states would refrain from depriving other states of their independence.[27]

Consider the problem confronted by two equally matched states that have just succeeded in disarming the third. As already noted, if they divide the territory of the defeated state in a way that reflects the current distribution of power between them, then this division may no longer be an equilibrium if a change in their ability to mobilize military capabilities

---

27. This is the focus of Wagner 1986 and Niou and Ordeshook 1990. However, these works assume that the outcomes of wars are predictable, which makes it hard to explain why they would have to be fought.

leads to a change in that distribution, and in an environment in which such changes occur frequently such an agreement may therefore not last long.

Suppose, however, that they do not redistribute all of the third state's territory but leave it with a reduced amount. If all three states agree that no state should be allowed to become more powerful than the two victors have become, then no state will accept an agreement giving either more territory than it has, and both may prefer to accept the existing distribution to the expected value of trying to defeat the other two.

Moreover, if subsequently one were expected to become stronger, then the other two would have an opportunity to wage a preventive war against it. McKay and Scott wrote of the balance of power:

> In practical terms the balance of power meant simply that no one state, or alignment, should become too powerful; and that if it did, the other European states would join together to reduce its power. (1983, 211–12)

It makes little sense to think that two states would attack a third because the third state was too powerful, as this passage suggests, but two states might attack a third in order to prevent the third from becoming too powerful if it were expected to do so. If they did and were successful then they could divide the territory of the formerly powerful state between them in the same way, maintaining the independence of the victim as a way of securing their own possessions against an uncertain future.

Thus there appears to be a close connection between balance of power thinking and the incentive to wage preventive war: preventive wars are fought to protect states from expected future increases in the military capabilities of an antagonist, and maintenance of a balance of power, interpreted in this way, is designed to preserve the ability of states to cooperate in the waging of preventive wars. Immanuel Kant wrote, for example, that "an alarming increase of power" in another state "which has acquired new territories"

> is an injury to the less powerful state by the mere fact that the other state, even without offering active offence, is *more powerful;* and any attack upon it is legitimate in the state of nature. On this is based the right to maintain a balance of power among all states which have active contact with one another. (1797, 167; emphasis in original)

An agreement between two successful aggressors that leaves some of the military capabilities of their victim intact is therefore like depositing some of the military capabilities at their disposal in an escrow account that can be used against either of them, protecting both against the possibility that their agreement might be overturned by a subsequent change in their relative military capabilities.[28]

But we have already observed that, in a world of three evenly matched states, the expectation that two states, if victorious, could reach an agreement about how to divide up the territory of the third would increase the expected value to them of an attempt to disarm it. And therefore, if "balancing" provides a means of enforcing an agreement that would otherwise be unenforceable, it would not be inconsistent with what Waltz called "bandwagoning" (i.e., states ganging up on other states to deprive them of their territory) but would actually make it possible.[29]

The extent to which the expectation of balancing could be used to support the forcible redistribution of territory depends on how powerful each state is willing to allow other states to become, since obviously the more territory that must be left with the third state, the less attractive is a military contest to capture the rest. If balancing is the result of a willingness to sacrifice some territory in order to make possession of the remainder more secure, it is like buying insurance, and the amount of insurance rulers will choose to buy will depend on both their attitudes toward risk and the amount of it they believe they are exposed to. But this implies both that no definite answer can be given to the question of how powerful other states should be allowed to become and that the leaders of different states may give different answers to it.

If, then, in response to the description of balance of power policies by McKay and Scott just quoted, we ask how powerful is "too powerful," the answer would have to be that there is no general answer to this question. Moreover, there is no guarantee that all states will buy enough insurance to protect them from the possibility that a single state will become powerful enough to coerce the others into relinquishing their independence.

Recall that McKay and Scott claimed that states were concerned not just that a single state might become "too powerful" but that an "alignment" might as well. We have seen that in a three-state world an unwillingness to allow another state to become as powerful as the other states combined can be explained as a way of controlling the risks that states are exposed to when the distribution of military capabilities is believed to be unstable. But this implies that when there are more than three states they all must also be concerned about the power of potential two-state coali-

---

28. Compare this to Avner Greif's (1998) argument that warring clans in late medieval Genoa solved the problem of enforcing cooperation between them by creating a third party that would provide a balance of power.

29. For a discussion of balance of power thinking in the eighteenth century that emphasizes its close connection with predatory behavior, see Schroeder 1994.

tions, since a two-state coalition could secure its winnings by eliminating all but one of the other states, which would be expected to "balance" between the two winners. And therefore all states must worry that two states, and not just one, might become optimistic enough about their ability to disarm all the others to try it. Thus the interpretation of balance of power thinking offered here can easily be extended to coalitions in a world of more than three states.

When violent conflicts are about the distribution of territory, then, and the distribution of territory affects the distribution of military capabilities, there appears to be a close connection between the sort of behavior emphasized in the literature on the balance of power and the fact that agreements among states must be self-enforcing. However, these conditions do not always hold. Moreover, "moderation" in the behavior of states (as Gulick called it) could also just be a consequence of the ability of states to reach negotiated settlements when they are all relatively evenly matched. And therefore it is not clear how important this factor is in explaining the historical behavior of states, and it is possible that most of the time international politics is best understood as a complex multiactor bargaining process.[30]

Extended Deterrence and the Balance of Power

The balance of power reasoning just analyzed also casts some light on what is commonly called the problem of "extended deterrence" and helps explain why it received so much attention during the cold war.

The problem of extended deterrence is the problem of how to make credible one state's commitment to defend another, which was the main preoccupation of U.S. foreign policy during the cold war.[31] Thus there are at least three states involved: a defender, a potential aggressor, and a third state that the defender is committed to defending. It is commonly assumed that the defender's goal is to deter an attack on the client state by the

---

30. Consider, for example, commentaries that portray recent efforts by Russia and China to thwart the "hegemony" of the United States by acting in concert as examples of modern-day balancing. Such actions are more likely designed to influence the terms of agreements that will be reached by all three states than to reflect the role either Russia or China would play in an all-out war with the United States in the future.

31. During the cold war, the problem of extended deterrence led to the problem of how to make threats to use nuclear weapons in defense of client states credible, but the former problem would have existed even without the latter. Indeed, initially nuclear weapons were seen as a way of solving the problem of extended deterrence, since they made it possible for the United States to devastate the USSR at little cost to itself. This changed when the USSR acquired missiles that could transport nuclear warheads to the United States. For a discussion of extended deterrence with citations to the literature, see Huth 1988. For a discussion of the debates about how to make extended nuclear deterrence credible, see Daalder 1991.

potential aggressor by threatening war against it if it attacks and that avoiding war by making a concession would be unacceptable. What is in doubt is the willingness of the defender to respond in this way, and the problem of extended deterrence is how defenders can credibly reveal their willingness to do it when they have an incentive to bluff. Left implicit in debates about this problem is the assumption that the reason for the defender's interest in preventing an attack is the fact that both a successful attack and any possible concession would increase the power of the aggressor and that both defenders who were bluffing and defenders who were not would have an interest in persuading the potential aggressor that an attack would be unacceptable for this reason.

The analysis offered here explains why these assumptions might be true, but it also shows that there are many circumstances in which they would not be. What is required for extended deterrence to be relevant is that (1) concessions would increase the military capabilities of an aggressor and (2) the potential aggressor is on the verge of becoming "too powerful" (as McKay and Scott put it). But not all concessions will change the relative power of states, and even when they would, a state will have an incentive to go to war just to prevent another state from making one only if the concession would make a third state unacceptably powerful.

I pointed out in chapter 4 that the fact that bargaining does not end when war begins poses a problem for much of the cold war literature about deterrence, which assumed that it did. The analysis offered here provides a possible justification for that assumption. Paradoxically, the inability of a dissatisfied state to commit itself not to exploit the increase in its bargaining power that a concession would give it implies that a potential victim, which might have wanted to make a concession to avoid war, can commit itself not to make one. And therefore a dissatisfied state cannot hope that an attack will lead to a concession. This is an example of the more general paradox already noted more than once that the possibility of a negotiated settlement as an alternative to war can make war more likely, not less.

However, the unwillingness of a state to allow another to become more powerful cannot be inferred from a knowledge of the distribution of military capabilities among states alone. And therefore the problem of extended deterrence is to find a way to reveal that information without actually fighting.

Situations in which some states believe that another state is already on the verge of becoming unacceptably powerful prior to war are unusual, and this is a plausible way of characterizing what was distinctive about international politics during the cold war. The cold war period was different, for example, from the periods prior to both the two world wars, when Britain was concerned about two potentially expansionist states, Germany and Russia (or the Soviet Union), did not want to encourage either, but could not oppose both simultaneously.[32] Moreover, Germany did not reach the position of potential dominance that the Soviet Union achieved by helping defeat it until after a long process of expansion in Europe. And therefore, instead of joining a "balancing" coalition against Germany during the 1930s, the United States later fought a preventive war to prevent it from exploiting its control over Europe after it had defeated France.

But there is no objective way of distinguishing between distributions of power like the one prior to World War II and distributions like the one during the cold war. The only reliable indicator of when some state has crossed the threshold of tolerance of other states is the behavior of the other states, which is why the problem of extended deterrence exists.

What Next?

With the help of Clausewitz, we have seen that the explanation for the recurrence of war among the predatory rulers of early modern Europe was repeated changes in their relative military capabilities, which provided frequent opportunities for renegotiating the distribution of valuable territory but left many of them able to maintain their independence. Expectations of such changes could make it difficult to construct self-enforcing agreements among competing predators, which might, paradoxically, actually reduce the frequency of war and help preserve the independence of states. But the price was to make war more severe when it occurred.

Many of these changes in relative power were the result of competition among rulers. But even if rulers had been willing to agree to restrict their competition, changes in relative power would still have occurred as a result of domestic political and economic developments, nothing could have prevented the beneficiaries from taking advantage of them, and often the only way of resolving disagreements about their effect on the relative bargaining power of states was by fighting.[33]

These wars could have been avoided had all the rulers been willing to give up their independence and subject themselves to a common ruler. But they were all too optimistic about how they would fare in future competition to agree to this, and if they had agreed, the result might have been to establish a super-predator and thus to eliminate one of the most important constraints on predatory rule in Europe.

Kant's answer to the problem of recurring warfare among predatory

---

32. Since the end of the cold war, this has also been true of U.S. relations with Iraq and Iran and with Taiwan and China. For an argument that it was this feature of the cold war that Waltz tried to explain by his distinction between bipolar and multipolar systems, see Wagner 1993.
33. This is the main theme of Blainey 1988.

rulers was to eliminate the connection between rule and predation, and this answer is arguably implicit in Hobbes's limited discussion of relations among rulers as well. Structural Realists claim this would not work, but none has offered a valid argument in support of their skepticism. In the next chapter, I will reexamine this question in light of this discussion of how to explain wars among predatory rulers.

CHAPTER 6

A World of Commonwealths

It seems obvious to many people that if no state hopes to gain from aggression there will be no war, and therefore to eliminate war one does not require a world government but only states without territorial ambitions. What is not obvious, one might think, is what sort of institutional arrangement, if any, will reliably produce such states.

This is what Kenneth Waltz, in his book *Man, the State, and War* (1959), called the "second image" of the causes of war. The main thesis of that book is that this view is wrong, because it overlooks the effect of the anarchic nature of the international system (the "third image") on the behavior of states. This is the basis for what has been dubbed "structural Realism," which I discussed in chapter 1.

However, we have seen that Waltz's "third image" was derived from Rousseau and Rousseau's ideas about international politics were based squarely on the incentives of predatory rulers. Rousseau wrote, "The whole life of kings, or of those on whom they shuffle off their duties, is devoted solely to two objects: to extend their rule beyond their frontiers and to make it more absolute within them" (1991b, 90). Kant, who was also much influenced by Rousseau, concluded that the solution was not to eliminate "anarchy" but to eliminate predation.

This view is consistent with what Hobbes wrote as well. Hobbes said that "in all places, where men have lived by small families, to rob and spoil one another, has been a trade, and so far from being reputed against the law of nature, that the greater spoils they gained, the greater was their honour," and "as small families did then; so now do cities and kingdoms which are but greater families" (1957, chapter XVII, 109–10). The role of Hobbes's sovereign, we saw, was to provide his subjects with security not only from the "injuries of one another" but also "from the invasion of foreigners." With security, Hobbes thought, the "passions that incline men to peace" would prevail.

The claim of structural Realists, however, is that the desire for security alone is sufficient to cause wars among rulers who are not themselves subject to a common sovereign. But the only justification of this claim that has been offered is the security dilemma, which, as we saw in chapter 1, means simply that attempts by one ruler to increase the security of his subjects will diminish the security of others. And the only basis for believing in the existence of the security dilemma is that, unless there is a complete differentiation between defensive and offensive capabilities, measures taken by one ruler to diminish the probability that he might be disarmed by foreigners also increase the probability with which he could disarm them. It is not clear why this should lead to war or even why it must lead to mutual insecurity.

As we saw in the previous chapter, what makes this incomplete reasoning plausible, apart from the mistaken belief that it implies that rulers are trapped in a Prisoner's Dilemma, are two facts: in a world of predatory rulers, states may have an incentive to wage preventive wars; and there may be a connection between control over territory and military power. These facts seem to imply that even rulers interested only in providing security for their subjects would be interested in territorial expansion and have an incentive to attack other states.

But we have seen that rulers might think twice before waging a preventive war, even if they were certain that a ruler who was expected to benefit from an expected future increase in his military capabilities was a fellow predator. If the beneficiary of an expected increase in military capabilities is unlikely to be a predator, it is not clear why a nonpredatory ruler would want to wage a preventive war against him.

Moreover, in early modern Europe the connection between territory and military power was largely the result of the connection between territory and wealth and therefore was inseparable from the incentive for predation. Thus, as we saw, its effect was not to motivate territorial expansion, for which ample motive already existed, but to make negotiated settlements prior to war more difficult.

If the connection between territorial expansion and wealth is broken, then expansion can lead to greater security for a ruler's subjects only if the territory to be absorbed directly affects the expected outcome of future military contests and control over it can be acquired and maintained at a lower cost than mobilizing greater military capabilities from within the territory a state already controls. Since one of the costs of trying to acquire more territory would be the risk of defeat, and therefore a loss of power, these conditions are hard to satisfy. And if other rulers are not likely to be predators, it is not clear how they ever could be.

Thus, when it is common knowledge that rulers are predators, the possibility of preventive war and the connection between territory and power provide additional incentives for contests in forcible disarmament beyond those implied by opportunities for predation. But in a world in which it is common knowledge that no ruler is a predator, these additional incentives would not exist.

The grain of truth in structural Realism is that if it is not common knowledge that rulers are not predators then preventive wars may occur, even if in fact no rulers are predators. But Kant, as we saw, apparently agreed:

> the state of peace must be *founded;* for the mere omission of the threat of war is no security of peace, and consequently a neighbor may treat his neighbor as an enemy unless he has guaranteed such security to him. (1795, 436; emphasis in original)

As we saw in chapter 1, structural Realists assume that such guarantees are impossible, since no state can ever be sure that other states are not predators. But none has offered a reason for believing this to be true.

One reason might be that predation is simply a reflection of the preferences of rulers, which they have an incentive to misrepresent. One might also think that, whatever the preferences of a state's current leaders, they may change over time, and no leader can commit his state not to engage in predation in the future. Thus, one might conclude, one should always prepare for the possibility that other states will take advantage of opportunities to engage in predation.

But this is also a reason for a ruler's subjects not to trust their ruler. And one of the central insights of European raison d'état thinking is that it is possible to guard against predatory rulers by the construction of institutions such that, as Kant put it, the "private attitudes" of conflicting individuals "mutually impede each other in such a manner that the public behavior . . . is the same as if they did not have such evil attitudes" (1795, 453). Thus trust might be based on an institutional structure, which can be publicly known, and not on the idiosyncratic preferences of particular rulers, which are reliably known only by them.

Some people have hoped to duplicate at the global level the institutional arrangements with these properties that were developed within European states. Others have thought that the balance of power among independent states, like a competitive market, might conceal an "invisible hand" that would be sufficient to accomplish the same thing.[1] Kant's idea seems to have been that the institutional mechanisms that make competing interests serve the common good within states can, if the way they work is common knowledge, simultaneously perform the same function among states.[2]

---

1. These possibilities are the focus of Claude 1962.

2. Kenneth Waltz claimed that Kant contradicted himself, since he believed both that in a state of nature no state can be secure and that a world state was both impossible and undesirable (1962, 338). He concludes that Kant just meant to say that world peace, like moral behavior, was an ideal that could never be fully achieved and thus "Kant makes understandable and in a sense excuses the failures of men and their rulers to achieve moral rectitude" (340). But Waltz's justification for claiming that Kant believed states could never be secure without a world state is a passage in which Kant says that states have a right to engage in preventive wars (338).

In recent years, Kant's ideas have been used to explain what is often called "the democratic peace": the observation that democratic states do not fight democratic states. But Kant did not actually say that democratic states would not fight democratic states, and his statement that peace requires some sort of guarantee implies that they might.[3] The absence of wars among democracies is often offered in support of Kant's ideas, while Kant's ideas are offered as reason for believing that the absence of wars among democracies is not just a coincidence. What is missing is a valid argument deriving the observed absence of wars among democracies from Kant's ideas. But without that neither of these inferences is justified.[4]

Following a pattern we observed in chapter 1, Kant's ideas have been appropriated by Liberalism, one of the "isms" that dominate the study of international politics, and Liberalism, like other "isms," is supported indirectly by the flaws in opposing "isms." For example, Michael Doyle, a defender of Kant's ideas, has written that

> In the end, as with most theoretical disputes, the debate will turn on the alternatives. Liberal theory should not be compared to the statistical residual or to a richly described case study, but to the comparative validity of other theories of similar scope. (1995, 183–84)

But the lack of validity of somebody else's argument cannot make one's own argument valid.

We have seen that wars are inefficient even for predators and are the consequence of a lack of common knowledge of military capabilities or the inability to reach self-enforcing agreements to divide the spoils of predation. And therefore democracy could reduce the incidence of war not because democratic states would have no interest in predation against the residents of other states but because bargaining between democracies is more efficient than bargaining between nondemocracies.[5]

---

3. Indeed, Kant said that democracy was just a form of despotism and that peace required that states be what he called republics (1795, 437–41). This does not necessarily contradict the claims made by writers on the democratic peace, but it illustrates the fact that it is difficult to define what the democracy that is supposed to lead to peace consists of.

4. The seminal work on the connection between Kant's ideas and the democratic peace is Doyle 1983. For an influential presentation of the empirical evidence for the democratic peace, see Russett 1993. For a critique of the evidence, see Gowa 1999. For a representative selection from the literature and an extended bibliography, see Brown, Lynn-Jones, and Miller 1996. A recent survey can be found in Morrow 2002.

5. For an argument in support of this proposition, see Schultz 2001. See also Lipson 2003. The seminal work on the importance of these factors in explaining the occurrence of war is Fearon 1995b.

Moreover, while the wars we have focused on were contests in forcible disarmament among rival predators, wars might be the result of other motivations as well and take many different forms. A war is just any contest in killing and destruction that results in some minimum level of damage or harm. We saw that a contest in forcible disarmament, even if carried to completion, might be followed by a countervalue contest between the armed forces of the winner and elements of the population of the territory it had occupied, and contests of that sort are possible even if not preceded by a contest in disarmament. Thus it is at least possible not only to reduce the frequency of war without eliminating predatory rule but also to eliminate predatory rule without eliminating wars.

These are reasons for taking seriously Geoffrey Blainey's claim that most attempts to explain the occurrence of wars focus on the wrong question. They try to identify what states fight about, he said, not explain why they fight, and they are therefore really explanations of conflict, not wars. But conflict is pervasive, while wars are relatively rare, and therefore what is important is not to identify what might occasion disputes but to explain why disputes turn into wars (Blainey 1988, 291). Much of the literature on war in recent years has followed this advice, and neither Realists nor Liberals have challenged it. While my discussion of bargaining and war in chapter 4, for example, focused, as did Clausewitz, on territorial conflicts among predatory rulers, the contemporary literature on which that chapter is based aims to be more general than that, and territorial conflicts are intended merely as examples.[6]

Nonetheless, there is good reason to think that eliminating the incentives for predation would reduce the incidence of interstate wars. Changes in relative bargaining power among predators will always occur, and thus there will be recurring opportunities to renegotiate territorial boundaries. It seems as unrealistic to think that this could always be accomplished peacefully, even by democratic predators, as it is to think that strikes might never occur even though labor and management are free to bargain over the terms of a contract between them. And expectations of changes in relative bargaining power would continue to provide a possible motive for preventive wars.

Of course, as long as states are independent, disagreements among them will still have to be settled by bargaining, and bargaining will always be inefficient to some degree. But it is possible that, in the absence of incentives for predation, states would find it easy to settle other disagreements peacefully.

Thus it is worth investigating what institutional arrangements, if any,

---

6. If the issue in dispute is not a divisible good such as territory, then compromise settlements may be more difficult. This point is discussed further later in this chapter.

might reliably reduce the incentives for predation among states and what role, if any, democracy might play in doing that.

Taming Predators

The incentive for predation by the great families of early modern Europe was twofold: predation was a means of securing their control over their existing wealth and also a means of increasing it further. But this was true only because there was enough wealth to make robbing and spoiling a valuable trade, as Hobbes put it, and because the people who produced the wealth lacked the means of resisting. Thus the only source of resistance to a family of predators was other predators, and since none was able to eliminate its competitors, continuing competition was required merely to maintain control over what one already possessed.

Two related developments in Europe helped change all that. One was an increase in the bargaining power of the prey. The other was the development of alternative means of acquiring great wealth, first through trade and overseas empire and then through industrial production. An increase in the bargaining power of the prey meant that predation against foreigners became less profitable, since the foreigners had greater means of resistance. And the increased bargaining power of subjects, together with the development of new forms of wealth, meant that rulers acquired alternative means of securing their positions within their own territories—they could supply public goods to their subjects in exchange for taxes. But the result was that the profits from rule were drastically reduced, and it became merely one occupation among others.

These changes were related, because the development of new forms of wealth contributed to the increased bargaining power of the producers of wealth. And since predators needed increasing amounts of wealth in order to protect themselves from competitors, at least some of them had to accept this reduction in their bargaining power in order to maintain their positions.[7]

Others, however, succeeded in mobilizing great wealth and popular support without having to accommodate the interests of the producers of wealth or of the larger population that supplied their armies. And they did this by capturing and controlling one of the mechanisms that in other circumstances could be used by ordinary people to protect themselves from powerful predators: mass political movements.

By coordinating the selective incentives such as praise and blame or

---

7. As we saw in chapter 2, many of these developments were described and explained by Kant.

honor and dishonor that all human groups have available to influence the behavior of their members, such movements enable ordinary people to overcome the collective action problem that would otherwise inhibit their ability to pursue common interests. Religion and what are commonly called political ideologies are among the means by which such coordination can be achieved, as is illustrated today by radical Islamic political movements.[8]

The more a ruler's subjects prefer him to foreign competitors, the more willing they will be to provide him with the resources necessary for defending himself against them. Mass political movements based on race, religion, ethnicity, or ideology provide a potent means of differentiating an existing predator from his opponents and creating expectations of attempted predation by them. And given such means of attracting support, predation against foreigners can then be justified as a preventive attack for the common defense. Thus the very mechanisms that make a mass political movement a powerful force against its opponents weaken the ability of its members to protect themselves against its leaders. Leadership of such a movement can therefore also become a "trade," which can make predation possible on a far larger scale than was feasible in early modern Europe. Thus it is still possible, as Rousseau claimed of rulers in the eighteenth century, for predatory rule and mutual insecurity to be mutually reinforcing.[9]

However, mass political movements based on a common commitment to the defense of a well-defined territory will have the opposite effect. If it is common knowledge that the rulers' subjects will provide support only for protection of their existing territory, then the ruler's incentive for predation is diminished. And if foreign populations can be mobilized to defend their territory against intruders, then their resistance to attack from outside their territory will not end even if their army is destroyed, and therefore the gains from disarming them will be drastically reduced. Finally, if trade provides a way of jointly benefiting from the economic resources in all territories, then the comparative benefit from predation against foreigners is reduced even further. In those circumstances, non-

---

8. For some recent examples and a discussion of how this is done, see Stern 2003. See also the discussion of the motivations of the early Christian martyrs in Stark 1997, 163–89. For a more extended discussion of the role of religion in making collective action possible, see Wilson 2002. For a classic discussion of the role of political ideas in collective political action, see Mannheim 1936.

9. With the religious conflicts of early modern Europe in mind, this is why neither Hobbes nor Kant thought that morality or social norms could be relied on to prevent predatory rule or organized violence. Note that this also implies that debates about whether mutual insecurity or predation explain ethnic civil wars may, like debates about whether insurgency is best explained by "greed or grievance," pose a false antithesis.

predatory rule and mutual security would appear also to be mutually reinforcing.[10]

Democracy merely requires that wars be popular. The reasoning just
outlined implies that, for democracy reliably to promote peace between
two states, it must provide a means of mobilizing support in each state for
the defense of a well-defined territory, and opposition to the extension of
rule to areas outside that territory. When this is true of two states and is
also commonly known between them, democracy can help sustain a peaceful equilibrium.

Virtually all discussions of the relation between democracy and peace
tacitly assume that democracies are characterized by such territorial commitments. But they are not implied by the notion of democracy alone, and
how they develop is not well understood. This is an important research
frontier in the study of international politics.[11]

Since insecurity can foster predatory rule, democracy may be hard to
sustain when the basis for mass mobilization is race, ethnicity, or religion.
Thus one might observe a correlation between pairwise democracy and
peace and conclude that the former causes the latter. But, like driving on
the right-hand side of the road and the absence of collisions, they may
both instead be the product of a more complex set of equilibrium expectations.

For example, the absence of war between Britain and the Weimar
Republic might be offered as an illustration of the democratic peace.[12] But
Hitler came to power under the Weimar Republic and had a significant
amount of popular support—support that was based on claims that non-
Jewish Germans everywhere were threatened by Jews and their foreign
allies. And had the possibility of his coming to power been more widely
anticipated, then the Weimar Republic, even though arguably democratic,

---

10. See the discussion of the difference between civic and ethnic nationalism in Snyder 2000.
11. See, for example, the recent discussion in Lipson 2003, which is largely based on Fearon
1995b. In addition to claiming, like Schultz 2001, that democracies have an advantage in
revealing information about their interests and capabilities, Lipson claims that democracies
have an advantage in making long-term commitments (2003, 100–104). But such an advantage, if it exists, is far more obvious for territorial commitments than for any other, and it is
far from clear that breaking commitments that prove to be inconsistent with territorial security would always be unpopular in democracies. One reason for the ability of democracies to
make territorial commitments may be that democracies are usually based on some system of
geographical representation. However, because students of domestic politics, like students of
international politics, tend to take states (and therefore territorial boundaries) for granted,
the relation between democracy and territorial commitments has been little studied. For a
discussion, see Linz and Stepan 1996, 16–37. For a general discussion of how to explain the
development of territorial commitments, see Goemans 2006 and the literature cited there.
12. As it is in Doyle 1983.

would not have been able to commit itself not to pose a future threat to the territorial security of other European states. Or consider how stable democracies could exist in both Israel and a Palestinian state independently of an agreement about what territory belonged to Israel and what territory belonged to the Palestinian state.[13]

Unfortunately, like the example of the rule of the road that I discussed in chapter 2, the proposition that both mutual insecurity and predatory rule, on the one hand, and mutual security and democracy, on the other, might be supported by a self-enforcing equilibrium, even if true, does not tell us anything about how to get from one to the other.[14]

Moreover, violent bargaining will always be possible, both within states and among them. In a world in which the territorial security of all states was guaranteed, groups within states might want to secede, and for all we know that could lead to violence. And even states in a world of territorially satisfied democratic states might conceivably find something besides territory to fight about, though if bargaining between democratic states is efficient enough that need not happen. I do not have any clear ideas about how to think about such questions and therefore leave them as an exercise for the reader.

However, that is not the world we live in. But neither does the world we live in much resemble eighteenth-century Europe. As a result of the development of European states since Kant's time and the incorporation of the entire globe into the European state system, we live in a world that contains some states that might be able to give each other Kantian guarantees of mutual security but more that would not. Moreover, many entities that have the legal status of states do not actually exercise effective control over all the territory that international agreements have allocated to them and therefore may not really merit the appellation of "state" at all. Thus parts of our world resemble Hobbes's state of nature, parts resemble the predatory states described by Rousseau, and parts, perhaps, resemble

13. Consider also the relations between India and Pakistan, where a combination of religious and ethnic conflicts with conflicting territorial commitments puts pressure on India's democratic institutions and inhibits the development of democracy in Pakistan. Lipson writes that "issues of race and ethnicity rarely surface in diplomacy among democracies" (2003, 54). But this leaves open the question of whether democracy diminishes the importance of issues of race and ethnicity or whether racial and ethnic conflicts make problematic the establishment of democratic institutions. For reasons to take the latter possibility seriously, see Fearon 1994.

14. Nor is it clear whether a common understanding of economics and political science is required for mutual security. Socialists, for example, have been skeptical of the idea that democracy alone could prevent predation and have claimed that peace required a world of socialist states. However, the socialist peace has fallen out of fashion. For an interesting discussion, see Viner 1944.

the world that Kant hoped would eventually emerge out of Europe's recurring wars.[15]

I used Clausewitz's analysis of eighteenth-century warfare as a way of understanding the recurrence of wars in a world of predatory rulers. Kant's ideas are, perhaps, relevant at most to a world in which it is common knowledge that no rulers are predators. It is important to consider what the consequences might be if some rulers and would-be rulers are predators and some are not.

A Mixed World

In exploring the implications of Clausewitz's explanation of warfare in chapter 4, I assumed that, no matter how much territory rulers already controlled, they would want to acquire more. If for some reason a ruler wanted no more territory than he already controlled, others would expect not to lose any territory if they were disarmed by him. But this would reduce the risk they faced in an absolute war and therefore increase their bargaining power. Thus satiation might diminish the ability of a ruler to hold onto the territory he already possessed—his adversaries could assume that "what's mine is mine and what's yours is negotiable."[16]

I also assumed that a state that was attacked would try to disarm the attacker rather than merely try to prevent the attacker from disarming it. If it is feasible to do the latter then one might think that a satiated state would be satisfied with doing so. However, this would reduce the risk to the attacker even further and therefore further increase his bargaining power.

Finally, I assumed that the object in dispute was divisible territory that was valued only because it provided private goods for consumption and that military defeat made possible the capture of all the enemy's territory. These assumptions have two consequences: they imply that everyone is in conflict with everyone else, even if they might ally temporarily, but also that compromises are possible, even if they do not last.

Thus the analysis of the relation between bargaining and war between predatory rulers offered earlier implies that domestic opposition to territorial expansion diminishes the bargaining power of states confronted

---

15. See the description of the post–cold war world in Cooper 2003. Cooper calls these "premodern," "modern," and "postmodern" states, respectively.

16. There is a difference between being satiated and being satisfied. A satisfied state is one that prefers its current allocation of territory to the expected consequences of trying to increase it by the use of force; it might become dissatisfied if the distribution of military capabilities changes in its favor. A satiated state is one that would decline more territory if it were given to it.

with predatory rulers. Domestic opposition to territorial concessions restores some of that bargaining power, as does any connection that may exist between territory and military power: they both enable states to make credible commitments not to accept territorial compromises as an alternative to war. This might, as we saw, actually make wars with would-be predators less likely. But the price of this effect is that any wars that occur will be more severe.

Nonetheless, if a state is expected to restore the independence of an aggressor that has been disarmed then it is less dangerous to attack it than it is to attack a state that is not satiated.[17] One way a satiated state can compensate for that is to threaten to divide defeated aggressors into smaller states, thereby depriving their rulers of some of their territory without paying the costs associated with absorbing it. Ex post this can be represented as a form of "balancing," since the relative power of each of the successor states will be less than the power of the original aggressor. But ex ante the expectation that this will be done will increase the ability of a satiated state to deter an attack by a dissatisfied one and therefore also serves as a punishment strategy for deterring aggressors.

However, to punish an aggressor a satiated state must first disarm it, and to do that it must fight it. A satiated state will resist forcible disarmament if attacked by two dissatisfied states. But if it is the only satiated state, how should it respond if one of the other two attacks the third? Since neither of the other two is satiated, if territorial expansion leads to greater power then the satiated state will confront a much more dangerous adversary in the resulting two-state world no matter which side wins. But the only way to avoid this outcome is to join one side or the other and, if successful, bargain with its ally, and therefore a satiated state might join a predator in an attack on another state, even if it plans to partition its winnings into independent states in order to avoid the costs of controlling them.

But it is also possible that the dissatisfied state might become satiated without absorbing all the territory of its victim. Perhaps, then, the existing satiated state could avoid the costs and risks of war by standing aside and allowing the dissatisfied state to expand. If so, then, in spite of the fact that concessions would only strengthen the dissatisfied state, the third state might prefer making concessions to fighting, since if the dissatisfied state becomes satiated it will no longer be a threat and if it does not then the satiated state will be more likely to fight as well.

Of course, satiated states need not remain satiated, and thus there are risks associated with allowing states to expand until they are satiated, just

---

17. Think of the movie *The Mouse That Roared*, about a tiny state that attacked the United States in order to be defeated by it, hoping thereby to get economic assistance for postwar reconstruction.

as there are risks associated with allowing them to expand until they are satisfied. The optimal policy for the satiated state therefore depends on its evaluation of the risks associated with allowing each of the other two states to increase in size and therefore power, as well as the expected costs of war in alliance with either one. Since neither the satiation point of the potential aggressor nor the satiated state's willingness to tolerate its expansion is likely to be common knowledge, the likelihood of mistaken expectations is great.

Moreover, the optimal outcome for the satiated state is the continuation of the status quo. Thus it may have an incentive to conceal its own true preferences if it believes that the result will be that each of the other two states will overestimate its willingness to support its opponent. Perhaps this helps explain the failure of Great Britain to make clear what it would do in response to German expansion prior to both World War I and World War II, as well as controversies about what is called "strategic ambiguity" in debates about contemporary U.S. policy toward Taiwan.[18]

Note that if two of the three states are commonly known to be satiated then each would benefit from cooperating with the other to disarm the third, since neither would want to acquire more territory and both would gain by dividing the third state and thus reducing the military capabilities of any single potential adversary. However, each would also need to consider the probability of success in a military contest between the two of them and the third state. If it is sufficiently low, one or the other might prefer to come to terms with the predatory state.[19]

These are the properties of a world in which (1) some states are only interested in maintaining the territorial status quo, while others might be predators; (2) it is not clear what it might take to satisfy potential predators; and (3) no potential predator has reached the point at which territorially satisfied states might consider waging a preventive war against it. They imply that the ruler of a Hobbesian commonwealth who is interested only in providing his subjects with security from foreigners faces a more complex and less well-defined set of problems than does a predatory ruler in a world of predators, whose decisions were analyzed in the previous two chapters. His problems are made even more complex if, unlike Hobbes's sovereign, he has to justify his decisions to his subjects.

---

18. See the discussion in Fearon 1997, 84–85.
19. Joanne Gowa (1999) has argued that the data that support the idea of a democratic peace merely reflect the fact that democracies have been allies during the twentieth century. Others have argued that alliances among democracies are implied by the idea of a democratic peace and therefore should be counted as evidence in its favor (see the discussion in Morrow 2002). But there are no complete arguments that tell us what sort of alliances territorially satisfied democracies should be expected to form.

Domestic and International Politics

As noted in chapter 1, Waltz claimed that the theory of international politics that he sketched in his famous book with that name was "closely identified with the approach to politics suggested by the rubric, *Realpolitik.*" He wrote:

> The elements of *Realpolitik,* exhaustively listed, are these: The ruler's, and later the state's, interest provides the spring of action; the necessities of policy arise from the unregulated competition of states; calculation based on these necessities can discover the policies that will best serve a state's interests; success is the ultimate test of policy, and success is defined as preserving and strengthening the state. . . .
>
> *Realpolitik* indicates the methods by which foreign policy is conducted and provides a rationale for them. Structural constraints explain why the methods are repeatedly used despite differences in the persons and states who use them. (Waltz 1979, 117)

We saw that the approach Waltz had in mind was raison d'état, and writers in the raison d'état tradition did indeed assume that it was in the interest of rulers to preserve and strengthen the state. But this was a means to the end of maximizing the wealth of rulers and their extended families and supporters.

Waltz claimed that what he called realpolitik implied the possibility of constructing a theory of international politics analogous to the theory of market competition in economics: states were like firms, which could be assumed to be maximizing something in a competitive environment (1979, , chap. 5). If we think of ruling families as organizations in the protection business, this makes a lot of sense, and it was the basis for the analysis of recurring warfare among predatory rulers in the previous two chapters. It is perhaps a good basis for understanding international politics in Europe during the eighteenth century, when, as McKay and Scott said,

> Rulers and statesmen strove ceaselessly to increase the power, and therefore the wealth, of their state. State power was everywhere measured in terms of territorial extent and population, which in turn determined revenue and the size of the army. . . . Additional territory was everywhere the aim of policy. (1983, 211)

But this "unregulated competition" among rulers required that all rulers find ways of mobilizing ever increasing amounts of domestic support. And in order to protect themselves from being overthrown by foreign competitors, some rulers had to give up the ambition of absolute rule at home and compromise with subjects who had no interest in territorial expansion.[20] Moreover, the combination of trade and industrialization meant that maximizing state revenues no longer necessarily entailed maximizing the territory a ruler controlled.

These changes raise the question of whether it still makes sense to think of all states as trying to maximize something in a competitive environment. The security dilemma has apparently led some Realists to believe that one might think of them as maximizing their security in an environment in which no state can be certain whether other states are predators or not. But there are several problems with thinking of international politics in these terms.

One is that, if all states really are security maximizers, then the only wars that can occur are preventive wars, and one must wonder why states could not reveal that their only concern was security (Kydd 1997, 2005). A second problem is that it is implausible to assume that anyone would want to maximize security. Much of life involves a trade-off between risk and reward, and no one simply minimizes his risks. If individuals do not do this, it is not clear why states would. And finally, we have just seen that in a world of multiple states in which it is unclear which are predators and which are not, or what it would take to satisfy a state that was, there may be no clear answer to the question of what a state that just wanted to maximize its security should do. These facts make the relation between the sovereign and his subjects in a Hobbesian commonwealth much more complex than the relation between ruler and ruled described by Rousseau.

Predatory rulers, like the leaders of democratic states, must be concerned about maintaining the support of their followers. But territorial expansion not only enriches the ruler; it also enriches his followers and provides resources that can be used to intimidate his opponents.[21] Thus successful predation is self-supporting: it provides the resources to maintain the ruler's position in the present and sustains the expectation that he will be able to control such resources in the future.

Hobbes apparently thought that, if a ruler's subjects gave him a secure license to rule and enough resources to protect both him and them from foreigners, his own self-interest would be sufficient to guarantee them all peace, justice, and prosperity. This is the reasoning of the Italian monarchist quoted in chapter 3, who said that

> the king is . . . the owner of the country. Like the owner of a house, when the wiring is wrong, he fixes it. (Banfield 1958, 27)

---

20. See the description of this process in England in Brewer 1989.
21. See Rousseau's discussion of all this in Rousseau 1991b, 92–93.

Many discussions of issues pertaining to national security within democratic countries involve reasoning similar to this. If every citizen is interested in maintaining the political independence of his country, one might think, then any political leader drawn from the general population will have the same interest in conducting foreign policy as any other, which seems to imply that questions of national security are different from domestic political issues, which require the resolution of conflicting interests among citizens. If this were true, democratic states would be similar to states with predatory rulers, in that the interest of the ruler would always be identical with the interest of the state.

Two ideas developed by economists can help us understand both why this reasoning is not universally accepted and some of the consequences of rejecting it. They are the concepts of a public good and of a principal-agent relationship.[22]

Security as a Public Good

The concept of a public good is best understood by comparing a public good to the goods that we might buy in a grocery store, which are private goods. If I eat a loaf of bread, for example, it is gone and no one else can eat it. This property is called "rivalry in consumption." And if I possess a loaf of bread, you do not have access to it—though you could take it away from me, and then I would not have access to it. This property is called "excludability." A public good is something of value that is characterized neither by rivalry in consumption nor by excludability. If I magically cleaned up the air in Los Angeles, for example, no one in that city could breathe deeply enough to limit the amount of clean air that other people could breathe, and the only way to prevent them from breathing it would be to kill them or expel them from the city. Cleaning up the air in Los Angeles is thus, for the people in Los Angeles, a public good.[23]

There are three problems associated with the provision of pure public goods. The first is how they can be provided at all, since their two defining properties imply that no one may have an incentive to do it. This question is the basis for what came to be known as the collective action problem,

---

22. A recent introduction to these and other ideas developed by economists, with references to the literature, can be found in Sandler 2001.

23. The two defining properties of a public good can vary independently of each other, and each really refers to opposite ends of a scale, along which there can be intermediate possibilities. A public swimming pool, for example, can be shared by many people, but if too many try to use it then there begins to be rivalry in consumption. And therefore, while it could be open to anyone, it makes sense to exclude people from using it who do not pay an admission fee.

after Mancur Olson's (1965) influential book on the subject.[24] Economists have traditionally said that this is why we need governments, since public goods cannot be supplied by markets. But that raises the question of where governments come from and why they would have an incentive to supply them.[25]

A second problem associated with the provision of pure public goods is how, if they are supplied at all, they can be supplied efficiently. This problem is closely associated with the third problem, which is the main reason for discussing public goods here: the provision of public goods requires the resolution of conflicting interests among the people who are to contribute toward the cost of supplying them.

One might think that people would not disagree about public goods, since if they are goods then everyone must want them. And it is true that if they are free then everyone would be happy to have them.[26] The problem is that they are not free and the conflicts are the result of the necessity of having to pay for them. There are two sources of such conflicts. One is that, while everyone may value a public good, not everyone will value it equally—for example, some people will find air pollution more bothersome than others, and richer people may be more willing to pay money to eliminate it than poorer people. Another is that, even if everyone placed the same monetary value on every quantity of the good to be supplied, everyone would have an interest in having others bear most of the cost of supplying it.

Decisions about the supply of private goods also entail both issues of efficiency, which benefits everyone, and the distribution of welfare, where increasing one person's benefit entails reducing someone else's. But decisions about these issues can in principle be divided between markets, which can be efficient, and governments, which can redistribute income. This is not possible with public goods, and some people may end up being asked to pay more for some quantity of a public good than they are willing to pay. Thus, at the price they are asked to pay, these people will want less of the good, while others might want more. And since tax burdens are distributed independently of decisions about the amount of various public goods to be supplied, conflicts over the distribution of costs can lead to conflicts over the level of supply of a public good.

National security is a public good, and since it is expensive, one should expect neither that everyone will want to maximize the supply of it nor that everyone would find it easy to agree about how much should be

---

24. I discussed the collective action problem in chapter 3.
25. I discussed this question in chapter 3 and will return to it in the next section.
26. However, it is possible that what is considered a good by some people would be considered a "bad" by others.

supplied and how the costs of supplying it should be distributed. And thus, even if everyone within the territorial boundaries of a state wants only to preserve the state's control over that territory but not acquire more, it does not follow that the interest in security of every political leader chosen from within that territory will be the same as everyone else's.

In addition, the cost required to maintain some level of security depends on the size of the threat that a state confronts. Since payments for weapons to provide security lead to transfers of income from some citizens to others, everyone has reason to worry that politicians may have an interest in exaggerating the size of the threat.[27]

Principals and Agents

A king who owns a country might, as we have seen, find it in his interest to supply many benefits to his subjects, just as a dairy farmer may have an interest in making life good for his cows. And every king would want to protect his subjects from other kings. The political leader of a democratic state, however, does not own the country but is hired by its citizens to supply them with public goods, among them security from foreign rulers. Thus a democratic political leader is not the owner but an agent (Grossman 2000). And therefore citizens of democratic states must find ways not only of resolving conflicts among themselves about how much security to buy and how to divide up the costs of supplying it but also of preventing their agent from simply doing what he prefers.

This is an especially complex example of the principal-agent problem. A principal is just anyone who has an agent, and an agent is someone who acts on behalf of someone else. The principal-agent problem is that the interests of the agent and the principal are not identical, and therefore the principal must find a way of inducing his agent to act in accordance with the principal's interests and not the agent's. The principal, therefore, will try to specify what he wants the agent to do and provide him with an inducement to do it. The problem is that the principal is not fully informed about the agent's interests or about what the agent actually does, and there may therefore be some gap between what the agent does and what the principal would have done had he acted for himself. Thus the principal-agent relationship, like the bargaining problem, is affected by the fact that

---

27. There are also other, more complex ways in which exaggerating threats to national security can serve private interests. For example, measures to protect national security may enhance the security of foreign investments. And there is the connection between insecurity and predatory rule discussed earlier. It perhaps helps explain why many people on the left are reluctant to provide support for interstate conflicts but have a soft spot for revolutionary violence. This gives nonstate predatory organizations an incentive to portray themselves as revolutionaries, which helps fuel the "greed versus grievance" debate referred to earlier.

people may have private information that they have an incentive to conceal.[28]

For example, suppose you hire a lawyer to defend your interests in a lawsuit and you lose. Does this mean your lawyer did a bad job? To answer that question you might have to know as much about the law as a good lawyer would know. But the reason you hired a lawyer in the first place was that you do not. Similar problems arise if you hire a doctor to treat your child and the child dies or your stock broker recommends you buy a stock whose value then plummets. The problem is that knowing the outcome is not enough to determine whether the agent acted as you would have acted, since even the best lawyers sometimes lose, patients of even the best doctors may die, and the best-informed investors sometimes lose money.

Similarly, the U.S. intervention in Vietnam was notoriously unsuccessful. Nonetheless, there are still people who maintain that it was the right thing to do. And President Kennedy was spectacularly successful in getting Soviet missiles out of Cuba without the use of force. But there were people who argued that the method he chose to accomplish that goal, a naval blockade of Cuba, was very unwise and that he was merely lucky that the outcome was a good one.

The simplest way of aligning the interests of a principal and his agent is for the principal to contract to pay for the performance of the agent. But when the principal cannot judge the performance by the outcome, this is not enough. Among the ways of overcoming this problem are procedures for supervising what the agent does; mechanisms for screening out agents who might be incompetent or whose preferences are very different from those of the principal; and hiring other agents to check up on the performance of the agent doing the job.

Medical doctors, for example, must be trained by certified medical schools and pass examinations to receive a license to practice. One can also try to pick doctors who have practiced medicine for a while and therefore have reputations that can be checked and hire other doctors to review their recommendations. And if things go wrong, a doctor's performance is subject to review by committees of other doctors and ultimately by courts where he can be sued for malpractice.

However, the mechanisms that principals use to control their agents may have perverse consequences. If you hire a painter and pay him by the hour, you may discover that it takes a long time to paint your house. If you decide next time to pay him by the job, you may discover places where the

---

28. See the discussion of this problem in the context of bargaining in chapter 4. For an application of these ideas to an issue that is pertinent to this discussion, see Peter Feaver's (2003) recent analysis of the problem of civilian control of the military as a principal-agent problem.

paint is applied in rather thin coats. A doctor who knows his decisions will be reviewed if the patient does not do well may perform unnecessary tests so that he cannot be accused of negligence or may fail to prescribe risky medicine that might have saved the patient but at the risk of serious side effects. And agents that one hires to check up on other agents may claim to find fault when none existed in order to demonstrate that they have earned their money.

These are problems that characterize all principal-agent relationships. They may help us understand the ambivalent attitude that people in democratic countries have about the relation between public opinion and foreign policy. Political leaders are sometimes criticized for making decisions just to curry popular support and at other times are criticized for making decisions that are contrary to public opinion. For example, once it became clear that the U.S. intervention in Vietnam was not going well and opposition to it began to emerge, President Lyndon Johnson was criticized both for deciding to intervene in Vietnam merely in order to maintain public support (he did not want to be the president that "lost Vietnam") and for failing to withdraw U.S. troops once it became clear that the war was very unpopular.

If we think of the constitution of a democratic country as a very complex contract between voters and political leaders that is designed to align the decisions of leaders with the interests of voters, we may be able to resolve the seeming inconsistency between these criticisms. A doctor, for example, is supposed to act in the best interests of the patient, and the certification and review procedures to which he is subjected are just a means to make sure that he does. A doctor who failed to follow prescribed procedures can be criticized, even though he acted as he did because he thought that was best for the patient. But a doctor who just follows procedures in order to protect himself from adverse consequences, even though it would have been better for the patient had he not done so, could be criticized for following the procedures. The parallel with the criticisms of President Johnson seems obvious, and what the two examples have in common are the problems inherent in any principal-agent relationship.

The more reliable are the procedures for aligning the interests of principals and agents, the smaller should be the difference between an explanation of the agent's actions based on the interests of the principal and an explanation of his actions based on his own interests as shaped by the institutional constraints to which he is subjected. This may be a useful way of thinking about the relation between "national interest" and "domestic politics" explanations of foreign policy decisions by democratic governments.

However, there is a deeper issue here as well, which is that both the principal's interest and the national interest may be poorly defined. When the principal's interest, for example, concerns a risky prospect, then, as we saw in discussing the choice between a gamble and a sure thing in chapter 4, there is an inherently subjective element in his choices. A broker may give you a questionnaire to determine your attitude toward risk, but if the whole country had to buy the same portfolio, it is not clear how it could determine its collective attitude toward risk.

Moreover, collective choices of both the level of supply of a public good and the distribution of its costs are at least to some extent arbitrary. A familiar proposition about distributive issues in the public choice literature, for example, is that for every possible distribution of some divisible good a majority can be found that would prefer some other distribution.[29]

When we combine these results with the indeterminacy of the problem faced by the Hobbesian sovereign, who just wants to provide his subjects with security from foreigners in a world in which other rulers may be predators, then it may be impossible to distinguish between the national interest and the decisions that emerge from whatever collective decision procedures a democratic state follows.

Nonetheless, the fixed geographical location of states implies that each state will confront similar choices over time and politicians will have an incentive to offer competing interpretations of current issues that can be made to sound plausible in light of prior experience. There may be people who disagree, but if they are unable to coordinate their actions sufficiently to compete effectively with the dominant competing interpretations, they will be ignored. Thus the combination of recurring problems with stable political organizations may give democratic states fairly stable conceptions of their national interests, but not necessarily one that could be inferred from the goal of military security alone. How this is done is little understood and is therefore an important research frontier in the study of international politics.[30]

It remains true, however, that foreign policy is different from domestic policy, in that the agent hired to make foreign policy must do so by engaging in (possibly violent) bargaining with the leaders of other states. In such bargaining, the political process in democratic states may reveal information about the interests of the state that rulers of nondemocratic states cannot reveal, while the rulers of nondemocratic states may be able to conceal information that the leader of a democratic state could not conceal even if it would be in the state's interest to do it. The interaction between domestic politics and interstate bargaining is also something that

---

29. See the discussion in Sandler 2001, chap. 5.
30. This is perhaps what Constructivists have in mind when they speak of a state's "identity." However, this terminology adds nothing to our understanding of how states determine their interests.

is little understood and is therefore another important research frontier in the study of international politics.[31]

Writing the Global Constitution:
Top-down or Bottom-up?

Kant wrote:

> Just as nature wisely separates the nations which the will of each state would like to unite under its sway either by cunning or by force . . . , so also nature unites nations which the concept of a cosmopolitan or world law would not have protected from violence and war, and it does this by mutual self-interest. It is the *spirit of commerce* which cannot coexist with war, and which sooner or later takes hold of every nation. . . . states find themselves impelled . . . to promote the noble peace and to try to avert war by mediation whenever it threatens to break out anywhere in the world. . . . In this way nature guarantees lasting peace by the mechanism of human inclinations; however the certainty [that this will come to pass] is not sufficient to *predict* such a future. . . . But for practical purposes the certainty suffices and makes it one's duty to work toward this (not simply chimerical) state. (1795, 454–55; emphasis in original)

There are two propositions of interest here. One is that a just and peaceful world order is not simply chimerical. We have seen that there are reasons to believe this to be true, though we still cannot confidently predict that it will come to pass. The other is that an interest in commerce will impel some states to cooperate with others in promoting the development of such an order. But since the foundation of a peaceful international order, according to Kant, is the institutional structure of the component states, it is not clear how this could be done.

As we saw, Western intellectuals have given contradictory answers to this question since the European state system first began to emerge, and it is still the source of great controversy. These controversies can usefully be divided into two parts: controversies about the role that international institutions might play in preventing war, on the one hand, and controversies about state building, on the other.[32]

---

31. For a pioneering analysis, see Schultz 2001. See also Lipson 2003.
32. For an extended discussion of the evolution of the "global constitution" that complements the analysis offered here, see Bobbitt 2002.

International Institutions

As we saw in chapter 2, in the eighteenth century the Abbé de Saint-Pierre proposed an agreement for collective security among the rulers of Europe as a kind of halfway house between a universal European monarchy and what would now be called an anarchic system of independent states. This idea has appealed to many people ever since and has influenced the structure of both the League of Nations and the United Nations.[33] But E. H. Carr's argument that the idea was utopian was the occasion for the introduction of the word *realism* into the academic study of international politics.

Rousseau's fundamental criticism of Saint-Pierre's proposal was that Europe's predatory rulers would never give up the option of using force to acquire more territory, since that would undermine the basis for their own rule.[34] But territorially satisfied democratic states share a common interest in maintaining their own territorial boundaries, and the only interest they might have in altering other states' boundaries would be as a means of weakening potential predators. Thus one might think they would be interested in a scheme like the one Saint-Pierre proposed, even if the predatory rulers that Rousseau described would not.

However, we also saw in chapter 2 that, even if the predatory rulers of eighteenth-century Europe had been willing to agree to Saint-Pierre's scheme, it would provide no further incentive for each of them to oppose the use of force than they would have had without it. But each predatory ruler actually had a greater incentive to oppose the use of force by others than a territorially satisfied state might have, since a predator would want to join an alliance against a competing predator in order to gain a share of the spoils. But actions taken to defend one state's territory can protect another's as well, and actions taken to weaken a potential predator will benefit all the predator's potential victims, and therefore the citizens of a territorially satisfied democratic state may hope that some other state will act to protect it. Thus territorially satisfied states confronted by the use of force may confront a collective action problem in opposing it.[35]

Because the Prisoner's Dilemma game has often been used to show why public goods lead to a collective action problem, one might think that this finally justifies the claim that it is a useful way of thinking about the consequences of anarchy.[36] But note that, if there is a Prisoner's Dilemma

33. For a survey of much of the literature on this subject, see Claude 1962, chaps. 4 and 5.
34. See the discussion in chapter 2.
35. For further reading on the collective action problem among allies, see Sandler 1992, 96–106, and the references cited there. Note that the collective security equilibrium discussed in Niou and Ordeshook 1994 is based on the incentives of predators.
36. For the connection among public goods, the collective action problem, and the Prisoner's Dilemma game, see Sandler 2001, 70–71.

here, it has nothing to do with either the security dilemma or the possibility of preventive war. Rather, it may inhibit the cooperation of territorially satisfied democratic states in waging war, and thus if it helps explain war it is only because the expectation of noncooperation among territorially satisfied states may encourage predators. The collective action problem among territorially satisfied democratic states therefore contributes further to the bargaining weakness of such states in dealing with potential predators that I described earlier.

However, while territorially satisfied states may be unwilling to commit themselves to automatic cooperation in a collective security scheme, there are two reasons why they may nonetheless be able to cooperate in defending themselves. The first is that they need not, like the two prisoners, decide independently of each other but can negotiate agreements arranging for conditional cooperation in the form of alliances. And the second is that territorial security is not often a pure public good. During the cold war, for example, protecting West Germany from the Soviet Union meant that France was protected as well. But it was possible to compromise West Germany's territorial integrity without compromising France's, and actions taken to protect West Germany could make Germany a threat to France in the future. And therefore not everything done to protect West Germany was necessarily in France's interests. Thus, like predatory rulers, territorially satisfied states cannot necessarily rely on other states to protect their interests.

But the example of France and West Germany also illustrates the fact that, since the interests of even territorially satisfied states are not identical, such states face a more complex problem in cooperating for their common defense than merely deciding how to share the costs of providing a public good. They must also agree on a common course of action that may not be identical to what each of them would prefer.

Cooperation among territorially satisfied democratic states is further complicated by the fact that democratic political leaders must persuade voters that their decisions are required to protect the state's security and do not merely serve the interests of one group at the expense of others; and they must reassure the leaders of other territorially satisfied states that they are not predators in disguise. This may be difficult if military preparations against potential predators can be interpreted as motivated by predatory interests. Controversies about the second U.S. war against Iraq illustrate the fact that it is especially difficult to provide such reassurances if what is contemplated is a preventive war.[37]

Thus territorially satisfied democratic states must negotiate agree-

---

37. But this war also illustrates the fact that democracy does not make preventive wars impossible.

ments for collective action in the common defense in a way that (1) satisfies each state's conception of what is required to protect its political independence and territorial integrity, (2) provides reassurances to all states about the defensive nature of each state's interests, (3) maintains domestic political support for whatever measures are agreed upon but (4) does not make potential predators optimistic about what they might accomplish by the use of force. This obviously poses an enormously complex coordination problem. Unfortunately, the first three conditions may not always be compatible with the fourth.

Since World War II, a variety of international organizations have been instrumental in helping territorially satisfied democratic states cooperate in defending themselves.[38] Until the end of the cold war, cooperation was made easier by the threat posed to many states by the Soviet Union and by the role of the United States as the central coordinator.[39] Since the end of the cold war, and under the more recent stimulus of the attacks on U.S. territory by radical Islamists, many of these arrangements have begun to be renegotiated. It is too early to say where this will lead. One of the issues in these recent conflicts has been the role that international institutions can or should play in state building.

State Building

Whatever international institutions states decide to create, as long as there is no global government with a monopoly of the legitimate use of force, the states themselves will constitute the most important part of the institutional structure of the global order, and the existence of governments in those states with a monopoly of the legitimate use of force is a necessary condition for peace at the global level. Kant, as we have seen, seems to have thought that a sufficient condition for peace was that the institutions of each state be designed to support a generally recognized commitment to defend a well-defined territory but not to extend it by the use of force.

Whether Kant was right or not, it is clear that most people in territorially satisfied democratic states would prefer that other states have those properties, for at least three reasons. First, they would imply security from foreign predators. Second, they would imply the existence of governments with which it might be possible to reach agreements for the mutual protection of property rights, which would facilitate commerce. And finally, they would satisfy the humanitarian impulses of democratic publics.

There are two ways a government might fall short of meeting these

38. For a recent discussion with citations to much of the relevant literature, see Ikenberry 2001.
39. As I noted earlier, these are arguably the attributes of the cold war period that Herz and Waltz tried to explain by the concept of bipolarity.

conditions: (1) it might not have a monopoly of the organized use of force within the territory that other states want to assign to it, and (2) it might exercise such effective control over its territory that it is a menace to other states. Unfortunately, correcting one of these problems might just lead to the other. Moreover, it is not clear how a government can participate in the construction of a state outside its own territory without depriving the residents of the foreign territory of their political independence.

As a result of the civil wars in the Balkans that accompanied the collapse of Yugoslavia after the end of the cold war, as well as a variety of civil wars in Africa, these questions have moved to the center of policy debates both within the United States and between the U.S. government and its allies. They have led to controversies about the role of the United States, its allies, and international institutions in mediating civil wars, as well as debates about whether the U.S. government, NATO, or the United Nations should engage in state building (or nation building, as it is often called). A closely related literature is devoted to explaining state failure or state collapse. Unfortunately, the division of intellectual labor between students of international politics and students of domestic politics has left us with few intellectual resources for thinking about these questions. This is therefore another important research frontier in the study of international politics.[40]

A state, let us remember, consists of a well-defined territory, the people who inhabit that territory, and a government. A government is an organization that uses force to collect economic resources from the people in its territory, which it uses to regulate their behavior, and to defend its position against competing groups either within its territory or from outside it. To build a state, therefore, one must put together an organization capable of supporting itself by forcible means from the economic resources available within a territory and of resisting challengers from both within and without. Acceptance of such an organization by people within its territory constitutes a government's internal sovereignty, and acceptance by people outside it constitutes its external sovereignty.[41]

Two sovereign states can fight a war with each other, but a government that fought a war within its territory would be said to have lost its

---

40. Examples of the literature on civil war termination include Licklider 1993; Stedman, Rothchild, and Cousens 2002; and Walter 2002. On state failure, see, for example, Zartman 1995 and Rotberg 2004. There is virtually no serious analytical literature on state building.

41. A nation is a collection of people with some characteristics in common (e.g., language or religion) who also share a sense of common interests—properties that facilitate their organization for large-scale collective action. A nation-state, therefore, is a state whose territory coincides with a nation. Nation building may be the consequence of state building or may precede it. Preexisting nations make the peaceful negotiation of the territorial boundaries of sovereign states difficult. But wars are one of the main ways by which the people governed by a state who were not already a nation become one.

internal sovereignty. Yet a sovereign government might regularly use force against individuals or small groups within its territory. The difference lies in the degree of organization of the people against whom the government uses force. Sometimes people say that internal sovereignty requires that the government have a monopoly of the use of force, but that is true of few governments, if any. Internal sovereignty requires, rather, something close to a monopoly of the *organized* use of force.

Thus a government can lose its internal sovereignty not because it has "collapsed" but because new organizations emerge to challenge it. That would be true of the government of Colombia, for example, whose control over its territory, which was never complete, has been challenged by a variety of organizations that have emerged in remote areas. In those areas these organizations might be said to be stateless governments: they do what governments do, but they lack both internal and external sovereignty over the territories they inhabit.

As we have seen, it is useful to think of a government as an organization in the protection business, an expression whose ambiguity exemplifies the range of possible relations between governments and the people they govern.[42] At one extreme an organization in the protection business might be a company that supplies armed guards to protect a piece of property. At another it could be a mafia that makes offers that people cannot refuse and protects them primarily from itself. Similarly, the governments of states range from what Jared Diamond has called "kleptocracies," which own and exploit the people they govern, to governments employed by the people they govern to provide them with public goods (1997, 265–92).

To explain the difference, one must think about the relative bargaining power of organizations in the protection business and their customers, which is in turn largely a function of how well organized each of them is. Even if a government has a monopoly of the organized use of force, it still requires the cooperation of its subjects to accomplish its ends, and therefore, as Thomas Schelling once wrote,

> the tyrant and his subjects are in somewhat symmetrical positions. *They* can deny *him* most of what *he* wants . . . [a]nd *he* can deny *them* just about everything *they* want—he can deny it by using the force at his command . . . [while t]hey can deny him the economic fruits of conquest. . . . It is a bargaining situation in which either side, if adequately disciplined and organized, can deny most of what the other wants; and it remains to see who wins. (quoted in Ackerman and Kruegler 1994, 9; emphasis in original)

---

42. The seminal discussion of governments in these terms is Lane 1958. The idea is developed in Tilly 1985. See also North 1981; Levi 1988; and Glete 2002.

Moreover, a government must worry about the possibility that it will lose its monopoly of the organized use of force, as happens in revolutionary civil wars.

Governments can be profitable for their members, but the benefits supplied by organizations formed to influence what a government does are often public goods, and therefore people who want to protect themselves from a government may have difficulty organizing themselves to do so. Moreover, once a government exists it can use the force available to it to punish people for organizing and can inhibit their ability to coordinate their actions. Thus it is easier to build a state than to organize people to protect themselves from it.

We saw that there are three main mechanisms that prevent governments from being pure kleptocracies. One is that, like any parasite, even kleptocracies have some interest in the well-being of the people they exploit. A second is that since kleptocracies are profitable they attract opposition from both within their territories and outside them. This may indirectly increase the bargaining power of the people they exploit, since the need to protect themselves from actual or potential opponents makes rulers more dependent on the resources their subjects control than they otherwise would be. And a third is that a government's subjects may be able to overcome the collective action problem and organize to oppose it by coordinating the selective incentives such as praise and blame or honor and dishonor that all human groups have available to influence the behavior of their members.[43]

There are limitations to each of these mechanisms, however. A parasite's interest in the well-being of its host may benefit the host a lot or a little. For example, a government that controls a territory with few valuable resources may have an interest in fostering the development of a commercial society in its territory to create wealth that it can then tax, while a government that controls a territory with a large supply of oil may have little interest in the well-being of the people with whom it happens to share that territory. Competition from other potential rulers may not be great, and if it is it may lead to recurring violence rather than to benefits for the people being exploited.[44] And political movements based on religion or political ideology can be captured and exploited by kleptocrats, leading to even more effective and profitable tyrannies. Thus organizations that satisfy the defining characteristics of a state have long existed, but states whose governments are genuinely controlled by the people they govern are historically rare.

---

43. For an analysis of how variations in the bargaining power of the residents of rural areas in Africa have influenced the terms of bargains struck between rulers and ruled in African states, see Boone 2003.
44. See the recent discussion in Skaperdas 2002.

The French Revolution and the wars that followed it, the U.S. Civil War, the Bolshevik Revolution and subsequent civil war in Russia, and the Spanish and Chinese civil wars are all examples of state building. The cold war was largely a conflict between the USSR and the United States about state building in Germany, and the ongoing conflict between India and Pakistan over Kashmir is a conflict over state building in the aftermath of Britain's abandonment of its empire in South Asia.

With the exception of the U.S. role in Germany after World War II, however, these are not examples that figure prominently in recent policy debates about state building, and when Germany is mentioned in that context it is rarely emphasized that World War II was part of the process that produced the current German state or that the cold war was the result of the ambition of both the United States and the USSR to reconstruct Germany after World War II. Moreover, the collapse of the ancien régime in France, the pre–Civil War federal government of the United States (which tolerated slavery), the czarist regime in Russia, the Chinese or Ottoman empires, or the Soviet Union do not figure prominently in the literature on state failures, in which state failures are typically portrayed as bad things, not good ones.

Rather, the implicit aim of state building in recent policy debates is to prevent the sort of violent conflicts that led to the building of the powerful states that might engage in it. Humanitarian catastrophes like the French Revolution are to be avoided, and if they occur their participants may be prosecuted for crimes against humanity; civil wars like the U.S. Civil War are to be ended early by compromise settlements, and their participants perhaps prosecuted for war crimes; and little Bismarcks seeking to redraw territorial boundaries are not to be allowed.

The contrast between contemporary debates about state building and the historical literature on the subject might lead one to ask: If state building is the answer, what is the question? And the question seems to be not how does one construct something like a European state where none exists but rather how does one construct some sort of institutional arrangement in such places that will protect the interests of the powerful states, avoid conflicts among them, and not require the expense and conflict associated with direct rule? It is an open question whether the answer to that question can provide a substitute for the long, violent process described by Kant that led to the development of modern democratic states.

Contemporary debates about state failure, civil wars, and state building are best understood as part of the long history of relations between the powerful states that first developed in Europe (which were then exported to parts of the rest of the world by colonization and imitation) and areas where such states do not exist. Sometimes the advantages enjoyed by European-style states led to various forms of direct and indirect rule over other territories, but even when they did not, relations between the powerful states and residents of other territories posed special problems, since there was no equivalent state in those territories with which one could make an agreement with any confidence that it would be kept.[45] One consequence of this fact was further imperialism, as one European government intervened preventively or preemptively in such areas to forestall possible intervention by another.[46]

Eventually the European empires proved too costly to maintain, a fact that posed the problem of what to do with those territories that the powerful states did not want to rule. The solution was for the powerful states to reach agreements among themselves and such organizations as existed in those territories that defined the boundaries of the territories and assigned responsibility for their governance to organizations within them.

One might call the territory assigned to some collection of people by such an agreement a "country." But while the negotiation of such agreements may be enough to create a country, which can be given a country code and admitted to the United Nations, it is not enough to create a state that resembles the former colonial powers.[47] And therefore the creation of such countries has not eliminated the problems that once were among the causes of European imperialism and which the European colonial empires were primarily responsible for coping with. It is not surprising, therefore, that some people have called for a resurrection of imperialism.[48]

But territorially satisfied democratic states are not interested in imperialism. Efforts to foster the negotiated settlement of civil wars and interventions leading to temporary rule (also known as "peace enforcement") are both present-day attempts to find a substitute for it.[49]

Mediating Civil Wars

As we saw in chapter 3, a state can be thought of as a bundle of contracts that define the organization of a government and its relation to the people

---

45. This was also a problem for the Romans in working out a relationship between their empire and the barbarians on their European frontier.

46. The U.S. government did this in Central America and the Caribbean as well. For recent discussions, see Smith 1981 and Abernethy 2000. For a seminal discussion of the relation among trade, political order, and imperialism, see Gallagher and Robinson 1953. For an interesting discussion of thinking by Europeans about the normative and legal foundations of relations between them and territories that lacked European institutions, see Keene 2002. Keene argues that, contrary to what many people assume, the problems these relations pose for writing a global constitution have not gone away.

47. This point is developed at length in Herbst 1996–97. Postcolonial governments often resemble the governments of the premodern world. For a systematic description of their properties, see Crone 2003, especially chaps. 3 and 4.

48. See, for example, Ferguson 2003.

49. For a recent discussion of the parallels between humanitarian interventions since the end of the cold war and imperialism, see Marten 2004.

it rules and to other states. All these contracts are subject to renegotiation by means of violence, and a civil war might be part of an attempt to do that. It is natural to think, therefore, that if outsiders can help the parties to such conflicts settle their disagreements, they can promote the development of the sorts of states that will provide the basis for a peaceful global order.

An evaluation of such an inference requires us to think about two questions. One is why outsiders would be able to promote the settlement of a conflict when the participants were unable to reach an agreement by themselves. The other is whether every conflict customarily identified as a civil war is really just a dispute about the terms of an agreement that, if accepted, would define a government capable of exercising internal sovereignty. Our discussion of contests over valuable territory among predatory rulers in chapters 4 and 5 is a useful place to begin thinking about both these questions.

We saw in those chapters that among the factors inhibiting predatory rulers from reaching peaceful agreements dividing valuable territory among themselves were conflicting expectations about the distribution of the cost of a contest in disarmament or its likely outcome, the existence of private information about rulers' preferences, and expectations of changes in the distribution of power that made it impossible for warring predators to commit themselves to abide by the terms of an agreement in the future.[50] Thus one possible role that third parties might play in fostering the peaceful settlement of violent conflicts would be to provide a means of overcoming these barriers to agreement.

A third party might, for example, try to make the adversaries' beliefs about their military capabilities and preferences more consistent by providing them with independent information. However, they may not believe what the third party says, and the third party may not want to share all the information it has. Moreover, the most important factor about which adversaries have conflicting expectations may be the behavior of the third party itself.

The source of all these problems is that it is unlikely that a third state's only interest in a conflict will be in arranging for a nonviolent outcome. Given the distribution of military capabilities between the adversaries, for example, an early settlement might require such adverse terms for the weaker side that a third party would not be willing to accept them and would instead prefer to intervene in the conflict to support the weaker side. Conflicting expectations about the circumstances that would be necessary

---

50. We also saw that writers influenced by game theory tend to assume that both the first two factors were just the result of the incentive of rulers to misrepresent private information—see, for example, Fearon 1995b.

to provoke such an intervention might themselves prevent a peaceful settlement of a conflict.[51]

Note well that, if such conflicting expectations lead to a military conflict and a third state does intervene, its intervention may lead to an end to the conflict, but only because the intervention reveals information about the third party's own capabilities or preferences. Thus it would be wrong to infer from the outcome of intervention that third parties can reliably manage conflict, since it may have been ex ante uncertainty about the eventual role that the third state would play that led to violent conflict, or its prolongation, in the first place. For the third state to have prevented the conflict would have required that it be common knowledge in advance what role it would play in the event that a violent conflict developed. But it is unlikely that this condition will usually be satisfied in the post–cold war environment.

Consider the recent conflict between NATO and Serbia over Serbia's treatment of ethnic Albanians in Kosovo. The U.S. government wanted simultaneously to deter the Serbs from harming the Albanians in Kosovo while convincing the Albanians that it would not support their independence. But the combined effect of these two messages may have been to leave both the Serbian leader Slobodan Milosevic and the Albanians uncertain as to what the United States would do if the Albanians insisted on secession and were on the verge of being decisively defeated by the Serbs, with the result that the conflict was prolonged until events provided an opportunity for the U.S. government to answer that question. Moreover, while the earlier U.S. intervention in Bosnia may have contributed to a more desirable resolution of the civil war there, uncertainty about what the United States would do may also have prolonged it.[52]

Similar problems inhibit the ability of third parties to act as enforcers of agreements. It is commonly assumed that enforcement of agreements consists mainly of confronting violators with superior force, an idea that is made plausible by the role that courts, police, and prisons play in enforcing laws within modern states and by the misuse of the Prisoner's Dilemma as a way of identifying what distinguishes international politics from domestic politics. The great disparity in military power between the United States and the parties to violent conflict in less fortunate countries might lead one to think that the United States can reliably promote nego-

---

51. See the recent discussion of third-party mediation in Rauchhaus 2003 and the literature cited there.
52. For a similar argument with other possible examples, see Kuperman 1999 and the June 2005 issue of *Ethnopolitics* devoted to moral hazard and humanitarian intervention. See also the discussion of the possible "moral hazard" resulting from attempts at extended deterrence, in Fearon 1997, 84–85. (Wagner 2005 argues that multiactor bargaining rather than moral hazard is the appropriate intellectual framework for thinking about these issues.)

tiated settlements of violent conflicts within and among them by serving as an enforcer of agreements.[53]

But, as we have seen, such reasoning rests on a misunderstanding of the role that force plays in preventing violent conflicts within states. It is true that law enforcement authorities confronting small groups of law-breakers can reliably make take-it-or-leave-it demands of them, and even when such demands do not work the scale of the resulting violence remains small so long as the miscreants remain less well organized than the authorities. However, the enforcement power of the state, when it is effective, is not the result just of the greater amount of force available to the state but also of the credibility of its commitment not to compromise with law-breakers and therefore its ability to make take-it-or-leave-it demands. This credibility is partly the result of the fact that the state does not just enforce agreements and will not enforce every agreement. It also enforces rules and will not enforce agreements that violate those rules. Thus in the United States the state is not available to enforce contracts between drug dealers and their customers, nor will it enforce contracts made under the threat of force. When this credibility is lacking it becomes possible to bargain with the enforcer, who then becomes just another party to the conflict.

One must therefore distinguish between the role of a third party as an enforcer of agreements made between the parties to a potentially violent conflict and its role as an enforcer of the rules of the game. Uncertainty about which role it will play is another source of potentially conflicting expectations about its behavior. The difference can be most clearly seen in the strangely split personality of Slobodan Milosevic as both war criminal and indispensable partner in the Dayton Agreement that ended the civil war in Bosnia. Some have argued that the Dayton Agreement rewarded Serbian aggression, while the reluctance of the U.S. government to accept negotiated settlements in Bosnia or Kosovo leading to a partition between the Serbs and their opponents seems to be the result of a desire to deter secessionist groups elsewhere.[54]

The problems just discussed are the result of a lack of common knowledge of when the third party will intervene and what agreements it will enforce. One might think that the probability of conflict would be diminished if the third party just succeeded in making clear that it would never intervene to support one side of a conflict or the other but would always enforce any agreement that the conflicting parties both accepted. Then the

---

53. For a recent discussion of the importance of third parties in enforcing civil war settlements, see Walter 1997.
54. Anecdotal evidence in support of such concerns has been supplied by Timothy Garton Ash, who was told by Albanians in Kosovo that what stimulated them to abandon nonviolent protest in favor of violence was the Dayton Agreement (Garton Ash 1999, 30).

third party could perhaps function as an impartial enforcer of agreements, which would enable the parties to conflicts to avoid violence by reaching negotiated settlements of their disagreements instead.

But, as we have seen in chapters 5 and 6, the availability of enforceable negotiated settlements may make violent conflicts more likely, not less, since the expectation of a negotiated settlement is what motivates violent bargaining over its terms—the fact that contracts between labor and management are enforceable does not, after all, prevent strikes from occurring. Governments prevent violence among their subjects not just by enforcing agreements among them but also by refusing to enforce agreements that have been extorted by violent means and punishing people who use force to get their way. That is part of what is meant by saying that a government has a monopoly of the legitimate use of force, and since there is no such monopoly at the global level, one cannot expect third parties contemplating intervention in a civil war to behave in the same way.

Thus there will necessarily be both uncertainty and conflicting expectations about the role that third parties will play in civil wars: third parties may be unable to commit themselves in advance either to intervene in a civil war or not to intervene. And therefore expectations about possible interventions may play a role in motivating an internal conflict even if outsiders never intervene in it.

I have so far assumed that the parties to a civil war would prefer a peaceful settlement if they could agree on its terms and be confident that they would be carried out. We saw in chapter 4 that this might be true if what was in dispute was a divisible good such as territory and the alternative to agreement was a costly contest in disarmament. But it need not be true even then, if one or the other of the adversaries is sufficiently risk acceptant.[55] And when the object in dispute is not a divisible good like territory, then a division of it between the adversaries cannot be the basis for a compromise settlement. Moreover, even territory may not be easily divisible for a variety of possible reasons.

A common way of making indivisible goods divisible in the literature on bargaining is to randomize over outcomes: instead of giving someone half the good in dispute, an agreement might give him a 50 percent chance at all of it. But we saw that a contest in disarmament is itself equivalent to a costly lottery, and if a lottery could be accepted as part of a negotiated settlement, one might think that there would always be at least one agreement that adversaries would prefer to fighting: a lottery that awarded the

---

55. It is important to remember that the terms *risk aversion* and *risk acceptance,* while seemingly referring to psychological properties of decision makers (their "attitudes toward risk"), really are just names for different points of indifference between a lottery giving them all of some valuable good and getting some of it for certain instead and therefore just refer to their preferences. These preferences might be explained in a number of different ways.

object in dispute to one of the adversaries with the same probability as a contest in disarmament but without the cost of fighting for it.

However, an agreement to accept a lottery as an alternative to war would likely not be enforceable: the outcome of the lottery would award all of the good in dispute to one or the other bargainer, and if the loser prefers fighting for it to allowing it to go to his adversary then he will not accept that outcome. That is a good reason for ignoring lotteries in thinking about negotiated settlements between warring predators, but lotteries illustrate a possible role that third parties can play in settling intrastate conflicts: third parties can sometimes help create a range of possible compromise settlements that would not otherwise exist and assist in enforcing them. While the notion of a lottery as part of a settlement of a violent conflict may seem fanciful, an agreement that some issues will be resolved in the future by a political process whose outcome is not predictable with certainty can be a functional equivalent, and a third party may be able to increase the adversaries' confidence that the outcome of that process will be implemented. Foreign aid and other side payments from a third party to one or both the adversaries that are conditional on reaching a peace agreement are more straightforward illustrations of the role third parties can play in creating a range of possible compromises where none would otherwise exist.[56]

Thus there are a variety of ways that a foreign state could facilitate the peaceful resolution of violent conflicts within the territory assigned to another state but also strong reasons to believe that a state that tries will not necessarily be successful. There are also good reasons to believe that the mere possibility of outside intervention can make it harder for the parties to a violent conflict to reach a negotiated settlement on their own. But even if all these difficulties are overcome and a negotiated settlement is achieved, such a settlement need not lead to the establishment of a government that is both capable of exercising internal sovereignty and incapable of posing a threat to the sovereignty of other governments.

Here again the discussion in chapters 4 and 5 of the relation between bargaining and war can be helpful in thinking about this question. In that discussion wars were contests in disarmament between competing organizations of economic predators, and the object in dispute was territory that was valuable to a predator. While the analysis in those chapters focused on agreements that divided the disputed territory between or among rival predators, I pointed out that, if there were economies of scale in predation, even equally matched predators might agree to join together and share the

---

56. See the discussion by Paul Pillar of package deals and agreements that leave the final resolution of some issues uncertain as ways of overcoming discontinuities in the bargaining space (1983, 224–31).

gains from exploiting the same territory, in which case a civil war might just be a conflict over how to divide the gains from predation.

But while an agreement that ended such a conflict might lead to an organization that could be called a state, it need not be enough to produce a state with the properties of a modern state. Not only would it not necessarily be either democratic or territorially satisfied, but it might not even be able to exercise complete control over the territory that other states were willing to concede to it. Indeed, conflicts commonly identified as civil wars may not actually be contests in disarmament between well-organized groups but may instead consist of recurring violence perpetrated by shifting groups of predators in areas that no organization exercises effective control over. In such conditions the problem is not to negotiate a peace settlement between or among competing organizations but to create an organization that would be capable of governing the territory that other states want to assign to it. And violence may be a means neither of defeating another organization nor of bargaining with it but may instead be part of the process by which the organizations that engage in it are created and maintained. In those circumstances, as in riots, there may be no one with whom to negotiate or reach a settlement.[57]

Temporary Rule
When mediation of a conflict is not enough to create an institutional arrangement in some territory that can keep the peace there, direct military intervention from the outside may be considered. But since territorially satisfied democratic states are not interested in permanently governing foreign territories, the question raised by such a possibility is whether such an intervention might lead to an institutional arrangement that would satisfy the interests of the intervening state or states after the occupation has ended.

That is a question that is also faced by any state that completely disarms another but does not want to govern its territory, as was true of the United States in its occupation of Germany and Japan at the end of World War II. But then whatever motivated the war that led to a state's defeat might be reason enough to confront this problem; and the defeated state will likely retain at least some of its previous organizational structure, which may make its reconstruction a straightforward task. Contemporary controversies about state building have focused instead on the question of whether intervention from the outside might be justified at least in part because it would give the occupying states or organizations an opportunity to create institutions that could keep the peace after the occupation had ended.

---

57. These can be properties of conflicts that, from one point of view, are called guerrilla wars and, from another, are called counterinsurgency operations.

This might be thought of as the problem faced by an imperial power that seeks to construct a temporary rather than a permanent empire. Thus there are important analogies between recent multilateral interventions in the Balkans and Afghanistan and such earlier halfway houses between empire and independence as the League of Nations mandates or the United Nations trusteeships (Helman and Ratner 1992; Caplan 2002). Of course, the European colonial empires proved to be temporary, but one might think that they would have been constructed differently had they been intended to be temporary at the outset. Moreover, when they ended, the colonial powers were typically in a hurry to leave. Had they prepared longer for their departure, perhaps the consequences would have been better. Besides the League of Nations mandates, the closest relevant examples might be the various interventions by the government of the United States in the Philippines and in Central America and the Caribbean between the beginning of the twentieth century and World War II. Unfortunately there has been little systematic analysis of this experience in the debates about state building since the end of the cold war.

Whether intended to be temporary or not, imperial rule is the result of a government's reliance on economic resources, organization, and technology that were developed in one territory to persuade the residents of another to acquiesce in its rule. Once established, of course, an imperial government can use the resources from its empire for the private benefit of its members or to solidify its control over its original territory. If this is the motivation for imperialism, it is yet another example of the close connection between economic predation and political order, which helps explain the ambivalent attitude many people have toward imperialism. Within democratic states, predatory rulers have been replaced by politicians hired by voters. Imperial rulers, however, have often been replaced either by less benign predators or by a condition resembling Hobbes's state of nature. If a substitute is to be found for imperialism, there has to be some mechanism to make sure that a temporary empire is not a predatory one or does not last longer than is necessary. One such mechanism is to organize temporary rule under the auspices of the broadest possible coalition of states. But without the incentives that motivated imperial rule, states may have little interest in joining such a coalition.[58]

Even with the requisite incentives for the occupying powers, however, there is still the problem of constructing a government that is both internally sovereign and temporary. If the temporary government is financed from outside the territory it governs and those resources are withdrawn when the government's mandate ends, then its replacement may not be able to raise the resources necessary to govern and its attempt to do so may

---

58. See the recent discussion in Fearon and Laitin 2004.

lead to violent opposition. If, however, the replacement government continues to be financed from outside its territory, then that will reduce the bargaining power of the replacement government's constituents.

If temporary rule is financed instead from within the territory it governs, this may increase the internal opposition that the temporary government must overcome. If it is resisted successfully, then the temporary government may be succeeded by a powerful predator when it departs; if not, then the temporary government may decide to depart rather than pay the costs of overcoming violent opposition to its rule, and the end of temporary rule may resemble the chaotic process that has often accompanied the liquidation of an empire. Thus there appears to be little reason to think that even beneficent temporary rule can be expected reliably to avoid the sorts of conflicts associated with the development of the most powerful states or with colonial empires and their aftermath.

The current interest in state building is based partly on the humanitarian impulse that leads people in rich and powerful states to hope that, having discovered the means of achieving peace, justice, and prosperity for themselves, they might transmit the secret to people in less fortunate places and partly on the common belief that the only sure remedy for recurring violence is a state. Thus if the problem in some place is organized violence the cure must consist of a Western-type state.

But an attempt to construct such a state where none existed before can lead to more violence than would otherwise exist. It was the need to fit all the former territory of the British empire in India into either postindependence India or Pakistan that created the conflict over the state of Jammu and Kashmir, which had formerly been an independent princely state only indirectly ruled by Britain. There was less violence in the Middle East under the Ottoman Empire than there has been among the states that replaced it. And just as the necessity of disposing of Germany after World War II led to conflict among the states that had defeated it, it is hard to see how a true Western-type state could be constructed in Afghanistan without resolving conflicts among the states that surround it, which include Pakistan, Iran, Russia, China, and India. Even if Europe and North America have already arrived at a destination that everyone else is bound eventually to reach, hastening others along the way may not be a way of preventing violent conflicts.

Nonetheless, upon occasion temporary rule will probably continue to seem better than the alternatives to one or more of the great powers, and it may also be necessary to think of more permanent possible substitutes for the European colonial empires. It would therefore be useful to try to understand both temporary and imperial rule better than we now do. This is therefore another important research frontier in the study of international politics.

CHAPTER 7

Summing Up

In his influential book *Theory of International Politics,* Kenneth Waltz claimed that "[t]o be a success," a theory of international politics "has to show how international politics can be conceived of as a domain distinct from the economic, social, and other international domains that one may conceive of" (1979, 79). His answer was that international politics consisted of interactions among units in a condition of anarchy and the interacting units were states. Thus a theory of international politics, he claimed, must be a theory about the working of a particular kind of social system, the system constituted by the collection of individual states of which it is composed. Theories of domestic politics, he claimed, were theories about the working of a different kind of social system, whose main common property was what he called "hierarchy."[1] While many criticisms have been made of Waltz's claims about the properties of international systems since his book was published, even many of his critics have accepted his definition of the subject of study.

One of the main theses of this book has been that this definition of the subject is misguided and has left us poorly equipped to understand the world in which we now live. If we are to understand international politics, I have argued, its study must be part of the more general study of the relation between political order and organized violence, as it was in the intellectual tradition from which modern-day Realism was derived. This is a puzzling and complex subject, in part because political order in complex societies *is* organized violence, and therefore one may wonder which is worse, the cure or the disease (Bates, Greif, and Singh 2002). This is the central question debated by early modern European political theorists as the European state system developed, and out of this debate emerged modern social science. The possibility of both interstate warfare and domestic repression was inherent in the development of that system, and, as we have seen, neither can be understood in isolation from the other.

Thus we cannot know what sort of political order is possible without understanding organized violence. But to do that we must understand

---

1. See Waltz 1979, chap. 5.

both violence and how people organize themselves to engage in it. Considered separately, each is an extremely complex phenomenon, and together they constitute a very difficult subject of study.

Violence is complicated in part because it can be used by some people to influence the behavior of others and therefore can be part of a bargaining process. Bargaining alone is hard to understand, and in spite of an enormous amount of intellectual effort that has been expended on it by economists and game theorists, there is still no generally satisfactory theoretical treatment of it. But violent bargaining is even more complex, because to understand it one must take into account several features of the bargaining situation that tend to be ignored by economists. First, variations in what is called the disagreement outcome in the bargaining literature will influence bargainers' relative bargaining power, and the disagreement outcome can not only be manipulated by the bargainers but also change as a result of exogenous factors. Second, one must consider how any agreements that are reached can be made self-enforcing. Third, bargaining among more than two bargainers is very complex and little understood. And finally, the extent to which people are organized will influence how much bargaining power they have.

Understanding how human beings organize themselves is a complex subject in its own right, because it requires an understanding of how they overcome both what is commonly called the collective action problem and the problem of coordinating their actions. Organizing for violence is especially complex, because it introduces the possibility of violent conflict between or among organizations seeking to profit from the threat of violence, as well as among the members of such organizations over how to divide the spoils.

Given the complexity of these phenomena, it is not surprising that people would try to ignore some components of them in order to analyze the effects of others, and for many purposes this is the only sensible way to proceed. Treating states as though they were individual actors bargaining with each other is an example of such a simplification, and much can be said about international politics in those terms.

If we want to evaluate the competing claims that have been made about the prospects for a peaceful global order, however, or about what the institutional basis for such an order might be, then such simplifications inhibit our understanding of the problem, since the modern state is at once the main example that we have of how violence can be organized to serve the common good and the basic institutional building block out of which a global order might be constructed. And one of the questions to be answered is whether peace requires some institution at the global level that resembles the modern state or whether properly constructed states alone would be a sufficient institutional foundation for it.

A state is constituted by the contracts that define the organization of a government and its relation to the people it governs and to other governments, and the collection of all such contracts defines the institutional structure of the global order. Force can be used to renegotiate any of them—an attempted coup d'état, for example, can lead to a popular revolt, which can lead in turn to a war with another government. And the barriers to the peaceful negotiation of agreements that define the relations among governments are not fundamentally different from the problems that inhibit the peaceful negotiation of agreements defining the organization of a government or its relation to the people it governs.

The terms of any agreement that might be accepted in lieu of violence will be influenced by the amount of force each party can inflict on the other. But this will be influenced in turn by the nature and extent of their organization. Thus the rise and fall of states is the product of the formation and dissolution of groups and forcible bargaining among them. The complexity of this process is magnified further by the fact that the terms of any agreements that might be reached may influence the subsequent relative bargaining power of the parties to the agreement. An agreement defining the boundaries between two states, for example, may influence their subsequent relative military capabilities. And an agreement defining the relation between a government and its subjects will usually require the disarmament of one or more of the parties to a conflict, which might be hard to reverse if the terms of the agreement are later violated.[2]

Thus the main problem in resolving violent conflicts is to define the terms of such contracts in a way that will reflect the current relative bargaining power of the antagonists without altering it. One barrier to agreement may be inconsistent estimates of what the parties' relative bargaining power actually is. Another may be the inability to craft an agreement that everyone is sufficiently confident will not place them at a disadvantage in the future. There is no guarantee that agreements that avoid both these problems and are also preferred to the continuation of a conflict by the parties to it always exist. And even if they do, they will be vulnerable to exogenous changes in incentives, expectations, or the technology of violence that can lead to subsequent renegotiation. The collapse of the Soviet Union is an example of how unpredictable such developments can be.

The complexity of these relationships makes it very easy to make mis-

---

2. This suggests a parallel between the problem of explaining the boundaries between states and the international system and the problem of explaining the boundaries between firms and markets: one of the themes of the recent literature on that subject is the fact that many contracts are necessarily incomplete and are subject to renegotiation. See, for example, Hart 1995. This parallel is briefly explored in Glete 2002, 55–58, and in Powell 1999, 216–22. However, contracts that define firms in the protection business are renegotiated in the shadow of organized violence.

takes in reasoning about factors that one happens to focus on and to over-look other factors that are also important. I have given examples of both in the preceding pages. A recitation of the mistakes I know that I have made, if I could remember them all, might be even longer, but they would be less interesting and important than the ones discussed here. And I do not doubt that critical readers will be able to find mistakes that I have unknowingly made in the preceding pages. Mistakes are inevitable. What is important is that they be spotted and corrected. And that requires that we be willing to check the validity of arguments and that arguments be constructed in such a way as to make that as easy to do as possible. We must be willing to use whatever tools are necessary to accomplish those goals.

Of course, given the difficulty of constructing interesting valid arguments about this subject, it is possible to be overly impressed by one. And therefore it is important to remember that the fact that an argument is valid only means that the conclusion must be true if the premises are true; and even if some facts that are known to be true can be derived from an explanation, there might nonetheless be another explanation that better explains all the known facts. That is why the progress of knowledge requires the development of competing theories, which are subjected to empirical tests. However, as Waltz wrote in his famous book:

> Many testers of theories seem to believe that the major difficulties lie in the devising of tests. Instead, one must insist that the first big difficulty lies in finding or stating theories with enough precision and plausibility to make testing worthwhile. Few theories of international politics define terms and specify the connection of variables with the clarity and logic that would make testing the theories worthwhile. Before a claim can be made to have tested something, one must have something to test. (1979, 14)

Unfortunately, the reader of Waltz's book is left with the impression that it is far easier to satisfy that requirement than it actually is.

References

Abernethy, David B. 2000. *The Dynamics of Global Dominance: European Overseas Empires 1415–1980*. New Haven: Yale University Press.

Ackerman, Peter, and Christopher Kruegler. 1994. *Strategic Nonviolent Conflict: The Dynamics of People Power in the Twentieth Century*. Westport, CT: Praeger.

Aoki, M. 2001. *Toward a Comparative Institutional Analysis*. Cambridge, MA: MIT Press.

Aoki, M., B. Gustafsson, and O. E. Williamson. 1990. *The Firm as a Nexus of Treaties*. London: Sage Publications.

Ashley, Richard K. 1986. "The Poverty of Neorealism." In Keohane 1986, 255–300.

Baldwin, David A., ed. 1993. *Neorealism and Neoliberalism: The Contemporary Debate*. New York: Columbia University Press.

Banfield, Edward C. 1958. *The Moral Basis of a Backward Society*. New York: Free Press.

Baron-Cohen, Simon. 1995. *Mindblindness: An Essay on Autism and Theory of Mind*. Cambridge, MA: MIT Press.

Bates, R., A. Greif, and S. Singh. 2002. "Organizing Violence." *Journal of Conflict Resolution* 46:599–628.

Bensel, Richard Franklin. 1990. *Yankee Leviathan: The Origins of Central State Authority in America, 1859–1877*. Cambridge: Cambridge University Press.

Berdal, M., and David M. Malone, eds. 2000. *Greed and Grievance: Economic Agendas in Civil Wars*. Boulder, CO: Lynne Rienner.

Berlin, I. 1998. *Many Thousands Gone: The First Two Centuries of Slavery in North America*. Cambridge, MA: Belknap Press of Harvard University Press.

Bingham, Paul M. 1999. "Human Uniqueness: A General Theory." *Quarterly Review of Biology* 74: 133–69.

Blainey, Geoffrey. 1988. *The Causes of War*. New York: Free Press.

Bobbitt, Philip. 2002. *The Shield of Achilles: War, Peace, and the Course of History*. New York: Alfred A. Knopf.

Boehm, Christopher. 1987. *Blood Revenge: The Enactment and Management of Conflict in Montenegro and Other Tribal Societies*. Philadelphia: University of Pennsylvania Press.

———. 1999. *Hierarchy in the Forest: The Evolution of Egalitarian Behavior*. Cambridge, MA: Harvard University Press.

Boone, Catherine. 2003. *Political Topographies of the African State*. Cambridge: Cambridge University Press.

Bowles, Samuel. 2003. *Microeconomics: Behavior, Institutions, and Evolution.* Princeton: Princeton University Press.

Bowles, Samuel, and Herbert Gintis. 2004. "The Evolution of Strong Reciprocity: Cooperation in Heterogeneous Populations." *Theoretical Population Biology* 65:17–28.

Brewer, John. 1989. *The Sinews of Power: War, Money and the English State, 1688–1783.* New York: Alfred A. Knopf.

Brooks, Stephen G. 1997. "Dueling Realisms." *International Organization* 51:445–77.

Brown, Michael E., Owen R. Coté Jr., Sean M. Lynn-Jones, and Steven E. Miller. 2004. *Offense, Defense, and War.* Cambridge, MA: MIT Press.

Brown, Michael E., Sean M. Lynn-Jones, and Steven E. Miller, eds. 1996. *Debating the Democratic Peace.* Cambridge, MA: MIT Press.

Bull, Hedley. 1977. *The Anarchical Society: A Study of Order in World Politics.* London: Macmillan Press.

Butterfield, Herbert. 1951. "The Tragic Element in Modern International Conflict." In *History and Human Relations,* 9–36. London: Collins.

Caplan, Richard. 2002. "A New Trusteeship? The International Administration of War-torn Territories." *Adelphi Paper* 341 (February 2002). London: International Institute for Strategic Studies.

Carr, Edward Hallett. 1946. *The Twenty Years' Crisis 1919–1939.* 2d. ed. London: Macmillan.

Cederman, Lars-Erik. 2001a. "Back to Kant: Reinterpreting the Democratic Peace as a Macrohistorical Learning Process." *American Political Science Review* 95:15–31.

———. 2001b. "Modeling the Democratic Peace as a Kantian Selection Process." *Journal of Conflict Resolution* 45:470–502.

Chandrasekhar, B. S. 1998. *Why Things Are the Way They Are.* Cambridge: Cambridge University Press.

Church, William F. 1972. *Richelieu and Reason of State.* Princeton: Princeton University Press.

Chwe, Michael Suk-Young. 2001. *Rational Ritual: Culture, Coordination, and Common Knowledge.* Princeton: Princeton University Press.

Claude, Inis L. 1962. *Power and International Relations.* New York: Random House.

Clausewitz, C. von. 1976. *On War.* Ed. and trans. Michael Howard and Peter Paret. Princeton: Princeton University Press.

Cooper, Robert. 2003. *The Breaking of Nations: Order and Chaos in the Twenty-first Century.* New York: Atlantic Monthly Press.

Copeland, Dale C. 2000. *The Origins of Major War.* Ithaca, NY: Cornell University Press.

Crone, Patricia. 2003. *Pre-Industrial Societies: Anatomy of the Pre-modern World.* Oxford: Oneworld Publications.

Culler, Jonathan. 1997. *Literary Theory: A Very Short Introduction.* Oxford: Oxford University Press.

Daalder, Ivo H. 1991. *The Nature and Practice of Flexible Response: NATO Strat-*

egy and Theater Nuclear Forces Since 1967. New York: Columbia University Press.

Derry, Gregory N. 1999. *What Science Is and How It Works*. Princeton: Princeton University Press.

Diamond, Jared. 1997. *Guns, Germs, and Steel: The Fates of Human Societies*. New York: W. W. Norton.

Doyle, Michael W. 1983. "Kant, Liberal Legacies, and Foreign Affairs." *Philosophy and Public Affairs* 12:205–35, 323–53.

———. 1995. "Reflections on the Liberal Peace and Its Critics." *International Security* 19:180–84. Reprinted in Brown, Lynn-Jones, and Miller 1996.

Elman, Colin, and Miriam Fendius Elman, eds. 2003. *Progress in International Relations Theory: Appraising the Field*. Cambridge, MA: MIT Press.

Falkenhayn, Erich von. 1920. *The German General Staff and Its Decisions, 1914–1916*. New York: Dodd, Mead.

Fearon, James D. 1994. "Ethnic War as a Commitment Problem." Paper presented at the annual meeting of the American Political Science Association, New York City, September 2–5.

———. 1995a. "The Offense–Defense Balance and War Since 1648." Paper presented at the annual meeting of the International Studies Association, Chicago, February.

———. 1995b. "Rationalist Explanations for War." *International Organization* 49:379–414.

———. 1995c. "Bargaining Over Objects That Influence Future Bargaining Power." Manuscript, Department of Political Science, University of Chicago, August 21.

———. 1997. "Signaling Foreign Policy Interests: Tying Hands versus Sinking Costs." *Journal of Conflict Resolution* 41:68–90.

———. 1999. "What Is Identity (As We Now Use the Word)?" Manuscript, Department of Political Science, Stanford University.

Fearon, James D., and David D. Laitin. 1996. "Explaining Interethnic Cooperation." *American Political Science Review* 90:715–35.

———. 2004. "Neotrusteeship and the Problem of Weak States." *International Security* 28:5–43.

Feaver, Peter D. 2003. *Armed Servants: Agency, Oversight, and Civil-Military Relations*. Cambridge, MA: Harvard University Press.

Fehr, Ernst, and Simon Gächter. 2002. "Altruistic Punishment in Humans." *Nature* 415:137–40.

Ferguson, Niall. 2003. "The Empire Slinks Back." *New York Times Magazine*, April 27.

Finer, S. E. 1997. *The History of Government*. Oxford: Oxford University Press.

Frankel, Benjamin, ed. 1996. *Realism: Restatements and Renewal*. London: Frank Cass.

Fraser, George MacDonald. 1995. *The Steel Bonnets: The Story of the Anglo-Scottish Border Reivers*. London: HarperCollins.

Frei, Christoph. 2001. *Hans J. Morgenthau: An Intellectual Biography*. Baton Rouge: Louisiana State University Press.

Fried, Morton H. 1967. *The Evolution of Political Society: An Essay in Political Anthropology.* New York: Random House.

Fukuyama, Francis. 1992. *The End of History and the Last Man.* New York: Free Press.

Fustel de Coulanges, N. D. 1956. *The Ancient City: A Study on the Religion, Laws, and Institutions of Greece and Rome.* Garden City, New York: Doubleday Anchor Books.

Gaddis, John Lewis. 1987. *The Long Peace: Inquiries into the History of the Cold War.* New York: Oxford University Press.

Gallagher, John, and Ronald Robinson. 1953. "The Imperialism of Free Trade." *Economic History Review,* 2d series, 6:1–15.

Gambetta, D. 1993. *The Sicilian Mafia: The Business of Private Protection.* Cambridge, MA: Harvard University Press.

Garton Ash, T. 1999. "Cry the Dismembered Country." *New York Review of Books,* January 14, 29–33.

Geanakoplos, John. 1989. "Game Theory Without Partitions, and Applications to Speculation and Consensus." Cowles Foundation Discussion Paper No. 914. Cowles Foundation for Research in Economics, Yale University, May.

———. 1992. "Common Knowledge." *Journal of Economic Perspectives* 6:53–82.

Gerth, H. H., and C. Wright Mills, eds. 1946. *From Max Weber: Essays in Sociology.* New York: Oxford University Press.

Gilpin, Robert. 1975. *U.S. Power and the Multinational Corporation.* New York: Basic Books.

———. 1981. *War and Change in World Politics.* Cambridge: Cambridge University Press.

Gladwell, Malcolm. 2006. "Troublemakers: What Pit Bulls Can Teach Us about Profiling." *New Yorker,* February 6, available at http://www.newyorker.com/printables/fact/060206fa_fact.

Glanz, James. 1998. "Putting Their Money Where Their Minds Are." *New York Times,* August 25.

———. 1999. "What Fuels Progress in Science? Sometimes, a Feud." *New York Times,* September 14.

Glete, Jan. 2002. *War and the State in Early Modern Europe: Spain, the Dutch Republic and Sweden as Fiscal-Military States, 1500–1660.* New York: Routledge.

Goemans, Hein E. 2000. *War and Punishment.* Princeton: Princeton University Press.

———. 2006. "Bounded Communities: Territoriality, Territorial Attachment and Conflict." In Miles Kahler and Barbara F. Walter, eds., *Territoriality and Conflict in an Era of Globalization.* Cambridge: Cambridge University Press.

Gopnik, Alison, Andrew N. Meltzoff, and Patricia K. Kuhl. 1999. *The Scientist in the Crib: Minds, Brains, and How Children Learn.* New York: William Morrow.

Gowa, Joanne. 1999. *Ballots and Bullets: The Elusive Democratic Peace.* Princeton: Princeton University Press.

Greif, A. 1998. "Self-Enforcing Political Systems and Economic Growth: Late Medieval Genoa." In Robert Bates, Avner Greif, Margaret Levi, Jean-Laurent Rosenthal, and Barry R. Weincast, *Analytic Narratives*. Princeton: Princeton University Press.

———. 2006. *Institutions and the Path to the Modern Economy: Lessons from Medieval Trade.* Cambridge: Cambridge University Press.

Grieco, Joseph M. 1988. "Anarchy and the Limits of Cooperation: A Realist Critique of the Newest Liberal Institutionalism." *International Organization* 42:485–507. Reprinted in Baldwin 1993.

———. 1993. "Understanding the Problem of International Cooperation: The Limits of Neoliberal Institutionalism and the Future of Realist Theory." In Baldwin 1993, 301–38.

Grossman, Herschel L. 2000. "The State: Agent or Proprietor?" *Economics of Governance* 1:3–11.

Gulick, E. V. 1955. *Europe's Classical Balance of Power.* New York: W. W. Norton.

Hardin, Russell. 1982. *Collective Action.* Baltimore: Johns Hopkins University Press.

———. 1991. "Hobbesian Political Order." *Political Theory* 19:156–80.

Harman, Gilbert H. 1965. "The Inference to the Best Explanation." *Philosophical Review* 74:88–95.

Harris, Marvin. 1977. *Cannibals and Kings.* New York: Random House.

Harsanyi, John C. 1967–68. "Games with Incomplete Information Played by Bayesian Players," parts 1–3. *Management Science* 14:159–82, 320–24, 486–502.

Hart, Oliver. 1995. *Firms, Contracts, and Financial Structure.* Oxford: Oxford University Press.

Haslam, Jonathan. 2002. *No Virtue Like Necessity: Realist Thought in International Relations since Machiavelli.* New Haven: Yale University Press.

Helman, Gerald B., and Steven R. Ratner. 1992. "Saving Failed States." *Foreign Policy* 89 (winter): 3–20.

Herbst, Jeffrey. 1996–97. "Responding to State Failure in Africa." *International Security* 21:120–44.

Herman, Arthur. 2001. *How the Scots Invented the Modern World.* New York: Crown.

Herz, John H. 1950. "Idealist Internationalism and the Security Dilemma." *World Politics* 2:157–80.

———. 1951. *Political Realism and Political Idealism.* Chicago: University of Chicago Press.

———. 1959. *International Politics in the Atomic Age.* New York: Columbia University Press.

———. 1981. "Political Realism Revisited." *International Studies Quarterly* 25:182–97.

Hirschman, Albert O. 1945. *National Power and the Structure of Foreign Trade.* Berkeley: University of California Press.

———. 1977. *The Passions and the Interests: Political Arguments for Capitalism before Its Triumph.* Princeton: Princeton University Press.

Hobbes, Thomas. 1957. *Leviathan: Or the Matter, Forme, and Power of a Com-*

monwealth Ecclesiasticall and Civil. Ed. with an introduction by Michael Oakeshott. Oxford: Basil Blackwell.

Hoffmann, Stanley. 1963. "Rousseau on War and Peace." *American Political Science Review* 57:317–33.

Hölldobler, Bert, and Edward O. Wilson. 1990. *The Ants.* Cambridge, MA: Belknap Press of Harvard University Press.

Holmes, Oliver Wendell, Jr. 1991. *The Common Law.* New York: Dover.

Holsti, Kalevi J. 1991. *Peace and War: Armed Conflicts and International Order 1648–1989.* Cambridge: Cambridge University Press.

Homans, George Caspar. 1950. *The Human Group.* New York: Harcourt, Brace & World.

———. 1967. *The Nature of Social Science.* New York: Harcourt, Brace & World.

———. 1984. *Coming to My Senses: The Autobiography of a Sociologist.* New Brunswick, NJ: Transaction Books.

Hopf, Ted. 2002. *Social Construction of International Politics: Identities and Foreign Policies, Moscow, 1955 and 1999.* Ithaca: Cornell University Press.

Howson, Colin. 2000. *Hume's Problem: Induction and the Justification of Belief.* Oxford: Oxford University Press.

Howson, Colin, and Peter Urbach. 1993. *Scientific Reasoning: The Bayesian Approach.* 2d. ed. Chicago: Open Court.

Hui, V. T. 1999. "Rethinking War, State Formation, and System Formation: Competing Logics in the Historical Contexts of Ancient China and Early Modern Europe." Paper presented at the annual meeting of the American Political Science Association, Atlanta, Georgia, September 2–5.

———. 2000. "Rethinking War, State Formation, and System Formation: A Historical Comparison of Ancient China (659–211 BC) and Early Modern Europe (1495–1815 AD)." PhD diss., Department of Political Science, Columbia University.

Hull, David L. 1973. *Darwin and His Critics: The Reception of Darwin's Theory of Evolution by the Scientific Community.* Cambridge, MA: Harvard University Press.

Huth, Paul K. 1988. *Extended Deterrence and the Prevention of War.* New Haven: Yale University Press.

Ikenberry, G. John. 2001. *After Victory: Institutions, Strategic Restraint, and the Rebuilding of Order after Major Wars.* Princeton: Princeton University Press.

Iklé, Fred Charles. 1991. *Every War Must End.* Rev. ed. New York: Columbia University Press.

James, Patrick. 2002. *International Relations and Scientific Progress: Structural Realism Reconsidered.* Columbus: Ohio State University Press.

Jaynes, E. T. 2003. *Probability Theory: The Logic of Science.* Cambridge: Cambridge University Press.

Jepperson, Ronald L., Alexander Wendt, and Peter J. Katzenstein. 1996. "Norms, Identity, and Culture in National Security." In Katzenstein 1996.

Jervis, Robert. 1978. "Cooperation Under the Security Dilemma." *World Politics* 30:167–214.

Johnson, Allen W., and Timothy Earle. 1987. *The Evolution of Human Societies: From Foraging Group to Agrarian State.* Stanford: Stanford University Press.

Johnson, Laurie M. 1993. *Thucydides, Hobbes, and the Interpretation of Realism.* DeKalb: Northern Illinois University Press.

Jones, E. L. 1987. *The European Miracle: Environments, Economies, and Geopolitics in the History of Europe and Asia.* 2d ed. Cambridge: Cambridge University Press.

Jones, Philip. 1997. *The Italian City-State: From Commune to Signoria.* Oxford: Oxford University Press.

Kahneman, Daniel, and Amos Tversky. 1979. "Prospect Theory: An Analysis of Decision under Risk." *Econometrica* 47:263–92.

Kamen, Henry. 2003. *Empire: How Spain Became a World Power, 1492–1763.* New York: HarperCollins.

Kant, Immanuel. 1784. *Idea for a Universal History with Cosmopolitan Intent.* In Carl J. Friedrich, ed., *The Philosophy of Kant: Immanuel Kant's Moral and Political Writings.* New York: Modern Library, 1949.

———. 1786. *Conjectures on the Beginning of Human History.* In Hans Reiss, ed., *Kant: Political Writings.* Cambridge: Cambridge University Press, 1991.

———. 1795. *Eternal Peace.* In Carl J. Friedrich, ed., *The Philosophy of Kant: Immanuel Kant's Moral and Political Writings.* New York: Modern Library, 1949.

———. 1797. *The Metaphysics of Morals.* In Hans Reiss, ed., *Kant: Political Writings.* Cambridge: Cambridge University Press, 1991.

Katz, Leonard D., ed. 2000. *Evolutionary Origins of Morality: Cross-Disciplinary Perspectives.* Exeter, UK: Imprint Academic.

Katzenstein, Peter J., ed. 1996. *The Culture of National Security: Norms and Identity in World Politics.* New York: Columbia University Press.

Katznelson, Ira, and Helen V. Milner, eds. 2002. *Political Science: The State of the Discipline.* New York: W. W. Norton.

Keen, Maurice, ed. 1999. *Medieval Warfare: A History.* Oxford: Oxford University Press.

Keene, Edward. 2002. *Beyond the Anarchical Society: Grotius, Colonialism and Order in World Politics.* Cambridge: Cambridge University Press.

Kelly, Raymond C. 2000. *Warless Societies and the Origin of War.* Ann Arbor: University of Michigan Press.

Kennan, J., and R. Wilson. 1993. "Bargaining with Private Information." *Journal of Economic Literature* 31:45–104.

Keohane, Robert O. 1984. *After Hegemony: Cooperation and Discord in the World Political Economy.* Princeton: Princeton University Press.

———, ed. 1986. *Neorealism and Its Critics.* New York: Columbia University Press.

Kincaid, Peter. 1986. *The Rule of the Road: An International Guide to History and Practice.* New York: Greenwood Press.

Kindleberger, Charles P. 1973. *The World in Depression, 1929–1939.* Berkeley: University of California Press.

King, Gary, Robert O. Keohane, and Sidney Verba. 1994. *Designing Social Inquiry: Scientific Inference in Qualitative Research.* Princeton: Princeton University Press.

King, Gary, and Langche Zeng. 2001. "Improving Forecasts of State Failure." *World Politics* 53:623–58.

Kolata, Gina. 2001. "The Genesis of an Epidemic: Humans, Chimps and a Virus." *New York Times,* September 4.

Krasner, Stephen D. 1999. *Sovereignty: Organized Hypocrisy.* Princeton: Princeton University Press.

Kratochwil, Friedrich V. 1989. *Rules, Norms, and Decisions: On the Conditions of Practical and Legal Reasoning in International Relations and Domestic Affairs.* Cambridge: Cambridge University Press.

Kreps, D. M. 1990. *A Course in Microeconomic Theory.* Princeton: Princeton University Press.

Kuperman, A. J. 1999. "Transnational Causes of Genocide: Or How the West Inadvertently Exacerbates Ethnic Conflict in the Post–Cold War Era." Paper presented at the annual meeting of the American Political Science Association, Atlanta, Georgia, September 2.

Kydd, Andrew. 1997. "Sheep in Sheep's Clothing: Why Security Seekers Do Not Fight Each Other." *Security Studies* 7:114–55.

———. 2005. *Trust and Mistrust in International Relations.* Princeton: Princeton University Press.

Lake, David A. 2003. "International Relations Theory and Internal Conflict: Insights from the Interstices." *International Studies Review* 5:81–89.

Lane, F. C. 1958. "Economic Consequences of Organized Violence." *Journal of Economic History* 18:401–17. Reprinted in Frederic C. Lane, ed., *Profits from Power.* Albany: State University of New York Press, 1979.

Lave, Charles A., and James G. March. 1993. *An Introduction to Models in the Social Sciences.* Lanham, MD: University Press of America.

Levi, Edward H. 1949. *An Introduction to Legal Reasoning.* Chicago: University of Chicago Press.

Levi, Margaret. 1988. *Of Rule and Revenue.* Berkeley: University of California Press.

Levy, Jack S. 1983. *War in the Modern Great Power System, 1495–1975.* Lexington: University Press of Kentucky.

———. 1987. "Declining Power and the Preventive Motivation for War." *World Politics* 40:82–107.

Lewis, David K. 1969. *Convention: A Philosophical Study.* Cambridge, MA: Harvard University Press.

Lichbach, Mark Irving. 1995. *The Rebel's Dilemma.* Ann Arbor: University of Michigan Press.

Licklider, Roy. 1993. *Stopping the Killing: How Civil Wars End.* New York: New York University Press.

Linz, Juan J., and Alfred Stepan. 1996. *Problems of Democratic Transition and Consolidation: Southern Europe, South America, and Post-Communist Europe.* Baltimore: Johns Hopkins University Press.

Lipson, Charles. 2003. *Reliable Partners: How Democracies Have Made a Separate Peace.* Princeton: Princeton University Press.

Lipton, Peter. 1991. *Inference to the Best Explanation.* London and New York: Routledge.

Lovejoy, Arthur O. 1910. "Kant and Evolution I." *Popular Science Monthly* 77:538–53.

———. 1911. "Kant and Evolution II." *Popular Science Monthly* 78:36–51.

Lynn, John A. 1993. "How War Fed War: The Tax of Violence and Contributions during the *Grande Siécle.*" *Journal of Modern History* 65:286–310.

Mannheim, Karl. 1936. *Ideology and Utopia: An Introduction to the Sociology of Knowledge.* New York: Harcourt, Brace.

March, James G., and Johan P. Olsen. 1989. *Rediscovering Institutions: The Organizational Basis of Politics.* New York: Free Press.

Marten, Kimberly Zisk. 2004. *Enforcing the Peace: Learning from the Imperial Past.* New York: Columbia University Press.

Mattingly, Garrett. 1964. *Renaissance Diplomacy.* Baltimore: Penguin Books.

Mayr, Ernst. 1991. *One Long Argument: Charles Darwin and the Genesis of Modern Evolutionary Thought.* Cambridge, MA: Harvard University Press.

McAdam, D., S. Tarrow, and C. Tilly. 2001. *Dynamics of Contention.* New York: Cambridge University Press.

McKay, D., and H. M. Scott. 1983. *The Rise of the Great Powers, 1648–1815.* London and New York: Longman.

McNeill, William H. 1980. *The Human Condition: An Ecological and Historical View.* Princeton: Princeton University Press.

———. 1982. *The Pursuit of Power: Technology, Armed Force, and Society since A.D. 1000.* Chicago: University of Chicago Press.

Mearsheimer, J. J. 1998. "A Peace Agreement That's Bound to Fail." *New York Times,* October 19, A21.

———. 2001. *The Tragedy of Great Power Politics.* New York: W. W. Norton.

Meek, Ronald L. 1976. *Social Science and the Ignoble Savage.* Cambridge: Cambridge University Press.

Meinecke, Friedrich. 1998. *Machiavellism: The Doctrine of Raison d'État and Its Place in Modern History.* New Brunswick: Transaction Publishers.

Milner, Helen. 1991. "The Assumption of Anarchy in International Relations." *Review of International Studies* 17:67–85. Reprinted in Baldwin 1993, 143–69.

Morgan, E. S. 1999. "Plantation Blues." *New York Review of Books,* June 10, 30–33.

Morgenthau, Hans J. 1948. *Politics among Nations: The Struggle for Power and Peace.* New York: Alfred A. Knopf.

Morrow, James D. 2002. "International Conflict: Assessing the Democratic Peace and Offense-Defense Theory." In Katznelson and Milner 2002.

Muthoo, Abhinay. 1999. *Bargaining Theory with Applications.* Cambridge: Cambridge University Press.

———. 2000. "A Non-Technical Introduction to Bargaining Theory." *World Economics* 1:145–66.

Niou, Emerson M. S., and Peter C. Ordeshook. 1990. "Stability in Anarchic International Systems." *American Political Science Review* 84:1207–34.

———. 1994. "'Less Filling, Tastes Great': The Realist-Neoliberal Debate." *World Politics* 46:209–34.

North, Douglass C. 1981. *Structure and Change in Economic History.* New York: W. W. Norton.

Olson, Mancur. 1965. *The Logic of Collective Action.* Cambridge, MA: Harvard University Press.

———. 1993. "Dictatorship, Democracy, and Development." *American Political Science Review* 87:567–76.

O'Neill, Barry. 1999. *Honor, Symbols, and War.* Ann Arbor: University of Michigan Press.

———. 2001. "Risk Aversion in International Relations Theory." *International Studies Quarterly* 45:617–40.

Osborne, Martin J., and Ariel Rubinstein. 1990. *Bargaining and Markets.* San Diego: Academic Press.

Osiander, Andreas. 1994. *The States System of Europe, 1640–1990: Peacemaking and the Conditions of International Stability.* Oxford: Oxford University Press.

———. 2001. "Sovereignty, International Relations, and the Westphalian Myth." *International Organization* 55:251–87.

Paret, Peter. 1985. *Clausewitz and the State: The Man, His Theories, and His Times.* Princeton: Princeton University Press.

Parker, Geoffrey. 1996. *The Military Revolution: Military Innovation and the Rise of the West, 1500–1800.* 2d. ed. Cambridge: Cambridge University Press.

Parsons, Talcott. 1937. *The Structure of Social Action.* New York: Free Press.

Perlez, Jane. 1998. "Feuds Rack Albania, Loosed from Communism." *New York Times,* April 14.

Pillar, P. R. 1983. *Negotiating Peace: War Termination as a Bargaining Process.* Princeton: Princeton University Press.

Pirenne, Henri. 2001. *Mohammed and Charlemagne.* Mineola, New York: Dover.

Porter, Bruce D. 1994. *War and the Rise of the State: The Military Foundations of Modern Politics.* New York: Free Press.

Posen, B. R. 1993. "The Security Dilemma and Ethnic Conflict." *Survival* 35:27–47.

Powell, Robert. 1991. "Absolute and Relative Gains in International Relations Theory." *American Political Science Review* 85:1303–20. Reprinted in Baldwin 1993, 209–33.

———. 1994. "Anarchy in International Relations Theory: The Neorealist-Neoliberal Debate." *International Organization* 48:313–44.

———. 1996. "Stability and the Distribution of Power." *World Politics* 48:239–67.

———. 1999. *In the Shadow of Power: States and Strategies in International Politics.* Princeton: Princeton University Press.

———. 2002. "Bargaining Theory and International Conflict." *Annual Review of Political Science* 5:1–30.

———. 2003. "Nuclear Deterrence Theory, Nuclear Proliferation, and National Missile Defense." *International Security* 27:86–118.

———. 2004. "The Inefficient Use of Power: Costly Conflict with Complete Information." *American Political Science Review* 98:231–41.

Press, S. James, and Judith M. Tanur. 2001. *The Subjectivity of Scientists and the Bayesian Approach.* New York: John Wiley.

Quester, George H. 1977. *Offense and Defense in the International System.* New York: John Wiley.

Rabb, Theodore K. 1975. *The Struggle for Stability in Early Modern Europe.* New York: Oxford University Press.

Raiffa, Howard. 1968. *Decision Analysis: Introductory Lectures on Choices under Uncertainty.* Reading, MA: Addison-Wesley.

Randle, R. F. 1973. *The Origins of Peace: A Study of Peacemaking and the Structure of Peace Settlements.* New York: Free Press.

Rashid, A. 2000. *Taliban: Militant Islam, Oil, and Fundamentalism in Central Asia.* New Haven: Yale University Press.

Rauchhaus, Robert W. 2003. "Asymmetric Information, Mediation and Conflict Management." Prepared for annual meeting of the American Political Science Association, Philadelphia, Pennsylvania, August 28–31.

Redlich, Fritz. 1956. *De Praeda Militari: Looting and Booty, 1500–1815.* Vierteljahrschrift für Sozial- und Wirtschaftsgeschichte, Beiheft 39. Wiesbaden: Franz Steiner Verlag.

———. 1964–65. *The German Military Enterpriser and His Work Force: A Study in European Economic and Social History.* Vols. 1 and 2. Vierteljahrschrift für Sozial- und Wirtschaftsgeschichte, Beihefte 47–48. Wiesbaden: Franz Steiner Verlag.

Reiter, Dan. 2003. "Exploring the Bargaining Model of War." *Perspectives on Politics* 1:27–43.

Riker, William H. 1962. *The Theory of Political Coalitions.* New Haven: Yale University Press.

Rochau, August Ludwig von. 1859. *Grundsätze der Realpolitik Angewendet auf die Staatlichen Zustände Deutschlands.* Stuttgart: Verlag von Karl Göpel.

Rogers, G. A. J., and Tom Sorell, eds. 2000. *Hobbes and History.* London: Routledge.

Rohan, Henri, Duke de. 1663. *A treatise of the interest of the princes and states of Christendome.* trans. Henry Hunt. London: Ric. Hodgkinsonne.

Rose, Gideon. 1998. "Neoclassical Realism and Theories of Foreign Policy." *World Politics* 51:144–72.

Rotberg, Robert I., ed. 2004. *When States Fail: Causes and Consequences.* Princeton: Princeton University Press.

Rousseau, J. J. 1913. *A Discourse on the Origin of Inequality.* Trans. G. D. H. Cole. London: J. M. Dent.

———. 1991a. *The State of War.* Reprinted in Stanley Hoffmann and David P. Fidler, eds., *Rousseau on International Relations.* Oxford: Clarendon Press.

———. 1991b. *Abstract and Judgement of Saint-Pierre's Project for Perpetual Peace.* Reprinted in Stanley Hoffmann and David P. Fidler, eds., *Rousseau on International Relations.* Oxford: Clarendon Press.

Rubinstein, A. 1982. "Perfect Equilibrium in a Bargaining Model." *Econometrica* 50:97–109.

Ruggie, John Gerard. 1998. *Constructing the World Polity: Essays on International Institutionalization.* London and New York: Routledge.

Ruse, Michael. 1998. *Taking Darwin Seriously.* Amherst, NY: Prometheus Books.

Russett, Bruce. 1993. *Grasping the Democratic Peace: Principles for a Post-Cold War World.* Princeton: Princeton University Press.

Sabra, Abdelhamid I. 2003. "Ibn Al-Haytham." *Harvard Magazine* 106, no. 1 (September–October): 54–55.

Said, Edward. 1999. "The One-State Solution." *New York Times Magazine,* January 10, 36–39.

Sandler, Todd. 1992. *Collective Action: Theory and Applications.* Ann Arbor: University of Michigan Press.

———. 2001. *Economic Concepts for the Social Sciences.* Cambridge: Cambridge University Press.

Schelling, Thomas C. 1960. *The Strategy of Conflict.* Cambridge, MA: Harvard University Press.

Schroeder, Paul W. 1994. *The Transformation of European Politics, 1763–1848.* Oxford: Oxford University Press.

Schultz, Kenneth A. 2001. *Democracy and Coercive Diplomacy.* Cambridge: Cambridge University Press.

Schweller, Randall L. 1994. "Bandwagoning for Profit: Bringing the Revisionist State Back In." *International Security* 19:72–107.

———. 1996. "Neorealism's Status Quo Bias: What Security Dilemma?" In Frankel 1996, 90–121.

———. 1998. *Deadly Imbalances: Tripolarity and Hitler's Strategy of World Conquest.* New York: Columbia University Press.

———. 2003. "The Progressiveness of Neoclassical Realism." In Elman and Elman 2003, 311–47.

Seabright, Paul. 2004. *The Company of Strangers: A Natural History of Economic Life.* Princeton: Princeton University Press.

Sheehan, Michael. 1996. *The Balance of Power: History and Theory.* New York: Routledge.

Skaperdas, S. 1998. "On the Formation of Alliances in Conflict and Contests." *Public Choice* 96:25–42.

———. 2002. "Warlord Competition." *Journal of Peace Research* 39:435–46.

Skyrms, Brian. 2004. *The Stag Hunt and the Evolution of Social Structure.* Cambridge: Cambridge University Press.

Smith, Adam. 1937. *An Inquiry into the Nature and Causes of the Wealth of Nations.* New York: Modern Library.

Smith, Alastair, and Allan C. Stam. 2004. "Bargaining and the Nature of War." *Journal of Conflict Resolution* 48:783–813.

Smith, Tony. 1981. *The Pattern of Imperialism: The United States, Great Britain, and the Late-Industrializing World since 1815.* Cambridge: Cambridge University Press.

Snyder, Glenn H., and Paul Diesing. 1977. *Conflict among Nations.* Princeton: Princeton University Press.

Snyder, Jack. 1991. *Myths of Empire: Domestic Politics and International Ambition.* Ithaca: Cornell University Press.

———. 2000. *From Voting to Violence: Democratization and Nationalist Conflict.* New York: W. W. Norton.

———. 2002. "Anarchy and Culture: Insights from the Anthropology of War." *International Organization* 56:7–45.

Snyder, Jack, and Robert Jervis. 1999. "Civil War and the Security Dilemma." In Walter and Snyder 1999, 15–37.

Stark, Rodney. 1997. *The Rise of Christianity: How the Obscure, Marginal Jesus Movement Became the Dominant Religious Force in the Western World in a Few Centuries.* San Francisco: HarperCollins.

Stedman, Stephen John, Donald Rothchild, and Elizabeth M. Cousens, eds. 2002. *Ending Civil Wars: The Implementation of Peace Agreements.* Boulder, CO: Lynne Rienner.

Stern, Jessica. 2003. *Terror in the Name of God: Why Religious Militants Kill.* New York: HarperCollins.

Strawson, P. F. 1952. *Introduction to Logical Theory.* London: Methuen.

Stueck, W. 1995. *The Korean War: An International History.* Princeton: Princeton University Press.

Swedberg, Richard. 2003. *Principles of Economic Sociology.* Princeton: Princeton University Press.

Thagard, Paul R. 1978. "The Best Explanation: Criteria for Theory Choice." *Journal of Philosophy* 75:76–92.

Thomson, Janice E. 1994. *Mercenaries, Pirates, and Sovereigns: State-Building and Extraterritorial Violence in Early Modern Europe.* Princeton: Princeton University Press.

Tilly, Charles. 1985. "War Making and State Making as Organized Crime." In Peter B. Evans, Dietrich Rueschemeyer, and Theda Skocpol, eds., *Bringing the State Back In.* New York: Cambridge University Press.

———. 1992. *Coercion, Capital, and European States, AD 990–1992.* Cambridge, MA: Blackwell.

Tomasello, Michael. 1999. *The Cultural Origins of Human Cognition.* Cambridge, MA: Harvard University Press.

Trachtenberg, Marc. 1999. *A Constructed Peace: The Making of the European Settlement, 1945–1963.* Princeton: Princeton University Press.

Tuchman, Barbara W. 1978. *A Distant Mirror: The Calamitous 14th Century.* New York: Ballantine Books.

Tuck, Richard. 1989. *Hobbes.* Oxford: Oxford University Press.

———. 1999. *The Rights of War and Peace: Political Thought and the International Order from Grotius to Kant.* Oxford: Oxford University Press.

Van Evera, Stephen. 1997. *Guide to Methods for Students of Political Science.* Ithaca: Cornell University Press.

———. 1999. *Causes of War: Power and the Roots of Conflict.* Ithaca: Cornell University Press.

Varese, Federico. 2001. *The Russian Mafia: Private Protection in a New Market Economy.* Oxford: Oxford University Press.

Viner, Jacob. 1944. "International Relations between State-Controlled National Economies." *American Economic Review, Papers and Proceedings of the Fifty-Sixth Annual Meeting of the American Economic Association,* March, 34:315–29.

Volkov, Vadim. 2000. "The Political Economy of Protection Rackets in the Past and the Present." *Social Research* 67:709–44.

————. 2002. *Violent Entrepreneurs: The Use of Force in the Making of Russian Capitalism.* Ithaca: Cornell University Press.

von Neumann, J., and O. Morgenstern. 1944. *Theory of Games and Economic Behavior.* Princeton: Princeton University Press.

Wagner, R. Harrison. 1980. "The Decision to Divide Germany and the Origins of the Cold War." *International Studies Quarterly* 24:155–90.

————. 1986. "The Theory of Games and the Balance of Power." *World Politics* 38:546–76.

————. 1993. "What Was Bipolarity?" *International Organization* 47:77–106.

————. 2000. "Bargaining and War." *American Journal of Political Science* 44:469–84.

————. 2001. "Who's Afraid of 'Rational Choice Theory'?" Paper, Department of Government, University of Texas at Austin, available at www.la.utexas .edu/~hw.

————. 2005. "The Hazards of Thinking about Moral Hazard." *Ethnopolitics* 4:237–46.

Walt, Stephen M. 1999. "Rigor or Mortis? Rational Choice and Security Studies." *International Security* 23:5–48.

————. 2002. "The Enduring Relevance of the Realist Tradition." In Katznelson and Milner 2002.

Walter, Barbara F. 2002. *Committing to Peace: The Successful Settlement of Civil Wars.* Princeton: Princeton University Press.

Walter, Barbara F., and Jack Snyder, eds. 1999. *Civil Wars, Insecurity, and Intervention.* New York: Columbia University Press.

Waltz, Kenneth N. 1959. *Man, the State and War: A Theoretical Analysis.* New York: Columbia University Press.

————. 1962. "Kant, Liberalism, and War." *American Political Science Review* 56:331–40.

————. 1964. "The Stability of a Bipolar World." *Daedalus* 93:892–907.

————. 1979. *Theory of International Politics.* Reading, MA: Addison-Wesley.

————. 1981. "The Spread of Nuclear Weapons: More May Be Better." *Adelphi Paper* 171. London: International Institute for Strategic Studies.

————. 1988. "The Origins of War in Neorealist Theory." *Journal of Interdisciplinary History* 18:615–28.

Weber, Max. 1946. "Politics as a Vocation." In H. H. Gerth and C. Wright Mills, eds., *From Max Weber: Essays in Sociology.* New York: Oxford University Press.

Weingast, B. 1998. "Political Stability and Civil War: Institutions, Commitment, and American Democracy." In Robert H. Bates, Avner Greif, Margaret Levi, Jean-Laurent Rosenthal, and Barry R. Weingast, *Analytic Narratives.* Princeton: Princeton University Press.

Wendt, Alexander. 1987. "The Agent-Structure Problem in International Relations Theory." *International Organization* 41:335–70.

————. 1992. "Anarchy Is What States Make of It: The Social Construction of Power Politics." *International Organization* 46:391–425.

————. 1999. *Social Theory of International Politics.* Cambridge: Cambridge University Press.

Wight, Martin. 2002. *Power Politics*. Ed. Hedley Bull and Jack Spence. New York: Continuum.

Wilson, David Sloan. 1998. "Game Theory and Human Behavior." In Lee Alan Dugatkin and Hudson Kern Reeve, eds., *Game Theory and Animal Behavior*. New York: Oxford University Press.

———. 2000. "Nonzero & Nonsense: Group Selection, Nonzerosumness, and the Human Gaia Hypothesis." *Skeptic* 8:84–89.

———. 2002. *Darwin's Cathedral: Evolution, Religion, and the Nature of Society*. Chicago: University of Chicago Press.

Wilson, Edward O. 1994. *Naturalist*. New York: Warner Books.

Winch, Peter. 1958. *The Idea of a Social Science*. London: Routledge & Kegan Paul.

Wittman, Donald. 1979. "How a War Ends: A Rational Model Approach." *Journal of Conflict Resolution* 21:741–61.

Wright, Moorhead, ed. 1975. *Theory and Practice of the Balance of Power 1486–1914*. London: J. M. Dent.

Wright, Robert. 2000. *Nonzero: The Logic of Human Destiny*. New York: Pantheon Books.

Wrong, Dennis. 1961. "The Oversocialized Conception of Man in Modern Sociology." *American Sociological Review* 26:183–93.

———. 1994. *The Problem of Order: What Unites and Divides Society*. New York: Free Press.

Young, H. Peyton. 1996. "The Dynamics of Convention." *Journal of Economic Perspectives* 10:105–22.

Zartman, I. William. 1995. *Collapsed States: The Disintegration and Restoration of Legitimate Authority*. Boulder, CO: Lynne Rienner.

Ziegler, D. 1997. "Ready to Face the World? A Survey of China." *Economist*, March 8.

Ziman, John. 2000. *Real Science: What It Is, and What It Means*. Cambridge: Cambridge University Press.

Index

abduction, 4n6
Abernethy, David B., 225n46
Ackerman, Peter, 222
agent-structure problem, 43
alliances, 19, 154–61. *See also* balance
  of power
anarchy, 21–33, 35, 39–40, 42, 44, 49,
  59, 120, 122–25, 127, 173, 183, 218
ant, social organization of, 8, 43–47
Aoki, M., 101n46, 121
appeasement, 186
arms race, 175–77
Ashley, Richard K., 42n62, 48n72

balance of power, 81–85, 155–70, 185,
  193–95
  balancing, 16, 17, 47, 165, 192, 207
bandwagoning, 16, 158, 159, 192
Banfield, Edward C., 119n210
bargaining, 106–12, 143–71, 174, 201,
  205, 222, 236. *See also under* war
  and force, 112–18
  Nash solution, 108
  and organization, 111–12
  and strikes, 106–7
  Rubinstein solution, 110–11, 112,
    145, 147, 160–61
Baron-Cohen, Simon, 10n21, 44n
Bates, R., 235
Bayess rule, 3n3, 3n5, 149, 153
Bensel, Richard Franklin, 127n30
Berdal, M., 118
Berlin, I., 113n
Bingham, Paul M., 96n39
bipolarity, 18–21, 195n32, 220n39
Blainey, Geoffrey, 20, 132n, 136nn3–4,
  144, 147, 162–64, 170, 195n33, 201
Bobbitt, Philip, 126n27, 217n32

Boehm, Christopher, 61n10, 64, 96n39,
  101n45, 118
Boone, Catherine, 223n43
Bowles, Samuel, 96n39, 101n46,
  117n15
Brewer, John, 76n, 90n33, 210n20
Brooks, Stephen G., 17n
Bull, Hedley, 123n23
Butterfield, Herbert, 106n3

Caplan, Richard, 232
Carr, Edward Hallett, 49, 50, 52, 53,
  58–60, 64, 79, 218
causality, 9
causal regularities, 5
Cederman, Lars-Erik, 96n39
Chandrasekhar, B. S., 5n12
choices, models of, 11–12
Church, William F., 74n23
Chwe, Michael Suk-Young, 55n3,
  101n46, 117n16
civil war, 33–35, 183, 221, 224, 225–
  31
  partition, 35, 183
Claude, Inis L., 18n33, 36, 85n31,
  161n44, 199n1, 218n33
Clausewitz, C. von, 133–71, 175, 176,
  179, 183n15, 184, 187, 195, 201,
  206
collective action, 112, 114, 115, 117,
  203, 211–12, 218, 223
collective security, 78–81
common knowledge, 54–55
commonwealth, Hobbesian, 70–73,
  105n, 208, 210
competition among predators, 90,
  93–94, 114, 119, 202, 222–23
constitution, global 125–27, 217–33